Christ Our Mother

Julian of Norwich

THE WAY OF THE CHRISTIAN MYSTICS

GENERAL EDITOR

Noel Dermot O'Donoghue, ODC

Volume 7

Christ Our Mother
Julian of Norwich

by

Brant Pelphrey

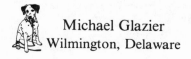

Michael Glazier
Wilmington, Delaware

First published in 1989 by Michael Glazier, Inc., 1935 West Fourth Street, Wilmington, Delaware 19805.

Library of Congress Cataloging-in-Publication Data

Pelphrey, Brant.
    Julian of Norwich/ by Brant Pelphrey.
      p cm.—(The Way of the Christian mystics;)
    Bibliography: p.
    Includes index.
    ISBN 0-89453-623-0
      1. Julian, of Norwich, b. 1343. 2. Mystics—England—Biography.
3.Mysticism—England—History. 4. Mysticism—History—Middle Ages,
600-1500.   I. Title.   II. Series.
BV5095.J84P45 1989
248.2'2'0924—dc19
[B]   87-82354
                                                           CIP

ISBN: *Way of Christian Mystics* Series: 0-89453-630-3
Cover Design by Brother Placid, OSB
Typography by Edith Warren
Printed in the United States of America by Edward Brothers

Contents

Editor's Preface

Up to quite recently mystics were either misunderstood or simply not understood. But now we are coming to see that, in T.S. Eliot's words, the way of the mystics is "our only hope, or else despair." As the darkness deepens, and the lights go out, those ancient lights begin to appear and to show us the way forward. They are not only lights to guide us, but are each a human countenance in which we can recognise something of ourselves—each is a portrait for self-recognition.

Unfortunately, the great Christian mystics have been generally presented as models of perfection or monuments of orthodoxy—sometimes, too, as inhumanly joyless and ascetical. Yet they were, above all else, men and women of feeling, always vulnerable, at times perhaps insecure and uncertain of the way ahead. For all that, they all shine with a special divine likeness and a special human radiance.

Each of the following portraits tries to present a true likeness of its subject, a likeness that comes alive especially in the ordinary and the everyday. In each case the author has been asked to enliven scholarship with personal warmth, and to temper enthusiasm with accurate scholarship. Each portrait hopes to be in its own way a work of art, something carefully and lovingly fashioned out of genuine material.

The main focus nevertheless is on the way in which each mystic mediates the Christian Gospel, and so gives us a deeper, richer, clearer vision of the Christian mystery. This kind of exposition demands the reader's full and prayerful attention. Each book is the story of a pilgrimage, for the mystic, the writer and the reader.

Noel O'Donoghue

Acknowledgements

Special thanks are due to Professor Valerie Lagorio, of the University of Iowa and editor/founder of *Mystics Quarterly* (formerly *14th-Century English Mystics Newsletter*), whose pioneer work with the *Quarterly* has done much to encourage scholarship in the mystics and to create interest in Julian of Norwich in particular; and to her co-worker, Sister Ritamary Bradley, SFCC, a Julian scholar and friend whose comments were invaluable in revising this manuscript. Their constant support and encouragement have made the writing of this book possible in the midst of heavy lecture responsibilities and much travel.

Any work about Mother Julian owes a debt to the scholarship of Julian's friends in Norwich and abroad, especially at the Julian Shrine on the site where Julian lived. These include the Rev. Canon Michael McLean, now at Norwich Cathedral; Fr. Robert Llewelyn, at the shrine; Mr. Frank Sayer, formerly at the Colman and Rye Library of Local History in Norwich; and above all the kind sisters of the Community of All Hallows, especially Reverend Mother Violet, who work adjacent to the shrine and who, over the years, have generously volunteered their time, their hospitality and their prayers. My wife and I rejoice to have been received into the Community as Associates.

Some of the material which appears here is condensed from my earlier work on Julian's theology and mysticism, and so is indebted to all the other friends who assisted in its publication. Many of these impressions of Julian ultimately spring from conversations with Fr. Roland Walls, founder of the Community of the Transfiguration in Roslin, Scotland; and from Fr. Noel O'Donoghue, a friend of Julian and the editor of the present series on the mystics. Responsibility for misinterpreting their advice must remain, of course, my own.

The Text

Quotations from Julian which appear here are all taken from the *Revelations of Divine Love*, Julian's only known manuscript. For the convenience of students, the Longer Version of the text as it appears in Marion Glasscoe's edition has been used, except where otherwise noted.[1] The translations are my own. However, inspiration has been drawn from time to time from the 1954 translation by James Walsh (a lyrical rendering which preserves the flavor of Julian's medieval English); from the beautiful version, recommended to first-time readers of Julian, by M.L. DelMastro; and from the unpublished translation by Sheila Upjohn, generously lent by the author.

The dramatic reconstruction of events in Julian's life, leading up to and including her sixteen supernatural showings in May, 1373—which appears in chapters one and two below—is based upon a close comparison of accounts in the Longer and Shorter Versions, and is the author's own conjecture.

The manuscripts are as follows:

The Shorter Version:	British Museum Additional MS 37790 (the "Amherst" MS). Probably the oldest text; mid-15th C.
The Longer Version:	1) Westminster Cathedral MS. Contains only selections from the text; late 15th/early 16th C.
	2) Bibliotheque Nationale, Paris, Fonds Anglais 40 (the "Paris" MS). Mid-17th C?
	3) British Museum Sloane MS 2499. Mid-17th C.
	4) British Museum Sloane MS 3705. Late 17th/early 18th C.
	5) St. Joseph's College MS, Upholland (the "Upholland" MS). Contains only selections from the text; c. 1650.

[1] In the rare instances where an alternate reading of the text has been preferred, the following notations have been given: P= Paris MS; CE= the "critical edition" of all MS by College and Walsh; Shorter Version= Shorter Version of the *Revelations* as rendered in CE.

Preface

Consider this book unfinished. Like Julian's own work, which she said was "begun by God's gift and his grace, but not yet performed," it represents a beginning rather than a task performed; an exploration rather than a destination.

Although it has been more than six hundred years since Julian wrote her *Revelations of Divine Love*—the only example we have of her writing—her spiritual journey has until recently remained largely unexplored. I have no doubt that Julian would have wanted it that way. A recluse who evidently preferred anonymity to fame, she would want us to fix our attention on the grace of God and not on her, especially not on her mystical experience. But she has much to say to us today, and it is only right that we should attempt to follow her a little way, at least, on the pilgrimage which was hers.

Writing this book has involved its own pilgrimage, some of it in Julian's Norwich and among present-day contemplatives and anchorites, and some of it in radically different surroundings in Asia and in America. It was at first difficult to write about the insights of a medieval English mystic while living in the noise and confusion of modern Hong Kong, far away from the unique atmosphere of spirituality and medieval history which are typical of Julian's Norwich even today. Yet in putting together these reflections now, a "new" Julian seems to have emerged who might otherwise have gone un-noticed. It has been impossible to write about Julian now without seeing

her in a wider context than before: among the poor, the
students, the tourists and merchants of Hong Kong; or more
recently, against the backdrop of Buddhist monasteries and
pilgrim hostels in China and Tibet.

I believe that if Julian were alive today we would find her
very much at home in this part of the world. Norwich was, in
her day, much like Hong Kong in our time. It was a bustling
center of world trade, overcrowded, teeming with languages
and a confluence of cultures from around the world. We can
imagine Julian living comfortably today in Hong Kong much
as she did centuries ago: hidden somewhere in the housing
estates of Kowloon, or among the boat-people in Aberdeen;
or perhaps in a tiny hut at the top of a nearby mountain in the
rural New Territories. She would divide her time, as before,
between silent prayer and worship on the one hand, and a
quiet ministry to the local poor on the other. She would wait
each morning at her window to visit with barefoot Hakka
women on their way to work at the garbage dump at the foot
of our road; or with street-sleepers stopping by near their
habitual meeting-place under a bridge downtown; or with Filli-
pina maids who gather on Sunday afternoons near the Cathedral to discuss their common experiences of economic
hardship, separation from their families, mistreatment or loneliness.

Julian's special calling was to be an anchoress, a type of nun
who traditionally lives in a tiny house—usually of one or two
rooms—and who never goes out. She gives herself entirely to
the exercise of prayer, both in contemplative silence and in
saying the psalms and set prayers (or "Offices") of the Church.
She also makes herself available to those souls in need of
comfort or advice, who come by to see her day by day.

This peculiar calling has never vanished completely from
the Church, though we would be less conscious of it today
than in former times. There are still anchorites (males are
traditionally known as "anchors") scattered here and there,
not only in Russia, Greece, or North Africa where they have
always been popular, but also in England and in Europe and
the Americas. However, they are not usually in the public eye,
typically known only to their confessors and to a handful of
poor among whom they live and pray. Most of us would be

startled to find them in nearby convents or housing projects, as well as in forest huts or remote deserts and caves (where there has in fact been a resurgence of life in recent years). Since it is not the business of an anchorite to attract attention, most of them will not usually write for publication. Julian herself seems to have been no exception. Therefore, attempts to persuade friends in this style of vocation to write about Julian have not, so far, met with any success. This book is offered, then, with a keen awareness that there are others who would be far more competent to tell about Julian's way of prayer, because they are living it continually in our own time.

Until recently there were not many scholars who demonstrated an interest in Julian. Only fifteen years ago, when I first began to learn about her way of spirituality, there was an unmistakable sense of stumbling onto new ground. Only one book had been written about her at all, dealing in a limited way with her understanding of prayer; and there were only a handful of articles. With a few exceptions, it seemed that only specialists in English medieval literature or the history of Christian mysticism knew very much about her, even though several translations of her book, or at least portions of it, had appeared in print in this century. Julian figured prominently, however, in the lectures and devotional life of several professors at New College, Edinburgh; especially those of Fr. Roland Walls, then lecturer in Divinity and Dogmatics at the college. These tantalizing references to Julian were a breath of fresh air for students and lent a completely new insight into our understanding of Christian theology and life. We wanted to hear more.

In those days whenever we attempted to follow up on Julian by asking about her in gatherings of clerics or theologians, someone was always bound to reply, "Julian who? Never heard of him!" Worse still, some educated boors managed to confuse our Julian with Julian the Apostate, the infamous emperor of Rome who lived eleven centuries before, and who distinguished himself for all time as a persecutor of the Church. We therefore had to rely on mostly antiquated translations or inaccurate paraphrases which were in themselves difficult to unravel for the uninitiated. We attended clandestine "Julian groups" in homes, to discuss Julian's book. We felt like members of a sort of theological underground.

Today the picture is changing rapidly. Julian is better known now, and in recent months several publications have appeared offering fresh translations of her book or commentaries on her way of spirituality. Although she was never officially canonized, she has been added to the calendar of saints for the Church of England. In the United States, a religious order in the Episcopal Church has been named after her. Numerous dissertations are being directed in universities around the world, either touching on her theology or inspecting her literary style from new points of view. A play has even toured England and America, dramatizing Julian's life as a solitary and mystic.

For purposes of scholarship a major breakthrough occurred with the publication ten years ago of an annotated text; and more recently with a smaller edition of the medieval text for use by students. As a result of efforts by many friends of Julian, she is being recognized as one of England's most important mystics—perhaps *the* most important—as well as a significant figure in the evolution of English literature. She may have been the first woman to write a book in the English language. In a relatively short time, then, Julian has emerged as a popular mystic and as one of the most important Christian theologians of all time.

In the Introduction, I have taken up some questions which are of special interest to scholars (such as Julian's possible sources, her relation to the development of medieval scholastic theology and mysticism, her literary style and so forth). Much more is being said about these things today—perhaps too much—in journals and at conferences and seminars, for those who wish to investigate them further. I have tried here only to set out the main points as an introduction to what Julian wrote in her *Revelations*.

There would be no need for any introduction to her, in fact, if it were not that Julian wrote in a language and culture which are unfamiliar to us today. She was herself a clear and lyrical writer who did not get entangled in the subteties and confusions of the scholastic theology of her day. She wrote, she said, for her "even-Christian"—meaning, I think, friends who were working people like herself and who for the most part had no opportunity for religious instruction or indeed for education of any kind at all.

Julian did not consider herself to be a theologian or expert or even a writer. She says, if she may be believed, that she was illiterate—implying that, in its initial stages at least, her book was dictated to someone else who could write. Nevertheless it is always a source of wonder for anyone who is familiar with the *Revelations* that she managed to say so much in so few pages, with such grace. Itself little more than a hundred pages in modern edition, the *Revelations* is a classic which would require a much larger book than would be useful to most readers, to be explored at any depth. Where through oversight or in the interest of economy I have failed to cover the ground adequately, I beg the pardon of readers, especially those who are already familiar with Julian and whose expectations for any new work about her will naturally be high.

Some readers of Julian may feel, as I have, that she wrote especially for women, and particularly for women who suffer from exploitation or from situations of hopelessness or help-lessness. More needs to be said along these lines than I have been able to do here. Julian will be especially helpful, too, to those readers who grieve for loved ones or who themselves face the prospect, as she put it, of "an end to this mortal life."

It has sometimes been remarked that, in spite of her own experience of suffering, Julian is a "positive mystic" who seems in some respects unrealistic in today's world. For her all things *are* well, in her Lord. It must be admitted that in these pages too much emphasis may have been given to the positive side of Julian's experience. She is able to write, for example, about the important experience of being "naughted," or literally, "nothing-ed," in her spiritual journey. About this experience I have said very little, in part because by its nature little can be said about it which makes sense; and in part because few of us have entered into the depth of Julian's way of prayer in which she spent the greater part of her life—perhaps fifty years—in contemplation of the mysteries of God.

Finally, too much attention may have been paid here to the *Christian* experience of faith, or to *Christian* mysticism or the basic tenets of *Christian* theology. Perhaps it was inevitable in a work of this kind, which appears in a series on Christian mystics and which assumes that the reader is familiar with the nature of Christian faith and prayer. Experience has shown, however, that Julian is of great interest not only to Christians but also to friends of other faiths or of no faith at all. Julian provides an excellent introduction to the basic material of Christian faith and life, presented humbly without any hint of judgment for those who do not share her experience as a "daughter of Holy Church." She has therefore provided interesting reading for many who have no particular religious orientation but who nevertheless struggle with the deep questions of life. She is beginning to figure prominently in dialogues between Christians and Buddhists here in Asia, especially with relation to our various understandings of the nature of compassion, love, and humanity. She has also been helpful to many who are preparing themselves for baptism into the mystery of Christ.

What is important for Julian is not the backgrounds from which we have come but whether we seek to know God and are willing to respond to God's love; that is, whether we wish to know genuine human life, for the two are, in her point of view, inextricably bound up with one another. For Julian, the path to life is one of humility and compassion, which she calls the "kindness" of God, built into our own nature as creatures of God, from the time that we were made. Julian calls us from whatever walks of life in which we find ourselves and draws us into the love which is in God and which is God, and which (she says) was intended for us from "before any time."

Introduction

Lady Julian of Norwich, better known in her native England as "Mother Julian," was an anchoress who lived through the latter half of the fourteenth century. An anchoress is a type of nun, or laywoman, who lives in a small enclosure, never going out, and never abandoning her commitment to prayer for those who live around her. Her whole life is given to silence, to worship and to deep contemplation of the mysteries of God. In Julian's case, this life of silent enclosure evidently also included another dimension, that of spiritual counselor to pilgrims who came to seek her advice. Although she is usually referred to in anthologies as "Lady Julian" or "Dame Julian" (or Juliana), she was probably not a "Lady" in the sense of nobility. The various titles which have been attributed to her since the Middle Ages are more likely titles of respect which reflect her spiritual calling as an anchoress—rather like the title "Sister" for a nun.

Very little is actually known about Julian herself. By her own account, she was born in the fall of 1342. As for where she was born, or whether she ever married, or when she finally died—or even what her name was in secular life—nothing at all is known about these things, and anything we could say about them would amount to little more than an educated guess. What *is* known about Julian is that at the age of thirty and one-half, on May 8th or 13th, 1373 (the exact date is not clear), following a severe chest infection which lasted for one week, she died.

Then followed an extraordinary series of sixteen revelations, or "showings," in an experience which today we might call "life after life."[1] The showings included visions—especially the vision of Jesus' face as he hung on the cross—voices, conversations which were conducted as it were without the need for any speech at all; vivid impressions and mental images of various kinds, and "ghostly" or "inward" teachings or explanations about what she had seen. She also seems to have experienced something like out-of-body travel, in that she found herself suddenly at the bottom of the sea, then transported to the highest heavens, and through the wounded heart of Jesus into a beautiful city which she took to be within her own soul. Most important, she saw a profound and puzzling vision of a great lord and his servant, a vision which she understood to occupy a central place in the revelations as a whole, but which she could not understand.

About eleven hours after the visions began, Julian awoke "with a loud sound and a bang" to find herself very much alive but in considerable pain. Actually, she had not been asleep during the time of her showings, according to her own account, but seems to have been in various states of awareness of the circumstances of the room around her, and of the people who were tending her in her illness. In any case, as the showings ended she found that it was the following afternoon, sometime past the hour of Nones or three o'clock. At some point, she was visited by a parson, and joked with him about the "ravings" which she had experienced through the morning hours. But the parson took her "ravings" seriously, and the indiscretion of making light of the visions plunged her suddenly into feelings of guilt and remorse. Sometime later she fell asleep.

Immediately the visions resumed, and continued through the night. Initially she was asleep for the experience—this time without any of the beauty and sense of joy which had accompanied the earier showings—but awakened in her fright, and was evidently conscious through the remainder of the night. Now she was brought face-to-face with evil in the form of a "fiend" who, it seemed, was attempting to assault her in her bed. Next she thought the room had caught fire; then she heard strange cackling and whispering. She struggled with the sense of utter abandonment and despair, which she took to be the pains of hell itself; and fought to regain her footing by rehearsing the substance of her faith. Finally, with a word of encouragement from her Lord, Julian awoke once again and found that it was the following morning, some thirty hours after the showings had begun. She was indeed alive; and she had been healed. But more important, the experience had left her with an entirely new appreciation for the love of God and indeed for life itself.

Although Julian understood from the beginning that the visions, with the central parable of the lord and servant, were teaching her about the love and compassion of God, she did not at first grasp what the visions meant, nor why she in particular had received them. The whole effect, certainly, was one of love: that God loved her as Father, Mother, Brother, Spouse, Lover, and Friend, and wanted to communicate that love to her and to others through her. But it required some twenty years before she could work out the full implications of what she had seen.

A "Devout Woman" in Norwich

Sometime after her recovery, it is not known when, the woman later called "Julian" withdrew from public life and enclosed herself in single cell at St. Julian's church, Conisford (the "King's Ford"), a suburb of Norwich near the Wensum River. So far as is known, she remained there for the rest of her life, spending her days in prayer and quietly offering spiritual advice to those who came to see her. She evidently gained a reputation as a "devout woman living in Norwich," as we shall see; but the circumstances of her life as an anchoress can only be guessed from what is known about anchorites in general in her time.

The term "anchorite" stems from the Greek *anachoreo*, "to retire." Although the word does not really derive from "anchor" in the sense of a ship's anchor, as it sounds, nevertheless the life of the anchorite reminds us of something which is firmly anchored in one place. The anchorite vows never to abandon prayer, just as he or she never abandons the place for prayer. Some anchorites were therefore sealed into their houses, called "tombs," with brick walls, in a special enclosure ceremony. They ate food handed to them through a window for the purpose; through another window (called a "squint") they could observe Mass in the church nave adjacent to the cell; and through a third window, covered with a curtain with a cross cut out of its center, they could chat during certain hours with visitors. Their visits were, however, subject to rules of extreme modesty, and they normally visited only with persons of the same sex.[2]

The life of the anchorite was a highly regulated calling in the Church, following a tradition which stretches back to the third and fourth centuries in the lives of the so-called Desert Fathers and Mothers in Egypt. By the fourteenth century almost every aspect of the anchorite's life was governed by rules. These concerned manner of dress (modest and plain, usually black and white in color); food (one simple meal each day in the afternoon, with fasts during certain seasons); times for prayer and the specific kinds of prayers to be said; and so forth. Some anchorites in medieval England probably had a degree of outdoor recreation in the form of keeping a garden; A few may even have owned livestock, since some rules prohibit it (it would not have been seemly for an anchoress to chase her cow down the lane, for example). Some anchorites were allowed to step out of their enclosures for the Eucharist, but others would have chosen to remain inside at all times.

While there was no single book of rules which was universally recognized for anchorites, some guidebooks began to be widely circulated in the Middle Ages. In Norfolk there was the *Ancrene Riwle*, composed in the thirteenth century by an anonymous priest for three well-born women who wished to live an ascetical life. The *Riwle*, which was probably still followed in Julian's time, allows us to know in some detail the features of an anchorite's life in her day—if indeed it was kept in full. Its theological justification was taken from a variety of sources besides the Bible, including St. Gregory the Great (540-604), Anselm of Canterbury (1033-1109), and St. Bernard of Clairvaux (1090-1153). The rite of enclosure itself is not discussed in detail, but enough accounts have survived to give us an idea of what was required. The anchoress vowed herself to celibacy, obedience, and stability. It is interesting that she was not vowed to "poverty," although evidently most anchorites had only modest means. She would proclaim herself "dead" to the world, and after suitable readings and prayers by the Bishop, would be sealed up forever inside her dwelling.

It has long been a tradition in the Church that anyone who wished to follow a special calling such as that of a hermit or anchorite would be required first to "test" the calling through years of life in a monastic community. However, there were exceptions to this rule; and the anchorite need not have belonged to any of the established religious Orders in Julian's day. Because the anchorite vow was considered an Order to itself, subject to no one except the local bishop, it has sometimes been suggested that this arrangement would allow a degree of freedom which otherwise would not have been possible within the "system." An anchoress could talk with visitors, for example, while a nun could not. She lived in absolute isolation, with all the hardship that implies, but her life was on the other hand self-regulated and more or less unsupervised. In this way she enjoyed the blessing of the Church without having to conform to the wishes of the abbots and abbesses of the local convents. And the life of the anchorite could, more than any other calling in the Church, allow both for silence and solitude over long periods of time, and the opportunity to tell others about one's own understanding of the gospel and the Christian life.

It is known that through the early part of the fourteenth century, for a period of at least fifty years, there were no anchorites in Norwich. Exactly why is not known. Perhaps the vocation had simply died out as spiritual fervor waned. Some of the convents had, for example, become havens for the rich: a kind of finishing-school for well-born young ladies who would not, for whatever reasons, marry; or a place to go in early widowhood which could provide security. While the Benedictine convent at Carrow maintained an anchorhold and another one in nearby Conisford, it seems likely that these had fallen into dereliction. All this changed, however, towards the end of the century—perhaps following the example of a single anchorite who inspired others to take up the same vocation. This is exactly the time when Julian is first mentioned in historical documents as an anchoress in the city.

A will written in 1393 or 1394 mentions Julian as a beneficiary, as do several wills following at various intervals, sometimes referring to Julian by name and sometimes referring only to an anchoress who lived at "St. Julian's church" in Norwich. One will in 1404 mentions her servant Sara; another in 1415 refers to Sara as well as to Alice, "sometime her maid." A will in 1416 refers only to "Julian, recluz a Norwich;" hence we may assume that, if in 1416 Julian were not the only recluse in town or even the first in recent memory, she was at least well known, so that she did not require lengthy identification.

How long Julian remained at her cell next to St. Julian's is unknown. A confusion has sometimes been made between our Julian and another woman by that name who may have been one of the Benedictine sisters at Carrow, not far from Conisford. Julian Lampyt lived at the anchorhold at Carrow from 1426 until 1478, and is thought to have died around 1483. Although the two are easily confused in historical accounts, it seems safe to say that they could not have been the same woman—not unless our Julian lived to be 140 years old. More likely, Julian died soon after 1429, when the last will mentions an anchoress at St. Julian's in Conisford. She would have been 86 by that time.

Finally, it is natural to assume today that the little church in Conisford was named after Julian of Norwich, a local saint. Residents of Norwich will sometimes tell visitors that this was the case, especially as Julian is becoming better known. But this cannot have been because the evidence of the wills is that the little church was already "St. Julian's" before our Julian chose to live there. Undoubtedly the anchoress—whose name in secular life is completely unknown—named herself after the church where she made her profession. The "Julian" for whom the church was named is equally mysterious, but was probably Julian the Hospitaler, a legendary saint who was revered in the Middle Ages as especially hospitable to travelers by water.

The Revelations of Divine Love

Eventually Julian wrote—or dictated, in the event that she could not write—a little book which became known as the *Revelations* (or *Showings) of Divine Love*. This book has come down to us in two versions: a shorter version, which is a simple account of what she saw and experienced in the sixteen "showings" themselves; and a longer one, which reads more like a mature theological work, and which omits nearly all the references to Julian herself or to the actual circumstances of the visions. By comparing the content of the two versions scholars have reached the conclusion that the longer one was written later, perhaps as the result of years of meditation. The shorter account, once thought to have been an abridgement of the longer, was in fact more like a diary. It would have been written down soon after the actual events so that Julian would not forget the details of what she had seen.

It is possible that, like St. Teresa of Avila, Julian was directed to write down everything by her confessor, because of the obvious spiritual value of her insights. On the other hand, she tells us only that initially she was afraid to say anything about what she had seen. She tells us nothing about the actual circumstances of the book itself. However, the scribe's introduction to the last chapter in the Longer Version—which may or may not represent Julian's own words—explains the reason for the two different accounts:

> The good Lord showed that this book should be completed in a different way than at the first writing. And he wills that we should pray for his work, this way: thanking him, trusting and enjoying [ourselves] in him. And how he made this showing because he wills to have it known, in which knowledge he will give us the grace to love him. For fifteen years afterwards, it was answered that the reason for all these showings was love—which may Jesus grant us! (ch. 86)

For even during the visions themselves, Julian recognized that they were meant to be shared:

> In all this I was greatly stirred to charity towards my fellow-Christians, that they might see and know the same things that I saw; for I wanted it to be a comfort to them. For this whole vision was shown [to everyone] generally. (ch. 8)

The longer version of the *Showings* is itself not very long, only about one hundred pages in a modern paperback edition, and in Julian's day must not have been difficult to understand. The language is plain, not that of the scholastics. Julian several times refers to her "even-Christians," or fellow-Christians, for whom the book was intended. Her meaning here is evidently not the Church in the sense of an exclusive group, but rather the ordinary believers like herself, perhaps especially women, who otherwise would have been excluded from theological study.

Julian's choice of words is significant: we are *even*-Christians, that is, all equal and alike before God. This theme is developed in the *Revelations* very deliberately, obviously to counter the prevalent notion that all believers are arranged in an elaborate hierarchy of "beginners," "proficients," and "perfects"—a hierarchy that inevitably excluded women from the "higher" things, and which placed the (male) priesthood above the laity, and, at least in theory, the cloistered monks above the ordinary priests. For Julian, the message of love which she received was intended from the start for those poor and uneducated who would have been most troubled by the questions of divine wrath, the judgment, of death and suffering, and how to live a decent life in the midst of a world full of turmoil and uncertainty.

In this longer work Julian mentions that she did not fully understand the visions for nearly twenty years. During this time she continued to experience supernatural assurances of God's grace, and teachings about divine love—and also about the original visions themselves. She refers obliquely to these supernatural events as "touchings"; but she does not tell us what kind of "touchings" she had, probably because she did not want to gain a reputation for unusual holiness or special favor.

> This showing does not make me good, unless I love God better. And if you love God more than I do, it is more [valuable] to you than it was to me. I am not saying this for those who are wise, because they know it well already; but I say it to you who are simple, for your ease and comfort, for we are all one in love. For in truth, it was not showed to me that God loved me better than the least soul that is in grace. And I am sure that there are many who have never had showings or visions, but only the common teachings of the Church, who love God better than I. (ch. 9)

A Theology of Kindness

If we could summarize Julian's contribution to theology in the *Revelations*, we would have to say that she formulated a theology of divine love. All Christians, of course, believe at least theoretically that "God is love," and to say that Julian's theology is distinctive in this respect needs further explanation. For Julian, the love of God was revealed in terms of divine *humility*; or, for want of a better word, what we may call the "kindness" of God.

We must not take "kindness" for granted here, because it is, in fact, significantly absent in much of popular theology today, as it must have been in Julian's time. For whatever we may say about the love of God, we live in an age which inevitably depicts suffering, death, and natural disasters as "acts of God." On the other hand, contemporary culture tends not to trust that God could be "kind," or that there is compassion in the Christian idea of the creator of the universe—a creator who is viewed, for the most part, as outside the affairs of this life altogether. When Julian speaks of the "kindness" of God, she does not mean it in an ordinary way. It is not "kindness" in the sense of a distant God who is benign but affectionate—an insipid kind of charity which, in popular religion today, is said to radiate from heaven. This would be kindness in a false sense, no more than a pretense at love which seeks to deny both the power of God and the necessity for human response.

For Julian, true kindness (or "kind-hood") is something else altogether, something which involves more than emotions or sentiment, and certainly more than a distant, if unpredictable, creator. True kindness implies, rather, a personal relationship with someone who cares for us and who has the power to affect our lives directly. It is a relationship in which there is no sense of superiority on one side or of guilt on the other; or else it is not really kindness, but patronization. Kindness involves our inner being: not "love" in the sense of sentiment or passing fancy, but a deep inbuilt disposition to charity which does not change through time. In this latter sense, Julian depicts "kindness," first of all in terms of the being of God, and then in terms of human nature itself, showing how human beings are meant to be transfigured in love, to share in the joy and outgoing charity which is God.

Julian's first premise, always more or less implicit in the *Revelations* and fundamental to her theological outlook, is that the love of God is identical with the being of God. Love, therefore, is not something which God *has* or *does*; it is not a "virtue" or a property of God. Nor is love something which God can decide to give here and withhold there. It cannot be uneven, or pass away. Love is, quite simply, what God *is*, in the mystery of the Trinity. It is defined by the way in which the Father, Son, and Spirit live in one another and work in one another, such that the Three are in fact perfectly One in their being.

Julian argues, then, that the love of God is shared with humanity in our creation, and that (therefore) we may be said to share the divine nature, which nature is always to love. Our lives are meant to be a process of growing into maturity in love, growing more and more into the likeness of God whose image we already bear in our creation. Julian's vision of divine love in relation to humanity is so far positive and ebullient. She frequently refers, for example, to the joy which is in God and of God's purpose for us to enjoy life. She is also fully aware, however, of the hideous reality of evil, and of the resultant suffering which is ours in this life. She understands these things, however, to be whatever is not-God—leading, ultimately, to death, which is the opposite of the life which is in God. Thus, Julian may be said, in the technical language of theology, to have constructed an argument about love which is *ontological* (from the Greek word for "being"), as opposed to the more psychological approach to love which we usually have today. We will see that love, for Julian, is built into the nature of God and of ourselves, our *being*, which is always in God and which God is.

It will be necessary for a moment to examine Julian's use of the word "kindness" because originally it had a double meaning which is valuable to us today. As English developed into its own language at about the time Julian was writing, the term *kynde*—borrowed from Anglo-Saxon, with parallel roots in Latin—had to do with "nature" or "family." We can still see its remnant in the German *Kind* ("child"), and in modern English conversation: as, for example, when we speak of our "kin" or of "human*kind*" or of a certain type of animal "and its kind," meaning of the same ilk or species. For Julian, "kind-hood" had to do, first of all, with nature, and especially with our own nature as human beings. At the same time, the word also had to do with goodness or gentleness, that is, being loving and humble (which Julian also identifies with "courtesy"). The link between the two meanings of "kynde" is not altogether clear, but perhaps it had to do with the idea that it is natural to be kind (*i.e.*, good-hearted); or that we are naturally kind to members of our own family (our own "kind"). In any case, the ambiguity of the word has survived into modern English, in that the noun "kind" means "type" or "species," whereas the adjective means "gentle," "good," and so forth.

We can ask, then, the philosophical question, "What kind of person is kind?" Julian would answer, "one who loves God"— because God *is* kindness, and in her words "the very mother [source] of kinds." Taking "kind" in its double sense, we may understand by this, first of all, that whatever we think of as "kindness" (goodness) is actually a reflection of the presence of God, who is working the divine will there; and second, that what we perceive as *true human nature*—that is, what we ought to be, our mature "self"—is also a reflection of God and is located in God. Julian goes further, to say that all species ("kinds") of creatures come from God, and in that sense share in the Being of God insofar as they have being at all. For it is God to whom we commonly refer somewhat unthinkingly as "nature;" and in fact God is at work in all things, continuously creating them and upholding them.

The implications of this line of reasoning are great, and so need to be understood carefully. For example, Julian's argument would mean not only that "God is love" in some distant or abstract sense, but that the love of God is immediately present in everything which *is*, simply because it exists. It would mean that everyone who loves, regardless of cultural or religious background, and whether conscious of it or not, has come into contact with God and indeed is experiencing something of God. It also means that human *nature* is of itself divine—or, as Julian puts it, is "knit" to the divine nature. Our true nature (our "kind") is hidden in God, and God is within our own nature. Julian's understanding of kindness, then, can be simply illustrated by saying that it is *natural* to be *kind*.

But what about sin—the obvious inhumanity, so to speak, of humankind? Julian would say that all cruelty, all injustice and whatever we commonly think of as "sin," is both *unkind* and *unnatural*. It represents a distortion of our true nature, a falling-short of our capacity to be something else. Our capacity, as human beings, is to live in the image of God. We are created for God's love. Instinctively we know this—as, for example, when we admire a mother's love for her nursing child, or when we "fall in love" ourselves. But we soon lose sight of our own nature at the slightest provocation, and the divine image is obliterated in us by sin, or what Julian calls "contrariness" and "wrath" in this life. It is joylessness, a blackness or heaviness which obscures what we really are and can be. Our true nature, however, is perfectly visible in Jesus, who is the image of God, whom we cannot see. In the same way, the true nature of sin—which is ultimately hidden from us, as created beings—is nevertheless clearly visible in the stained and battered face of Jesus on the cross.

For Christians, Julian's view of kindness has important implications for the way in which we understand the incarnation of the Son of God. First, we need not say that the Son of God became human in spite of his divine nature, as if divinity and humanity were opposites (the almost universal assumption of Western Christianity perhaps since Augustine, and at least since the Reformation). Rather, Jesus may be said to be fully human because of his divine nature, and vice-versa. Here a question which has sometimes plagued theologians, especially in the West, appears to be resolved. It has not always been clear to the faithful how to understand what is meant by St. Paul in Philippians 2:7ff., where he says that Christ "emptied himself." One interpretation, that the Son of God left behind his divine nature altogether, has been suggested from time to time, and found acceptance especially among certain Protestants in the last century; but it was condemned as heretical by the Church very early, on the obvious grounds that in the New Testament Jesus is regarded as divine. Likewise, the Church also rejected the opposite notion—popular among many pious Christians even today—that Jesus simply restrained himself from using his divine powers in public, that is, that he only *appeared* at times to suffer, or to doubt, or to be ignorant of future events and the like.

To this dilemma, Julian responds that there is no inherent contradiction between the "emptiness" of the Son of God and his divinity. Jesus is both fully God and fully man; but it is God's nature to be "self-empty" or, in her own words, "humble" and "courteous." Therefore, it was natural for the Son of God to empty himself, even to the point of death, without ceasing to be divine.

A second implication for our understanding of Christian faith is that salvation in Christ does not ultimately depend upon what we know about Jesus (called "saving knowledge" in many churches today), nor even upon what Jesus did on the cross, as a single act of salvation. Rather, salvation depends upon Jesus' identity as the true human being. He is *our* nature; in him our humanity is lifted up into the divine being, and in him we are "knit" to God. This "knitting" took place before we ever knew of it, even before we were born, and so it involves much more than our own decision or faith, or even the event of the crucifixion itself.

Julian's understanding of salvation differs here from what many of us will have learned in our upbringing in the Church , and so has to be investigated critically. For Julian, salvation is not an "either/or" category. There is no specific moment in which a person has "gotten saved," unless it is the moment of the incarnation of the Son of God. Rather, our own salvation is an organic process, something like growing up into adulthood.

While from the divine point of view our salvation could, perhaps, be said to take place as a single "event" in Christ, it is nevertheless a cosmic event which includes the creation of the world, the incarnation of the Son of God, his crucifixion and resurrection, and our own birth and coming-to-faith. For our part, salvation involves many things which together lead to our becoming one with God. Atonement is literally a process of at-one-ment (the original intent of the medieval word, which

Julian renders as "oneing"). It is a growth into one-ness with God, and also into the fulness of our own humanity.

All this takes the whole of our lives, however long or short they may be. It involves the joys and delights which we experience, as well as the sufferings and bitter disappointments; the things we take for granted, such as eating and drinking, tasting, seeing, touching, hearing—all of which teach us about God—as well as significant events such as birth, marriage, or death. In short, God is at work in everything, at every moment, drawing us into the divine nature in every possible way. God is in everything. "He is the ground," Julian says, of life and love, because God is life itself. It is interesting that this concept of salvation, as healing or wholeness, actually recaptures the biblical intent of the word, which inevitably refers to "healing" and "wholeness" in the languages of the scriptures and of early Church theology.

Another important conclusion of this line of reasoning is that, since God's own nature is to be "kind," it is impossible for God to be unkind (or not-God). Julian says, therefore, that in the whole of her visions she never experienced wrath from God. Indeed she says, "It is impossible for God to be wroth." Julian goes on to argue that usually, when we picture God as wrathful, harsh, condemning, or arbitrary, it is not a picture of God at all, but of ourselves. The blame which we ascribe so easily to God is blame which is generated by our own sinfulness or, as she calls it, our "contrariness" to the love of God.

Julian's assertion that she saw no wrath in God has sometimes been taken amiss by readers who insist that the God of the Bible—of the Old Testament, at least—is undeniably a "God of wrath." Their inference is that Julian either was unaware of what the Bible says about divine wrath, or else chose to ignore it—wanting, rather simplistically, for God to be "all love." But this is to miss the point both of Julian's theological insight, and also of the Bible itself.

As we explore Julian's understanding of divine love, we will see that she is not unaware of indignation in God. She says, in other words, that because God is Truth and Goodness itself, there is an eternal opposition between God and whatever is not-God: specifically, whatever would seek to destroy goodness and love in this life. This eternal opposition of divine love to evil is so great that, as Julian is suddenly warned at one point in her showings, she must make no mention of sin and evil in the presence of God—for mention is made neither of the devil nor of those who serve him, in God's sight. Julian is taught in fact to scorn the "fiend" altogether; not that God reviles Satan, but that we, as created beings, should not be afraid to scorn evil because it is hateful in God's sight. This is divine "wrath" in the biblical sense, and it is a necessary corollary to truth.

We may note here that if Julian composed her *Revelations* sometime after she began her life as an anchoress, she rehearsed the wrath of God every day more than once as she repeated the psalms which were part of her daily prayers. One of these is Psalm 6 (in modern enumeration). It is the first of the so-called "Penitential Psalms" which are part of the anchoress' daily Office or prescribed prayers. In a medieval English translation contemporary with Julian, it begins with the words:[3]

> Lord, repreue thou not [me] in thy strong veniaunce; neither chastise thou me in thine ire!

Another, Psalm 38, begins with the same words; and still another prayer which the anchoress would recite daily included these words:[4]

> Lord, when thou shalt come to judge the earth, where shall I hide from the face of thy wrath? For I have sinned full much in my life...I dread my trespasses, and I am ashamed before thee; when thou shalt come to judgment, condemn me not.

At least two points could be added here relating to Julian's understanding of divine wrath. First is that Julian is simply telling us what she did *not* experience in her visions. As we shall see, it appears that her expectation at the moment of death was to pass through judgment, which she took to be synonymous with "blame." But in her actual experience, God was not condemning and was not interested in blaming her for her sins. While it would appear that Julian took this generally to refer to the nature of God (that God does not blame sinners), it is also quite clear, as Julian says again and again, that she took her experience to refer to "those who are being saved." In other words, she cannot hazard a guess about what the "wrath" of God might be for those who serve the "fiend" and actively oppose the love of God; but she is quite clear that her own experience—and that for any soul who is in charity, who desires the goodness of God—was not of divine wrath, but of divine love and compassion. Second, Julian makes a distinction between "wrath" in the sense which we have described it above—the eternal hatred which God has for whatever would destroy life—and the "wrath" which is commonly ascribed to God, especially by those who do not trust the love and forgiveness of God.

In the popular imagination, it would appear that the "wrath of God" often means an arbitrariness on God's part: the willingness or even the desire of God to reward some creatures (perhaps without any basis) and to punish others eternally. While Julian will hold to the idea that eternal bliss, or salvation, ultimately depends upon God's own purpose, nevertheless she rejects the popular picture of God as a wrathful judge who is waiting to punish the helpless creature. She points out that in this sinful life, we sometimes experience rage—a frenzy of helplessness which leads to the desire for retribution and a loss of judgment. It is contrary, destructive, and self-centered. This kind of "wrath" always implies blame: we blame others, usually for the faults which are in ourselves. This is the sort of "wrath" which we attribute all too casually to God, whereas, in fact, it is something in ourselves, which is the product of our own sin. Thus, she concludes that it is impossible for God to be "wroth" in the sense which we know it in this life.

It is important to realize that the Church never understood the God of the Old Testament to be a God of wrath, and especially not in contrast somehow to the God of the New

Testament. The heretic Marcion, condemned by the Church in the second century, taught that there were actually two different gods: an evil one, evident in the stories of the Old Testament, and a good one, manifest in Jesus Christ. Marcion's ideas were never accepted by the Church, and could hardly be compatible in any case with Christian faith, on numerous grounds. For Julian, at least, faith is precisely to recognize that God is compassionate, and desires only for us to enjoy this life, and this life in God; and so to put aside our fears of retribution once and for all, in the name of Christ. This does not mean that we lose sight of sin as contrary to the nature of God or even to our own nature (to sin more, as the saying goes, so that grace might abound); but that we learn to hate sin and to love God, so that we might experience fully the joy of life both now and in the age to come.

Evil and Non-Being

A corollary to Julian's discussion about wrath (which she did not see in God) is her deep understanding of the reality of sin and of evil. We have said that for Julian sin represents a distortion of our own nature. However, Julian points out that she could not see sin itself, but only the negative effects of sin. This was because, as she understood it, sin does not have any positive "substance." It is not even, technically speaking, the wrong things we do in this life which we commonly call "sins." For Julian sin is, rather, a "non-deed." It is, in other words, the *absence* of joy and life in the Spirit of God. It is not what we do, but the condition in which we find ourselves in a world infected by evil. It is, therefore, a kind of sickness which affects our whole lives. With any disease, it is not actually the disease which we see, but the symptoms of the disease. In the same way, sin itself is hidden deep in our souls; what we call "sins" are the symptoms of the *sin* which has to be cured, if we are to live fully and joyfully.

Similarly, and somewhat paradoxically for the modern reader, Julian argues that evil itself does not actually have any being in the positive sense of sharing existence. This is because all that *is* shares in the being of God; but God is not evil. This is not to say that evil is only an idea in our minds, that it is an illusion—a concept which Julian is sometimes said to have taught, but which is actually foreign to the *Revelations*. What she does say is that evil is a dark and powerful force which has its power precisely in the fact that it *is not*. Evil, therefore, is impossible for us to understand because we cannot even see it and, as created beings in the image of God, have no real way to measure it for ourselves.

The idea that evil could be non-being (called *mē ōn* in Greek) was argued by theologians in the Church from earliest times. The Church soon recognized the dilemma, much discussed in Greek philosophy, that if God is both good and the source of all that exists, then God could not be the source of evil itself; otherwise, God could not be called "good." Some proponents of religion, especially in India and the East, were prepared to argue that God is indeed the source of evil, or that evil is mixed with good (insofar as it has being), or that there are essentially two Gods, one good and one evil; Christians were not prepared to argue this.[5] Julian put it simply in her assertion that "God does not sin."

It may be that Julian was familiar with the idea of evil as non-being as it derived from the works of St. Augustine. The idea, however, had also found its way into medieval thinking through the popular writings of an ancient mystic called "St. Denys" (thought in the Middle Ages to be the same "Dionysius" who is mentioned in the book of Acts, but now known as "Pseudo-Dionysius"). This writer, a Greek or Syrian monk who probably lived near the beginning of the sixth century produced a series of mystical treatises which were introduced to the West in Latin translation during the ninth century. Although his works did not become popular until after the twelfth century, they had a profound influence on Western theology and spirituality as a whole, including the thought of the great scholastics such as St. Thomas Aquinas. The idea that evil tends toward non-being is essential to Pseudo-Dionysius' thought, as it is to many early writers. Whatever Julian's source, she can be said on this point to have a more or less traditional point of view. A problem for the modern reader is that today the idea finds little place in our ordinary way of thinking.

To say that something *is* without having any real being is difficult to understand. The idea is actually important, however, in modern science, especially in the fields of astrophysics and (on the other end of the cosmic scale) of sub-atomic theory. For example, the recent discovery of "black holes" in outer space offers a sobering parallel to what Julian had in mind. Sin is like these pockets of darkness whose existence cannot be positively measured, but which paradoxically are dense concentrations of mass focussed entirely upon themselves, seeking to pull all other beings nearby into themselves. They emit no light; they are not "there," though their presence is absolutely destructive. Or, at the opposite extreme of existence, we may think of certain hypothetical particles in atomic theory such as anti-matter which for the purpose of calculation could be "there" and at the same time "not there," in the sense of having any measurable presence or positive being, as we can understand it.

It is significant that for Julian, sin and evil do not have any ultimate power. There are not two Gods, but only one; and the God who created all that is has the last word even over what "is not." Thus Julian can conclude, in a famous passage which is both comforting and disturbing, that even sin is "behovable"; that is, that sin and the suffering which results from it, though they are absolutely hateful in the sight of God, are nevertheless somehow useful and even valuable in the outworking of God's love and compassion in our lives. In the end, Julian says, we shall see that this arrangement was for the best. God will put all things right, and the time will come when we shall see for ourselves that

> all shall be well, and all shall be well, and all manner of things shall be well.

Having said that for Julian all things will turn out to be "well" in the end, and that even sin is within the control of God, and that God is all goodness and "kindness," we cannot say on the other hand that Julian's very positive theology tries to skip over human responsibility for sin, or even the existence of a hell. Julian understands hell, however, in terms of an estrangement from the joy and life which are in God. Hell is

an abysmal absence of divine love which, in a curious way, is
evidently willed by some human beings. The punishment which
is in hell is the pain of sin itself, chiefly blame and despair
which, as we have said, originate not in God but with ourselves.
Its end result is bitterness and an utter hopelessness which
cannot coexist with the joy and outgoing love which is in God.
"In hell," Julian is told, "there is despair"—a greater form of
suffering than any other in this life.

Although Julian tried in the course of her visions to pursue
the whole question of eternal damnation, she could not manage
to obtain any answers in the sense of proofs of hell's existence,
or visions of its exact nature. Julian notes too that she did not
see purgatory, although she leaves it unclear whether she means
to say that purgatory itself does not exist, or merely that she
did not encounter it. Furthermore, she is warned specifically
against trying to investigate the whole subject any further,
especially when she attempts to learn the fate of a beloved
friend. On the other hand, Julian does experience in the final
"showing" a sense of utter abandonment and the pains of
self-blame and hopelessness, which she takes to be like the
pains of hell. Through this experience she concludes that in
God there is no desire to blame us—which blame would not in
any case accomplish the healing of the sinner—but that, as we
have said, these things result from our own participation in
evil and can destroy the life and joy which God has intended
for us. Our aim, therefore, should be to discover the goodness
of God, and of life itself, and not to inquire into the things we
cannot understand, which must remain "secrets" in God.

The Judgment

These observations bring us to another central point in
Julian's theology, in which she appears at first somewhat
ambiguous. Since Julian says that our true nature is grounded
in God, and that God is only Good, and that God is at work in
all things—even to the extent of using our sin to work a divine
purpose—may we then say that all people are somehow
"saved" and are inevitably being drawn into God? Some critics
at least have understood Julian in this way, with the result that

she has sometimes been condemned for holding to an idea of "universal salvation;" or has been praised, on the other hand, by readers who see all religions as somehow equally valid or as leading to the same goals or salvation. Either point of view, however, would fail to represent Julian fairly. In fact she does not seem to answer the question of universal salvation at all, though we may say that the theme of the Last Judgment is absolutely central to the *Revelations* and is a question which she continually had in mind.

From what we have already said, it should be clear that Julian does not understand all persons to be equally "saved"—sharing, that is, in the process of salvation. It is true that for her, all who are being saved in Christ are equal in God's sight. But it is not true that all people are what she would call "lovers of God" or "souls-to-be-saved." Julian is aware of the coming Judgment, and of those whom she calls the "heathen," who are outside the Church. Perhaps in a different category are those whom she calls "servants of the fiend," who actively oppose the love of God. Julian is familiar, too, with the curious medieval notion that the number of the saved is equal to the number of fallen angels in hell, an idea put forward by St. Anselm.[6] On the other hand, she avoids the question entirely, in the sense that she is warned against seeking to understand who is being "saved" and who is not. She constantly reminds us that her visions were of "the souls to be saved;" in other words, of the Church on earth, which she understood to be some souls and not others. However, of those who are not being "saved" she is shown nothing at all. (An exception is her insight, significant for her time, that God does not despise the Jews any more than he does other sinners, even though they were popularly held responsible for the crucifixion of Jesus).

About the judgment itself, Julian concludes that we will see it to be right and fair; and that, moreover, in the final judgment all things *will be made right*. This last point deserves some attention in itself, because the argument is uniquely Julian's. Put simply, she argues that the "Doom" (as it was known in her day) is much more than a separation of the faithful from the unfaithful, or a condemnation of the unrepentant. It will involve a new divine act in itself, something comparable to what we already understand to be the act of salvation in the birth, death, and resurrection of Christ.

In this sense there are not one, but two "great Deeds" which God has accomplished in order to bring about our atonement. Julian hints that the first of these is understood only in part, in this life; it is the redemption which we have in Christ, as taught by the Church. But the other "Deed" is absolutely hidden from us. It is not even known in heaven, because it is "not yet." Nevertheless it is of equal importance with the atonement which is to take place in Christ. Thus, Julian elevates the traditional theological theme of eschatology (the "Last Things") to a much more important place than it usually occupies in theology; and she reminds us, somewhat bluntly, that whatever concepts we might hold about salvation, hell, the judgment, and so on, are ultimately inadequate. Even the teachings of the Church on these points, while they are absolutely true as Julian sees it, are nevertheless only true *insofar as they go.* They are necessarily incomplete, because the end is "not yet." We have not seen the end of the story, in which we shall see for ourselves that everything is well and that God has indeed made everything to be well.

Christ, Our Mother

Finally, we come to an element of Julian's theology which is as central to her thought as it is startling to the modern reader. It is the idea, touched upon earlier, that Christ is—in a very real sense—our divine Mother. While the Bible speaks of God as "Father" (specifically, for Christians, as the "Father of our Lord Jesus Christ"), Julian can say that "as truly as God is our Father, so just as truly God is our Mother" (ch. 59). To understand Julian here it will be important to recognize what she is *not* saying—for example, that there is either maleness or femaleness in the Trinity, or that we should think of the Father of Christ rather in female terms—as it is to recognize what she *is* saying about the nature of our creation and salvation in Jesus Christ.

The idea of God as Mother is in fact biblical, though it may be unfamiliar to many of us because it has been, for whatever reasons, consistently overlooked in modern times. Isaiah and others of the prophets, for example, refer to God as the Mother of Israel, and the theme is present in various strands of Jewish and Christian theology from the beginning.[7] It is possible that Julian was familiar with the works of St. Anselm, writing in the eleventh century, whose meditations touch on the idea that Christ is like a nursemaid to the faithful. Meister Eckhart, who taught in the century before Julian, had also referred to Christ as "mother." Julian, however, develops the idea carefully into a consistent theology of creation and salvation: a theology in which creation and salvation are not separated or viewed as distinct acts of God, but are seen as part of a single process of drawing the soul into God. Here, God is best understood (as Julian sees it) in feminine terms; for in creation God has given birth to us, so to speak; and in the flesh of Christ God has embraced us, seeking to heal us when we fall into sin, and to unite us with the divine nature as mature human beings.

For Julian, then, Christ is our "Mother" because he has given us birth and also re-birth. In the incarnation, our flesh is permanently bonded to God, and we are created "in" Christ. In the cross and resurrection, we are re-born and perfected. Jesus has given us mortal life, which is pre-eminently his to give. In the sacrament of the Church, he feeds us with his own blood, which pours from his side like milk from a mother's breast. Like a true mother, he seeks to take our pains from us by bearing them himself. All this he does in order to rear us to maturity, to share in the mystery of love which is God. While the "Motherhood" of God reflects primarily the role of the Son of God in the incarnation and in his intercession for us, Julian also sees it as intrinsic to the Being of the Trinity. To understand her thought here will require a chapter in itself, both because the idea is central to her theology and because it is easily misunderstood. But we can see immediately that if God is "Mother" for Julian, it is impossible for her to think of God as a distant or forbidding judge who seeks to condemn or destroy the creation which God has made.

A Joyful Mystic

As a mystic and theologian of the Church Julian ranks with

the most significant in the West, certainly in England. While some of her important conclusions may sound novel to us today because we are not used to hearing them, Julian's *Revelations* actually provides a concise summary of traditional Christan faith and spirituality. Julian presents this in terms of three dimensions of divine love, which are expressed in the individual who loves God: Love which is uncreated (the Holy Trinity); love which is created (in the incarnation of the Son of God); and love which is given or shared (the work of the Holy Spirit in the Church).

These three dimensions of divine love cannot be separated from one another, but represent a kind of "reaching out" or ecstatic movement of God, so to speak, in which the divine nature—which is the joy of shared Love—is shared with human beings. It is a movement "from Love, to love, in love." This sharing is the essence of Julian's mysticism, which we may call the ecstatic love of God.

Julian is indeed a positive mystic, full of light and joy. She speaks constantly of the delight of knowing God; of God's own desire for us to "enjoy" him and to enjoy life itself; of Jesus' delight in dying for us on the cross, and of his endless joy in sharing life with us, and even our pains. Throughout the text she refers more than fifty times to "joy," "bliss,""blessedness," "cheer," and their source in God. Thus, the normal Christian life, in her view, is one of affirmation and outgoing love, of praise, of thanksgiving, of grace, of peace (which is more than mere rest, but a kind of active enjoyment of God), and of "bliss." It is hardly life-denying—that is the activity of the "fiend"—but always life-affirming. It is honest, forthright, earthy and practical, sensual (in a positive sense, not "lustful"), and supremely natural.

Julian's emphasis on joy and light may be surprising to some readers who would otherwise associate Christianity with severity and gloom, or mysticism with an experience of the "dark night." Julian, however, is here typical of Christian mystics in general, especially as they may be seen in the Eastern Church, but also in the West, particularly in the tradition of English spirituality. She does describe the experience of intense doubt and temptation, of separation from God (which, later on in Western mysticism came to be known as a "dark night" of the soul); she says, for example, that some of her visions were "murky as night" or "mistily shown," and that she knew the experience of spiritual dryness. But she immediately moves on to the life which was given to her in the Holy Spirit. "Faith is a light," she says, "and this light is love." For her it is unthinkable that the God, who made all that is and who is life itself, should be known only in darkness or obscurity. As we will see, she identifies a kind of "dread" which sometimes passes for piety (fearing hell, and wanting to move on to the next life); but it is not really from God, though God may use it in drawing us to himself. True mysticism is to know the light and joy of God as surely as we know our own soul.

But now a word of warning is in order. It has become fashionable these days to read books about mystics, and especially about women mystics who were previously little-known or whose works have only recently been published in English. The desire to know about the mystics of the Church is commendable enough, but it is questionable whether we are prepared, culturally or spiritually, to receive what we find there. There is always a certain danger in reading books about mystics (including this one), for at least two reasons: we will almost surely misinterpret some of what the mystic has to say, even with the best of intentions; and we risk misunderstanding the Christian mystic altogether if we do not share something of his or her life in the Church.

The final pages of one manuscript of the *Revelations* contains a warning, probably written by a scribe but reflecting an intimate knowledge of Julian's own work:[8]

> I pray almighty God that this book will not fall into [any-one's] hands except those who will be his [God's] faithful lovers, and to those who will submit themselves to the faith of Holy Church, and obey the wholesome understanding and teaching of those men who are of a virtuous life, sober years and profound learning. For this revelation is high divinity and high wisdom, and therefore it cannot dwell with him that is a slave to sin and to the devil. And beware that you do not take one thing according to your affection and liking, and leave aside something else; for that is the sign of a heretic. But take everything together with the rest,

> and truly understand that all is according to Holy Scripture, and grounded in the same...

The advice is sound. Julian's ideas, as the scribe warns, can be easily misunderstood, especially without sound spiritual guidance and discipline. Here the scribe simply reiterates an ancient teaching of the Church, that we cannot hope to understand the things of God unless we commit ourselves to God first and are willing to live accordingly. Otherwise, we open ourselves to the dangers of spiritual pride, of misunderstanding, and of spiritual harm by attempting to walk where the mystics have gone, but without their grounding in faith and their practice in prayer.[9]

For the modern scholar there is, in addition, the danger of wishing for our favourite mystic or saint always to have been "right." Julian herself warns readers to test what they read against the teaching of the Church and against "holy writ." We must feel free to differ with Julian and to challenge her, or else we cannot expect to have read her carefully—nor to have understood her own principle, that love of God must always come before our interest in the point of view of one particular saint—in this case, a woman who saw herself as "feeble and frail."

Mystical Union with God

Having said this, we now turn to the essential point of Julian's understanding of union with God—a point on which she must be understood carefully. We have said that Julian calls the process of union with God "oneing," a forerunner of the modern word "atonement." Literally these terms mean at-one-ment with God. We may understand it as a mystery of "profound identification" (to borrow a term from Chinese Taoist tradition), in which we remain uniquely who we are, as creatures of God, but without any separation being made from God's side which would divide us from himself. We should be careful to note here that in the teaching of the Church, the model for this union of the soul to God is the mystery of the Trinity itself: a communion in which the creature is not confused with God, any more than the Persons of the Trinity (Father, Son, and Spirit) are confused with one another; and in which the creature and the Creator are not separated, any more than the divine Persons are separated from one another. Julian, then, describes her experience this way (speaking of the "soul-to-be-saved"):

> ...And I saw no difference between God and our substance; but, as it were, all God. And yet my understanding took it that our substance is in God: that is to say, that God is God, and our substance is a creature in God. (ch. 54)

It would be worth pointing out here that the great mystics of the Church have not been, for the most part, particularly unusual people. Contrary to what we may imagine, they are not usually people who have experienced strange things all their lives. They have ordinary vocations, grow up in the ordinary ways, and remain entirely human: a bit foolish, perhaps, but not removed from the world. Julian, as we shall see, articulates the desire—which is always the desire of the true mystic—to draw closer in love *to the world itself*, to experience it as a "grace" from God; to love "all that God loves," for God's sake. In this, the mystic is not likely to be vague at all. The so-called mystical experience is inevitably one which provides clear thought and a clarity of vision which may be startling or impressive even to the skeptical observer.

All great Christian writers and theologians have been mystics of this type, beginning with the men and women who figure in the New Testament. St. Paul, often characterized today in terms of modern theological ideas, is better understood as a Jewish mystic who saw in Jesus the presence of the unseen God. Paul asserted then that "it is no longer I who live, but Christ who lives in me."[10] Peter, the fisherman who left his nets to follow Jesus, also describes what is meant by Christian mysticism in the opening paragraphs of II Peter, which promise that we can "escape the corruption that is in the world ... and become partakers of the divine nature." St. John, called "the Divine" in the Eastern Church, is regarded as the mystic *par excellence*, as where he expounds the teaching that the Father and the Son would come to make their home in anyone who would believe. Similarly, Julian relates the experience of discovering the Trinity dwelling within her own soul, and the promise that the love of God created within her would shape her into the fulness of humanity which is in Christ. In this sense, she saw herself as an ordinary Christian, nothing more, sharing a message of divine love which is available to even the most ordinary believer.

With these points in mind, we may say that Julian's importance as a mystic is due not so much to her experience of extraordinary phenomena—including her visions of May, 1373—as to her theologial position. We have mentioned that Julian did evidently continue to experience signs of God's grace and presence throughout her life, following her recovery from near-death. It is possible too that, like Thérèse of Lisieux, Julian had a profound awareness of God even as a child. But she did not regard these things as very important, and so she does not tell us anything about them except to say that they did not make her better in God's sight than anybody else. They were not, in her view, signs of God's special favor, but simply graces which God had given in order to teach her, and others through her. Nor was she, so far as we know, one of those unusual persons who floated in the air or who manifested supernatural phenomena such as the stigmata or auras of light. Her feet were firmly planted on the ground, and in her writing she uses images from the daily chores which she evidently knew such as babysitting, washing clothes, mending, knitting, and the like. These things also make her typical, really, of the great mystics and, in her view at least, an "even-Christian."

Classifying Julian's Theology

Among the great writers and mystics of the Church, however it is not easy to classify Julian—not only because she was a woman, and not one of the scholastics of her time, but also because she evolved a style and point of view which, though soundly orthodox, are nevertheless refreshing and unique. She provides a kind of bridge between diverse styles and periods of theological writing. Experts in the theology of Augustine, for example, have tended to see in Julian a fair amount of Augustinian theology—although she never quotes from "St. Austin" directly, nor indeed so far as anyone can tell, from any other Doctor of the Church.[11] Carmelites, on the other hand, tend to think of Julian as Carmelite, prefiguring by some two hundred years the insights of Sts. Teresa of Ávila and John of the Cross on prayer and spirituality. Dominicans find in Julian strong echoes of St. Thomas Aquinas, in the *Summa Theologiae* and of Meister Eckhart, who died about sixteen years before Julian was born. Carthusians have noted strains (as they thought) of William of St.-Thierry; Benedictines point out apparent references to the works of St. Benedict; Franciscans most justifiably discern a Franciscan joy and technical vocabulary; and so on. We could give other examples which have been noted in the literature about Julian's possible sources, some of them preposterous in that she could not have known anything about them, given her historical circumstances. Perhaps it is good, then, that Julian did not leave behind any evidence of belonging to one or another of the orders, and indeed quite possibly never belonged to any, so that she might equally belong to all.

It is interesting to note, here, that in Julian's *Revelations* are certain ideas which were not strongly asserted (or which were not held at all) until the Protestant Reformation two hundred years afterward—even though, in other respects, she remains distinctly Catholic, as fits her own time and the tradition which she knew. At the same time, the basic structure and style of her theology closely resemble those of certain Eastern Orthodox saints, about whom Julian surely knew nothing at all.[12] These similarities do not help us to identify Julian's theological sources (although she does appear to be familiar with the content of much traditional Catholic theology), so much as to remind us that the main elements of Christian mysticism have remained the same in different times and places.

For many readers today, Julian will be more interesting as a spiritual writer who can serve as a personal inspiration than as a mystical theologian. Here she may be favorably compared to Thomas á Kempis, who is thought to have composed the *Imitation of Christ* in the Netherlands either towards the end of Julian's lifetime or immediately after. The *Revelations*, like the *Imitation of Christ*, is a spiritual classic. It may be read in small sections, without needing to read the entire book at one time. Some readers will find it most valuable taken in this way, with short passages for meditation—bearing in mind, meantime, the scribe's advice that the visions do make a whole, with which we should be familiar before attempting to weigh the book theologically.

The Revelations in Literature

As a writer of the English language, Julian is more significant than many of us would realize, especially if we are now learning about her for the first time. It appears that she was the first woman to compose a book in the English language, a surprising fact given that Julian's work is still relatively unknown in English literature. While many of us labored to memorize passages of Chaucer's *Canterbury Tales* in secondary school (perhaps failing to grasp why this piece should be thought so important to the evolution of our language), our teachers may not have pointed out—or even have realized—that Julian's work is exactly contemporary with Chaucer's, and is itself an important classic. To some modern ears, at least, Julian's prose sounds more attractive than Chaucer's couplets. The *Revelations* is composed in a lyrical style which retains, even in translation, a sense of inner rhyme and rhythm unique to Julian's part of England and to her own generation. In an age which is finally beginning to take note of the achievements of women in our cultural development, the *Revelations* has now become required reading in more than a few colleges and universities and even secondary schools in various parts of the world.[13]

Translation, however, still poses a problem when reading the *Revelations*. Although Julian's English (originally an East Anglian dialect) is not as radically different from our modern tongue as, say, the Anglo-Saxon which went before it, nevertheless the vocabulary can seem as foreign at times as Spanish is to Italian, or German is to Dutch. Thus, for the average reader, a translation into modern English is necessary. Even in translation, however, it is sometimes difficult to follow Julian's train of thought. For one thing, Julian—like many writers of her time—seems to wander a bit in telling her story, coming back again and again to the same themes rather than moving clearly from point "A" to point "B." For another, we may not readily understand what her words meant in the context of her own medieval society. We already have certain theological ideas firmly implanted in our minds which did not exist in Julian's day or which she at least did not share; and we are not accustomed to the conventions of story-telling and theology which she followed. Images of knights and lords, for example, or of the Plague or of medieval chivalry, have become stereotyped for us, and are probably often inaccurate. Other things to which Julian refers in passing, such as the cottage cloth-making industry or the plight of the serf at work on a great manor or the horrors associated with widespread death and war are often outside our experience in a modern, first-world society.

Translating an older form of English can also be misleading, even for the expert, simply because it *is* English—and so gives us the impression that we know it already. Many words in fact carry new meanings, and still others simply resemble words which we have today but actually have a different origin altogether. This is complicated by the fact that spelling (like pronunciation) had not been standardized in the fourteenth century, depending very much upon the local dialect and the whim of the scribe. Difficulties with the language, then, have sometimes led to interesting misunderstandings of Julian's theological position. A case in point will suffice.

Julian uses the term *soule*, which was probably pronounced in two syllables, with a Scandinavian sound [sǫ͝ʊːlə]. Unwary translators have sometimes assumed, quite naturally, that since this word appears in some manuscripts as a variant spelling of "soul," it would have this meaning in every case. Thus they have speculated about Julian's meaning where she says that

> A man goyth vppe ryght, and the soule of his body is
> sparyde as a purse fulle feyer. (ch. 6, P)

The word *sparyde* means "closed" or "enclosed"; hence the sense of this passage appears to be that the soul is enclosed in the body, which stands upright. The idea of the soul being enclosed in the body seems to be borne out when, later on in the same passage, Julian says that

> as the body is clad in cloth, and the flesh in skin, and the bones in flesh, and the heart in the breast, so are we, soul and body, clad in the goodness of God, and enclosed there. (ch. 6)

Scholars have recently pointed out, however, that the use of *soule* is not so straightforward as it might have been. Besides referring to the human soul (sometimes spelled *sawle*), it may also be a variant spelling of *sole,* which is a shoe or boot. This term was also used, as today, to describe certain flat fishes like halibut; and in a sea-faring society was used as a slang for "food." In that case, Julian is simply saying that human beings walk upright, but the food which we eat is—somewhat miraculously—contained in the body, and does not fall out. It is taken into the body like money into a purse, and at the proper time is let out again. She goes on to say, then, that

> ...when it is the time of his necessity, it [the "purse" or body] is opened and closed again, very neatly [or "firmly"]. That it is he [God] who does this is shown there, where he says that he comes down to us in the lowest part of our need; for he has no contempt for what he has made... (ch. 6, P)

For Julian, then, the point of the passage is that God is at work in everything, even the bodily function of digestion and using the toilet.

Overcoming difficulties in Julian's English is a relatively minor task when compared to the problems of translating other great writers of the Church from ancient languages such as Greek and Latin. It is therefore a curious fact that Julian has until recently remained comparatively unknown, even among scholars and theologians. The reason she is not better known has to do in part with the apparent disappearance of her book during the century or so after it was written.

Only four complete manuscripts of the *Revelations* survive

today. Three of these are of the so-called Longer Version, and one is of the Shorter. Of these, three are housed in the British Museum, but one, interestingly, surfaced in Paris and resides in the Bibliotheque Nationale. None of the manuscripts is, comparatively speaking, very old. The earliest (of the Shorter Version) is part of a collection of a dozen spiritual works which were contemporary with Julian. It appears to date from the mid-fifteenth century. In the introduction, however, the original scribe refers to a "woman named Juliana, who is a recluse at Norwich and is still alive in this year of our Lord, 1413." The other manuscripts appear to range in date from the late fifteenth century to the late seventeenth or early eighteenth centuries. The manuscripts show varying degrees of error in copying: even the date of Julian's vision, for example, is unclear due to a copyist's mistake in rendering "xiij Daie of May" for "viii" or the other way around. The Paris manuscript has been considered by most editors to be the most faithful, though its date (once thought to have been around 1500) has now been brought into question with the discovery that it appears to be a forgery of an earlier writing style.[14]

The *Revelations* was not actually brought into public literature until the publication in 1670 of a printed version, probably based on the Paris MS, by the English Benedictine Serenus Cressy. Recent scholarship suggests that Cressy made his version while in Paris, where he was acting as chaplain for the Benedictine nuns at Cambrai. It was here that he discovered a carefully preserved manuscript of the *Revelations*, now lost, which had been made under the direction of his predecessor, Fr. Augustine Baker. Apparently, of the two remaining manuscripts of the Longer Version, one was copied from the other at this same convent, as were the selections which appear in the "Upholland" Manuscript.

An Unwilling Heretic?

Why the *Revelations* was not more widely copied, or why any other copies have not survived, is not known. One theory is that Julian's book was suppressed during or immediately after her own lifetime—either to protect her from the suspicion of heresy or because the text itself was already banned. A careful reading of the *Revelations* suggests that Julian might have been regarded as heretical in her lifetime. Certainly there are passages which, if taken out of context or read in an inflammatory atmosphere, could be interpreted as going against the teachings of the Church in her day. The possibility of being accused of heresy was, in any case, no idle threat during Julian's years at Norwich.

Especially significant were the so-called "Lollards," a religious sect otherwise known as Waldensians, who were active in England during Julian's lifetime. They attracted attention by refusing to submit to the authority of local prelates on a number of points—chiefly demanding the radical reform of the clergy (whom they perceived, perhaps all too correctly, as immoral), and also the "unbinding" of the scriptures into English. Although some translation of the Bible was already going on within the approved structures of the Church (by the Dominicans, for example), it was evidently the manner in which the Lollards went about it that brought them into disfavor. Some, in a concern for biblical inerrancy, insisted on carrying Latin grammar and syntax (from the "original" Vulgate) over into English, thus distorting the meaning of the text. Others seemed to advocate a free-for-all in which every believer could interpret Holy Writ privately, on the basis of visions and the like, without the guidance of the Church.

It should be admitted, in all fairness, that there were elements of truth on both sides. The non-conformists' criticisms of the clergy were probably accurate, or so we must surmise from the literature of the time. Abysmal ignorance brought on in part by filling the ranks too quickly after deaths in the clergy roll due to plague, was beginning to be the rule rather than the exception. Well-meaning pilgrims fell victim to scheming prelates and petty officials, who saw an opportunity at the shrines: pilgrims, who hoped against hope for cures and spiritual enlightenment, frequently lost both their money and their faith. On the other side, it was becoming increasingly difficult to tell who was following the teachings of the Church and who was not. The question was not merely an academic one; some non-conformists were becoming organized into pathological cults, which were dangerous to society as a whole. The situation is not without its parallels in the various religious movements today, some of which might be viewed as "fringe movements" within Christianity, but others of which have obviously been founded by neurotic personalities or are engaged in deliberate mental and physical violence. The Church, in reaction to what it saw as growing spiritual anarchy, began to overreact to any deviations. These included the seeing of visions, supernatural experiences, or "private" teachings—all of which, obviously, form the background to Julian's *Revelations*.

However we might assess the situation today, the fact is that during Julian's later years in Norwich the Church brutally suppressed what it saw as a threat to the integrity of the faith and the fabric of the society. More than a few suspected Lollards were burned at the stake not far from Julian's cell; it would appear in fact that she could see the fires of the "Lollards' Pit" from her window. It is possible that in this atmosphere of suspicion, bordering on hysteria, Julian herself came under scrutiny for any of several reasons: either because of something in the contents of her book itself (such as her assertion that she did not see Purgatory; or the implication, in one passage, that the soul of an unbaptized infant might not go straight to hell); or because of her avowed aim to speak openly about spiritual matters to the uneducated laity; or because Julian, who was a woman and therefore not a "theologian," did not have permission to write about theological matters in the first place. Finally, it is at least possible that Julian had in her possession an English translation of parts of the New Testament—a translation which, perhaps without her knowing it, originated in the "underground" efforts of the local Lollards to disseminate scriptures in English.

That Julian may have had a contraband Bible can be argued from use of the scriptures in her book. Although Julian obviously composed the *Revelations* herself, it is possible that she could neither read nor write; in the text she describes herself as "unlettered." We will return to this point, because her exact meaning is unclear; however, it seems almost certain in any case that she means at least that she could not read Latin, the language of the Bible in her day. It is not surprising, then, that in the text she nowhere quotes directly from the Vulgate, even though she seems to have a wide knowledge of the contents of the scriptures. A careful analysis of scripture references in the *Revelations* would indicate that Julian was probably familiar with the Passion accounts in the gospels (although perhaps only in a "Gospel harmony"); and with at least some of the Pauline epistles (especially Romans, 1 & 2 Corinthians, Ephesians, and Galatians) as well as the Psalms. These passages coincide with portions of the scripture evidently favored in Lollard translations.[15]

Within the text of the *Revelations*, there are other indications that Julian was at least aware of the dangers of falling under suspicion. Several times, she takes care to say that she is a "daughter of Holy Church" and that she has no desire to add to, or take away from, the teachings of the Church which she had received from those in authority to teach. In the Shorter Version, too, there is one uncharacteristically defensive passage in which she hints at criticism of her efforts to put down in writing the content of her visions. Julian defends her right to speak out on theological matters even though she is a woman:

> God forbid that you should say, or take it, that I am a teacher... For I am a woman, uneducated, feeble and frail. But I know well what I am saying...
>
> Because I am a woman, should I therefore believe that I should not tell you about the goodness of God? Because I saw then that it is his will for it to be known. (Shorter Version, Ch. VI)

And we have already seen the scribe's notation at the end of one manuscript which warns against misinterpretation of the text "in the manner of an heretic."

It is possible that Julian was aware of instances in which other women like herself had been accused of heresy. There is a record, for example, of an anchoress who was summoned by her bishop out of her cell, found innocent of having taught wrong beliefs, and summarily walled up again. However, there is no direct evidence that Julian ever became the object of any official inquiry either during or after her lifetime. So far as we know, no harm every came to her in her years in Norwich. The Longer Version of the book, written some years after the visions, omits the passages we have quoted above. Certainly

Julian never betrays the slightest desire to go against the accepted doctrines of the Church, or to stand outside its sacramental life in any way.

Another theory suggested by students of the *Revelations* is that Julian's book was suppressed during the time of the English Reformation and perished in the dissolution of the convents. Certainly it is possible that her book was destroyed along with many of the existing libraries, and this theory would account for its presence in France—where it would have been brought by exiled Benedictines after the Dissolution. However, it remains a puzzle why, apart from Fr. Baker's lost text and the extracts in the Westminster MS, there were not more copies of the *Revelations* around. There are dozens of copies of extant works by Julian's contemporaries, in spite of the destruction of the libraries in the Reformation. Why not the *Revelations*? The answer may lie in a simpler explanation: Julian was simply not noticed, as only one in a field of many bright stars who published theological and spiritual works in her lifetime.

An Age of Writers and Mystics

Julian lived during a "golden age" of great writers, mystics, and theologians, both in England and on the Continent. We have already mentioned Geoffrey Chaucer, who was born just one year before Julian and whose *Canterbury Tales* was written at about the same time as Julian's *Revelations*. Chaucer had traveled widely, could speak several languages, and served in official capacities as a diplomatic agent. His translations into English of folk tales, Latin classics and Italian literature—including a multitude of references to theological and philosophical texts and newer works, such as Dante's *Divine Comedy*—made an invaluable contribution to the literature, and also to the English language itself. Besides, his most famous work, the *Tales*, is ribald and delightful to read aloud. Chaucer's works, too, are not without serious theological content; though this feature, apart from the lampoons of popular medieval piety and the abuses of spiritual pilgrimage, would for the most part be lost on readers today, as they may have been in Chaucer's own time.

A more sober attempt to address the spiritual ills of the Church was produced by William Langland. Langland's book, called *Piers Ploughman* ("Peter the Plowman"), is an extended parable which personifies the vices which he saw—lust, greed, and so forth—as slovenly characters with suitable names. It is difficult to say whether Langland made much social impact in his day, but his work is nevertheless important as a milestone in the English language, and can still be read in a modern edition.

An important writer and mystic from the north of England was a wandering hermit from Yorkshire named Richard Rolle. Rolle was a colorful figure, a kind of "free spirit," who left his home wearing only a home-made habit which he fashioned out of one of his sister's tunics. Educated at Oxford, he may have been for a while under the patronage of one John of Dalton; and, breaking with him, may have studied at the Sorbonne. For a time he associated with an anchoress, Margaret Kirkeby, at the town of Richmond. Later he directed a convent of Cistercian nuns at Hampole and died there of Black Death in 1349. Rolle wrote commentaries on scripture, poetic paraphrases of Psalms in English for layfolk, and several spiritual treatises which tell of his experience of "heat," "sweetness," and "song" in prayer. Although Julian was only six years old when Rolle died, he left behind a spiritual legacy. Efforts to canonize him shortly after his death probably failed only because recurrence of the Black Death interrupted the proceedings.

Another famous writer in Julian's lifetime was Walter Hylton (or Hilton), who is exactly contemporary with Julian. A Canon Regular of the Augustinian Order, he enjoyed the reputation of learning and spiritual maturity—so much so that he earned the position of inquisitor in the proceedings against the Lollards, whom he intensely disliked. Whatever we may think of his strong words against the nonconformists, there is no doubt that his personal piety was considered to be above suspicion. He produced several important theological works, including translations of older spiritual writings and commentaries of his own which were designed to help others in their spiritual walk. Like Julian's, Hilton's writings are decidedly christocentric: he uses the name of Jesus frequently, apparently sharing in a kind of "Jesus-movement" of his time. He seems, too, to have been especially interested in the questions which worried lay Christians most: about how to live decent lives in the midst of difficult times, or how to enjoy the deeper things of prayer in the midst of busy secular lives. One of his treatises therefore describes the "mixed life"—that is, how to pursue contemplative prayer and silence even while living the active life of a business administrator on a manor. Here he illustrates the interest which laypersons evidently held for spiritual development in Julian's time, and a typically English willingness to entertain the idea that the laity, no less than the cloistered monks, could know something about prayer and holiness. Hilton died in 1395, not many years before Julian, so their careers overlapped considerably. It is not impossible that they knew one another.

Undoubtedly the most important spiritual work to be produced in England during Julian's lifetime, apart from her own, was an anonymous treatise on prayer entitled the *Cloud of Unknowing*. This book, apparently one of several by the same author, is still regarded by many spiritual directors to be an unparalleled guide to advanced prayer and meditation, and finally what is known as "contemplation." Its theme is "pure" prayer, that is, prayer which seeks to move beyond the contemplation of earthly things to contemplation of the pure things of God.

Ultimately the *Cloud* is based upon the writings of the sixth-century monk whom we met earlier, known today as Pseudo-Dionysius. The author of the *Cloud* translated some of "St Denys'" works into English from Latin (they had already been translated into Latin from Greek), popularizing Dionysius' style of mysticism—or what, at any rate, was thought to have been his theology. It is questionable whether the author of the *Cloud* really understood Dionysius; or, for that matter, whether Dionysius was understood correctly in the West at all. In general, his works were taken in a Neoplatonic way: drawing a sharp distinction between body and soul, material and spiritual reality, this world and the heavenly world. It was argued, then, that spiritual development would require one to place a "cloud of unknowing" between the self and the world; and that, on the other hand, the true nature of God is above-knowing, and so hidden from us in a "cloud" of divine darkness. On this point in particular it seems that Dionysius may have been misunderstood; but the ultimate effect, in any case, of his writings on the West was to implant Neoplatonism solidly into Western spirituality. The *Cloud of Unknowing*, then, teaches a way of prayer which moves beyond the contemplation of images (the crucifix, for example) to the "pure" contemplation of God—assuming, meantime, that the inner being of God the Trinity is ultimately "beyond knowing" in this life.

It has sometimes been suggested that Julian borrowed her ideas either from Walter Hilton or from the author of the *Cloud*, or both, in composing the *Revelations*. As evidence there are at least two instances in which a significant phrase found in Julian's book is also found in one of Walter Hilton's.[16] (That the direction of influence might have worked the other way around has also been suggested, but seems unlikely in view of the dates of the works in question.) Julian also appears to share with Hilton his emphasis on the person and name of Jesus; and with the *Cloud*, the teaching that the inner nature of the Trinity is ultimately "secret." However, there are important reasons to suggest that Julian did not in fact borrow from either of her better-known contemporaries in formulating her own theological outlook.

As we outline Julian's theology in the following pages, we will see that most of her images are distinctive and unique, and are not actually found in the works of other contemporary writers. Thus, most of the ideas which make Julian an important theologian do not appear in either Hilton's works or in the *Cloud*. More to the point, there are important instances in which Julian appears to differ sharply with these two writers, not only in points of detail but in her general approach to theology as a whole. Julian, for example, rejects the idea that Christian spirituality is like a ladder on which we progress from one degree of perfection to another—an idea which is basic to Hilton, as illustrated in his book, the *Ladder of Perfection*. Julian will point out, perhaps with Hilton in mind, that her experience of God was of the Holy Trinity, and not merely of "ministering angels"—possibly a reference to Hilton's theological development of the role of angels in another of his works. Finally, and most important, Julian's theology argues directly against the Neoplatonic separation of matter and spirit. She says, for example, that in her revelations the dwelling-place of the Holy Spirit is shown to be the world of sense, which God has created. In another significant passage, Julian rejects absolutely the idea that she should attempt to contemplate God (or the nature of God) in "darkness," or apart from the incarnate Son of God, Jesus Christ.[17] Thus Julian concludes that to look to God apart from the crucified Jesus is not "higher" prayer, but a subtle temptation from the Fiend. In this, she can hardly be said to have borrowed from the *Cloud* at all.

However we might measure Julian against her better-known contemporaries, it remains that it would not have been difficult for scribes to overlook her slim volume in light of the publication of such significant works as the *Cloud* and Hilton's several books in her lifetime. And apart from these writers, there were many other famous theologians and mystics, both in England and on the Continent, who were gaining attention, some of whom were later canonized by the Church. We have already mentioned one illustrious teacher who was not canonized: Meister Eckhart, who died shortly before Julian was born in 1323. Eckhart's teachings were eventually condemned by the Church, at least in part, as heretical; but the condemnation proceedings were to some extent politically motivated and therefore questionable, and his influence never really diminished. His students, John Tauler (d. 1361) and Heinrich Suso after him (d. 1366) were to prove extremely important in the development of popular mysticism in Germany; as was John Gerson (d. 1427), writing in Holland. The Spanish mystic Ramon Lullo (d. 1315) bears some resemblance to Julian in portions of his writing, though it seems impossible that Julian could have known anything about it.

A list of the important women mystics and writers on the Continent is even longer, as the movement known as *frauen-mystic* ("women's mysticism") grew especially along the Rhine. Some of the women who were best known, or who published accounts of their own "revelations," were: Gertrude of Helfta (d. 1302), Angela of Foligno (d. 1309), Christina of Stommeln

(d. 1312), Margaret Ebner (d. 1351), Christine Ebner (d. 1356), St. Bridget of Sweden (d. 1373), Adeheid of Langmann (d. 1375), St. Catherine of Siena (d. 1380), St. Katherine of Sweden (d. 1391), Dorothea of Prussia (d. 1394), and St. Mary of Venice (d. 1399).[18] The canonization proceedings for St. Bridget, known as "Bryde" to Julian, was a highly publicized event which took place in Julian's lifetime, and which attracted pilgrims from England. It is interesting that her death occurred in the same year as Julian's experience of the showings. Pilgrims, who traveled constantly back and forth between the Continent and England, reported the marvelous stories of these women and their writings. In view of all these developments, what seems remarkable is not so much that Julian's book dropped temporarily from sight, but that it has emerged today from so large a field as a piece of lasting significance.

Julian Today

While Julian remained out of the mainstream of theological dialogue over the centuries, first-time readers of the *Revelations* will nevertheless sometimes discover a phrase here and there which sounds familiar—and which, in fact, they have encountered somewhere in modern literature. Some of these phrases have gone completely unacknowledged; others may or may not have originated with Julian. The phrase for which Paul Tillich is best known in contemporary theology, for example—that God is "Ground of Being"—is common to Meister Eckhart and to Julian; it has simply gone unrecognized. Julian develops the idea as fundamental to her theology, although she sees it in a christocentric way which we do not find in Tillich. Julian can say that

> Our reason is grounded in God.... Of this substantial nature [kind], mercy and grace spring and spread into us.... These are our *ground, in which we have our ... being.* (ch. 56, emphasis added)

or again,

> God, in his being, is nature [kind]. That is to say, the goodness which is kind, is God. *He is the ground*, he is the substance, he is the same thing as nature [kindhood]. (ch. 62)

The late Thomas Merton, the Trappist monk who did much to reintroduce the calling of the solitary life to the Church in recent decades, drew from Julian both in his personal life and in his published writings. Merton recognized the significance of Julian's theological concepts, especially in her discussion of the Last Things; and he praised her as one of the few Christian writers in modern times who understood eschatology correctly. Merton's lengthy reference to Julian in his book, *Conjectures of a Guilty Bystander*, undoubtedly did much to bring her ideas to the attention of theologians in our lifetime.[19]

Other publications, not so much theological as literary, have introduced Julian to popular reading. These range from a full-length historical novel based on the character of Julian's contemporary, Katherine Swynford (the mother of English kings), to contemporary science-fiction.[20] The most important recent work to draw from Julian directly, however, does not actually identify her as the source at all. It is the well-known poem by T.S. Eliot, entitled, *Four Quartets on Playthings in the Wind.*

It is arguable that Eliot's poem is an extended meditation, based directly upon Julian's *Revelations*—and perhaps prompted by a visit which Eliot paid to the site of Julian's cell in Norwich. Portions of the poem refer to Julian's illness, leading up to her death and the showings of divine love. Eliot refers to Julian's meditation on the suffering of Christ on the cross, and quotes from the *Revelations* several times in the body of the poem. Then the final movement, "Little Gidding," closes with a powerful reflection on the ascetical life and the end of time— two themes which are important to Julian. The passage, referring to Julian's vision of the crown of thorns on Jesus' head, is taken from the opening passages of the *Revelations* (in which Julian's visions began with the crown of thorns); and then from ch. 27 and elsewhere in the book, where Julian develops the meaning of the incarnation for humanity. Using a traditional English metaphor for the incarnation and suffering of Christ, the "rose," Eliot introduces into modern English literature the phrase for which Julian is now most famous:[21]

> Quick now, here, now, always—
> A condition of complete simplicity
> (costing not less than everything)
> *And all shall be well and*
> *All manner of thing shall be well*
> When the tongues of flame are in-folded
> Into a crowned knot of fire
> And the fire and the rose are one.

A Pilgrimage of Love

"All shall be well, and all manner of things shall be well." To understand Julian's words, we must enter with her, finally, into a pilgrimage; for she was, above all, a pilgrim and the object of pilgrimage herself. Her reputation as a wise spiritual counselor seems to have spread, at least in East Anglia, so that others came to see her on pilgrimage. One such pilgrim, called Dame Margery Kempe, recorded her visit with Julian in a lengthy autobiography. It is the only contemporary account we have of Julian, outside her own book and a few public records. In her account, Margery tells of a visit to Julian's anchorage sometime around 1415, when Julian was seventy-two.[22] Margery's words are worth quoting in full, because here we have the sense of meeting Julian in person. Speaking in the third person about herself, Margery tells how she was plagued by an abundance of tears during the times of her public devotion. Her outbreaks led to persecution and feelings of guilt, until she was able to consult with Julian:

> "Then she was called by Our Lord to go to an anchoress in the same city [Norwich], named Dame Jelyan, and so she did, and showed her the grace that God put into her soul, of compunction, contrition, sweetness and devotion, compassion with holy meditation and high contemplation, and

very many holy speeches and conversations which Our Lord spoke to her soul; and many wonderful revelations, which she showed to the anchoress to find out if there were any deceit in them, because the anchoress was an expert in such things, and could give good counsel.

"The anchoress, hearing the marvelous goodness of Our Lord, highly thanked God with all her heart for his visitation, counseling this creature to be obedient to the will of Our Lord God and to fulfill with all her might whatever he put into her soul, if it were not against the worship of God, and profit of her fellow-Christians; for if it were, then it would not be the moving of the good spirit, but rather of an evil spirit. "The Holy Spirit never moves anything against love, for if he did, he would be contrary to his own self—for he is all Love. Also, he moves a soul to all chasteness, for chaste livers are called the Temple of the Holy Spirit, and the Holy Spirit makes a soul stable and steadfast in the right faith, and the right belief.

"And a man who is double in his soul is always unstable and unsteady in all his ways. He that is always doubting is like the waves of the sea, which are moved and borne about with the wind, and that man is not likely to receive the gifts of God.

"Any creature who has these signs may steadfastly believe that the Holy Spirit dwells in his soul. And much more when God visits a creature with tears of contrition, devotion and compassion, he may—and should—believe that the Holy Spirit is in his soul. St. Paul says that the Holy Spirit intercedes for us with unspeakable mourning and weeping; that is to say, he makes us to ask and pray with mourning and weeping so plenteously that the tears may not be numbered. No evil spirit can give these signs; for St. Jerome says that tears torment the devil more than do the pains of hell. God and the devil are always at odds, and they will never live together in one place. And the devil has no power in a man's soul!

"Holy Writ says that the soul of a righteous man is the dwelling-place of God; and so I trust, dear sister, that you are. I pray God to grant you to persevere. Set all your trust in God and do not fear the language of the world, for the more despising, shame and reproof that you have in the world, the more is your merit in the sight of God. Patience is necessary for you, for in that you shall keep your soul."

These words, which reveal Julian's wide-ranging knowledge of the New Testament (especially Matthew 5:11, Romans, 1 Corinthians, and the book of James) as well as of Jerome and traditional Catholic theology, neatly summarize much of what we read in Julian's own book about the compassion of God. Margery left greatly cheered, and continued on her way to encounter both blessing and persecution in a rich career. Margery's account gives us, incidentally, a picture of pilgrimage in Julian's day. Margery traveled as far away as Italy, the Holy Land, and the Baltic Sea in her wanderings, even though she needed to walk only about forty miles—or two days' journey—from her home in King's Lynn in order to visit with Julian.

We said, however, that Julian was also a pilgrim. It is only a matter of conjecture today whether Julian herself ever managed to walk on pilgrimage as Margery did. Undoubtedly she ventured at least to local shrines in her lifetime, because it was the practice of her day to do so, and because we know from her writings that she was a pious soul even in her youth. Later on, as an anchoress, it was the tradition that she did not travel at all. We can say, however, that without a doubt at the heart of her mysticism is a joyful pilgrimage—a journey of the soul into the heart of God.

1

Beginnings: A Desire for God's Gifts

Julian's story—so much as we know of it—begins in East
Anglia, that part of England on the east coast which reaches
out into the sea and which, with its broad and flat fields of
tulips and daffodils and mustard, resembles Flanders or the
Netherlands as much as it belongs to the English countryside.
In the Middle Ages, it had its own distinctive dialect, a living
and constantly changing combination of Saxon and Latin,
Norman French (itself derived in part from Scandinavia, and
unintelligible in Paris), Danish and Flemish, together just
emerging into what we know today as "English." The center of
its culture—of its art and music, literature and commerce, and
indeed of its religion—was Norwich, a busy sea port in the
trade with the Flemings and the Dutch, Normandy and the
rest of Europe stretching to the Mediterranean Sea and the
door to the Far East.

By the beginning of the fourteenth century, Norwich had
become a major city, with its own charm and cosmopolitan
atmosphere. Here sea traders and merchants from every part
of the Christian world bartered with local craftsmen and
farmers for the finest goods the West had to offer. Artisans
and laborers were organized into guilds, many of which were
associated with the raising of sheep and cattle, or with the
woolen trade and parchment industries, at which Norfolk
excelled. The city market, known as "Tombland" (*tomb* meaning an empty space, probably, rather than a place of burial)
was one of the most modern and largest of its kind, well-
regulated, with permanent stalls across from the cathedral,

identifying the guilds which were responsible for their wares.

To some extent Norwich was considered to be a holy place. It was the "City of Churches," with more than two hundred of them within the city walls at the height of the Middle Ages. Every guild had its own chapel, the name and patron saint of which identified the guild which had built it and which hoped to be blessed by the offerings made there. Some thirty of these can still be visited today: St. Peter's Parmentergate, for example, built for parchment-makers ("parmenters"); St. Julian's, probably named for Julian the Hospitaler.

The religious atmosphere of the city was heightened by the presence of religious houses, wandering hermits and ascetics. Learned Dominicans called "Black Friars" because of the color of their habit, occupied a large friary. They maintained a library which, if it was not very large by our standards today, was nevertheless a fine example for its time. Benedictines occupied the cathedral and owned a hermitage in the suburb of Conisford, besides maintaining convents and schools. Franciscans ("Grey Friars") were there, as were Carmelites ("White Friars") and Augustinians, each with friaries of their own. By the end of the fourteenth century,nearly fifty of the churches or convents had hermitages nearby, which were occupied by persons living singly under vows. Pilgrims traveled to see the local shrines and to see the massive Norman cathedral, which dominated the life of the city with its stunning architecture, its tower clock (which rang out the hours), and its library. Tourists jostled up and down the narrow lanes, chatting in accents which were nearly mutually unintelligible, from the various parts of England.

While Norwich itself was a relatively prosperous city, involved as it was in the international trade, most of the people who lived there were not. Even the most modern dwelling would have seemed poor in our eyes: built of clay and bent poles, with straw, horsehair and twigs artfully woven in and out, the "wattle and daub" construction of the average house was flimsy at best. The roofs were made of straw; and since there were no fire-proof bricks with which to make chimneys, the hearth was more likely than not in the center of the earthen floor, sending up sparks to catch the ceiling on fire now and then. The streets were filthy. Wild boars, dogs, and cats prowled constantly in search of garbage, which was dumped unceremoniously out of windows onto pedestrians below. To negotiate these muddy lanes on foot meant avoiding at all costs the channel, or "kennel," which ran down the center of the wider thoroughfares which had been "improved." Actually, these were nothing more than open sewers which carried filth, rotted meat and general household trash away from the dwellings. Rats, always in evidence, had no difficulty gnawing their way through the walls of even the best houses. Owing to the dangers presented by wild boars, dogs, and stray cattle running loose within the city gates—not to mention stowaways from the ships and migrants who had long been out of work—men were constantly armed and did not go out after dark for any reason, if it could be avoided.

It is a commonplace that life in these times was filled with ignorance, superstition, and the fear of death; but it is difficult for us to imagine today the scale of suffering which presented itself in the great cities of this time. The Black Death—a form of pneumonic plague or bubonic plague, probably both—visited the city of Norwich three times in rapid succession from 1348 to 1369, killing about a third of the population of England in a single epidemic. The rampage of this killer disease affected every aspect of life. Fields lay idle because there was no one to work them. The economy spiralled downward with every new wave of infection; it was impossible to conduct business as usual, and ships, still laden with goods, turned away from the infected ports. Priests were overworked in their haste to grant absolution to the dying and to baptize the newborn before they, too, would die outside the grace of the Church. The dead could not all receive proper burial and in the worst of times, lay stacked in carts like so much cordwood, or in hastily-dug pits on the edge of town, or simply where they fell, in the streets. And meantime the Hundred Years War, an especially fruitless struggle with France which ran from 1337 through the end of the century, cost the lives of the nobility for three generations, following upon the magnificent failure of the Crusades.

The effects of unremitting hardship and mass death showed themselves in the culture in ways which we can only reconstruct from what we know of Auschwitz or the Russian Front in our own century. A strange form of mass hysteria appeared in the cities of England, a kind of corporate guilt which was accompanied by brutal self-punishment on the one hand, and gross immorality on the other. The so-called Flagellants descended upon town after town, whipping themselves with rods and proclaiming ominous warnings of Doom, or the Last Judgment, which was coming soon. Even reasonable people could think that the Judgment was near: the Moslems had conquered the Holy Land; all the known world was suffering from an incurable disease, from continual warfare, and mass starvation; and through the fourteenth century there came reports of strange floods and hailstorms, drought and earthquakes, which wiped out what few crops as could be raised in the face of economic ruin and a decimated work force.

The outbreaks of plague, with their devastation of the economy, had political repercussions. The first civil uprising of its kind in English history took place in Norwich in June, 1381. Workers had been frustrated by ruinous taxes, which were designed to support the wars overseas. In response to the fear that labor shortages would result in massive cost increases, the government froze wages with the infamous "Statute of Laborors." Then a poll-tax was levied in the spring of 1381. Whole towns refused to pay, and in May there was rioting. Finally a rebellion of sorts was organized under Wat Tyler, egged on by a preacher named John Ball, and marchers reached London with the evident aim of overthrowing the government. The leaders were eventually arrested and put to death; and when marchers reached Norwich, they were brutally destroyed by the army of the Bishop, Henry Depenser.

The scene was ugly on both sides. If it seemed necessary however for the local police, under the authority of the Church, to put down with arms the rioting of farmers carrying only pitchforks and stones, nevertheless it cannot have helped an already unfortunate image which the Church was acquiring by this time. In the fourteenth century, every dimension of social life was in some way bound up with the Church; but the authority of the Church had suffered permanent damage.

It was taught, for example, that the Church knew best how to interpret scriptures and how to relate the faith—and also how to govern the people in the context of God's will. At the same time, however, it was not even clear who governed the Church. The so-called "Babylonian Captivity" of the pope began in 1305, when Clement V became virtually a puppet of the French court, living at Avignon. This situation, the subject of heated debate and understandable outrage, continue until 1377. Gregory XI, urged on by the saintly Catherine of Siena, removed the papacy back to Rome but did not live to restore the place of the highest prelate in the Church. Following his death, two popes were elected at the same time in the dispute called the "Great Schism"—one serving in France and one at Rome. From 1409 to 1414 the situation deteriorated even further, as three popes claimed legitimate rights at once. This state of affairs could only serve to undermine permanently the confidence of the faithful in their spiritual leadership—outside of which, it was taught, there could be no salvation.

As confidence in the Church declined and hardships increased, the art of the time reflected a certain despair or hopelessness even among the faithful. It appeared that God was pouring out his wrath on the whole world. Who could avoid it? It is no wonder, then, that in every part of Europe the art of this period reveals a grim fascination with death. Devils and skulls grin at the pious worshipper. The Angel of Death takes his toll of unwary sinners, who pursue their lives of devil-may-care immorality. Strange sexual aberrations appear in church art, in anticipation of the fantastic scenes by the Fleming, Hieronymus Bosch.

The Paintings of Norwich

Alongside the darkness of the age, however, or in spite of it, there continued to develop a refinement and gentility which made this a period of romance and of spiritual growth. In Norfolk, a school of artists began to assert their hope in God— and not merely their fear of God—through their decoration of the churches. Here in Norwich, and especially around the cathedral, a new and distinctive style of art was growing up. Painters from as far away as Siena joined local artisans to produce frescoes and altar retables for the new cathedral, and for the guild churches which were located on the corners of the city streets. These frescoes, painted in delicate tempera over sketches of sienese brown, give no hint of the darkness of the times. The colors are bright and sunny; the lines are graceful and relaxed. Unlike paintings of this period in Flanders or Germany or Spain, Norfolk art is seldom somber. It is not a depiction of death, but of life: Christ rises from the dead as the conqueror of death. He steps from the grave with insensible soldiers at his feet, carrying a flag of triumph in his hands. A smile plays on his lips. The colors are emerald, ruby, and cobalt, surrounded by bright gold.

At about this time the paintings and carvings of the crucifixion also underwent a significant change. In the past, Christ had stared down from the cross impassively, as *pantocrator*— "ruler of the universe"—with stiff, wooden arms and rigid legs. The eyes looked past the viewer, into heaven. There was little of humanity here. Now, Christ is depicted as Man—the friend and intercessor who knows our sufferings. He is surrounded by the Virgin Mary, the Magdalene, and the Apostle John, as well as the soldier who said, "Truly, this is the Son of God." These paintings of the passion do not seem to tell us so much about Jesus' physical suffering (though it is there, with a new attention to anatomy and the features of the face), as about the miracle of life which is taking place here, for the sake of a miserable and suffering world. The passion has become *compassion*: Jesus is suffering with the world, not merely for it; and we see the agony of Mary for her Son.

Finally, we too are drawn into the drama as we look into the face of Christ. In earlier days, the staring eyes did not seem to engage the viewer at all. Now, they look into our hearts. Christ almost asks us to speak with him about the crucifixion. The thin body curves gently to the left, in the shape of a reverse-"S." The head inclines to one side, and when the eyes are open, they are gentle. The face is noble and serene. The crown of thorns, which was not inevitably depicted before the fourteenth century, is not so much an instrument of torture as a genuine crown, almost like a garland decorating the head. A slight trickle of blood wells up beneath the crown of thorns pooling above the brow and from there runs down to Jesus' beard, mingling with the blood of the wound in his right side; from there onto his white *kirtle* or kilt. The blood, however, is not grotesque. Somehow, the picture radiates an intense joy.

Who created these unique paintings, and why, is for the most part unknown today. Much of the art of the time was lost during the Reformation and may never be recovered. But in the cathedral at Norwich, we can still stand beneath retables which hung there or in churches nearby more than six hundred years ago. Some of these were rescued only recently from disrepair. (One was found nailed upside-down as a table top, the upper part sawn off and lost.) We are fortunate to have these paintings back, not only because there are no others quite like them in Christendom, but also because they bring us to the beginning of our story.

An Inspiration to Prayer

Sometime in the middle of the fourteenth century, a young girl whose name we do not know stood beneath such paintings and was transfixed by them. Two things in particular struck her: the sight of Jesus' suffering for her sake; and the suffering of the women who watched the crucifixion. She wondered at the suffering which the Mother of God had felt and reflected that, in a special way, these women shared the passion of Christ because of the love which they felt for him. Mary was granted the grace of participating in the passion, according to the prophecy at Jesus' circumcision ("a sword shall pierce through your own soul also"); the Magdalene, because she was Jesus' friend and had been delivered from devils. This young girl wanted to be there at the cross with the women, to experience what they felt and to share as much as possible in the passion of Christ.

Seeing the paintings of the crucifixion moved the girl to pray for two special gifts of God which, in later years, would form an important part of her spiritiual life. The first gift was "mind of the passion." This was not merely a request to keep the sufferings of Christ in mind, but to know the crucifixion as the women had known it. Whether suddenly, from the beginning, or gradually as she thought about it, the request grew into a prayer for something extraordinary: she wanted to have a vision of the Passion itself, as realistic as if she were really

70   *Beginnings: A Desire for God's Gifts*

there. In this way she hoped to share in the devotion of the holy women whom she saw in the altar paintings, but she knew that such visions were not for common people. She had been warned, no doubt, against seeking the things which were out of the ordinary graces of the Church, so she prayed for the vision "conditionally," that is, on the condition that it would meet with God's will.

The request for a second gift followed from the first. She wanted not only to have a vision of the suffering of Jesus on the cross, but to share in the suffering herself. Scripture, after all, urges us to "die in Christ." Thus, the desire came to her suddenly, without her seeking it especially, to pass through death—or at least to come to the point of dying—so that she would have shared as completely as possible in the passion of her Lord. This would, she thought, prepare her for death at a later time: she would already know beforehand what it is to leave the world behind; she would have dealt with the prospect of Doom before it became too late to mend her ways. She realized that this prayer, like the one before it, was extraordinary. Once again, she asked for this gift only on the condition that it would agree with God's will for her. Nevertheless, her prayer was specific: she wanted to experience an illness to the point of death, so that everyone (including herself) would believe that she was actually dying and did die, before she passed the age of thirty.

If the prayer for this second gift of grace seems strange to us today, we should bear in mind that this young woman, who was only five years old when the plague first visited Norwich, did not know what it was like to live without the continual specter of death. Apart from the plague, which haunted every family, there was the prospect of death in even the simplest accident or infection. A small wound could turn septic and result in hideous suffering and death; there were no antibiotics or anesthetics. Pregnancy carried with it not only discomfort and the prospect of great pain, but often resulted in the death of the mother; and every married woman could expect to remain pregnant more or less continually through the childbearing years. The average life-span for a woman is estimated to have been between thirty and forty years. It was not unreasonable, then, to desire to come to terms with death as soon as possible. A good spiritual discipline would be to face death every day, so that one might live more fully in the present time. The young woman asked, accordingly, that she might have this experience of the passion and of death while she was still young enough for it to be of use to her. It would, she hoped, "purify" her.

As she grew older, these two "conditional" prayers gradually passed from her memory. It may be that she thought they were childish or immature; or, possibly, they no longer seemed necessary to her. Or perhaps she was persuaded by her priest or confessor to let them go. In any case, she simply forgot about them. In the meantime, a third prayer began to occupy her and to form the center of her spiritual life for some time.

A Desire for Martyrdom

The prayer for a third special gift was not inspired, this time, by the paintings in and around Norwich, but by a story which was told to children in medieval England, and which she heard from a "man of holy Church." It is not a biblical story, but one of the many hagiographies, or "saint-stories," which were popular, and which had an air of historicity about them. Their real purpose was to teach a moral or to inspire the young listeners to a deeper piety and desire for God. In this case, the story was about the saint called "Cecily," or Cecelia, a legendary figure who does not appear in our calendar of saints today but whose story has been preserved for us by Chaucer in the *Canterbury Tales* as "The Second Nun's Tale." It has also been preserved, in a variety of forms, in other collections of folk stories from England and Scotland, demonstrating its popularity. The story may be paraphrased as follows:[1]

> Once upon a time, long ago in ancient Rome, there was a virtuous young woman named Cecily who had dedicated her life to Christ. She received baptism secretly, and pledged to devote her virginity to her Lord and Savior. Her father, a pagan, had however promised her hand to a suitor named Valerian, who also was not a Christian. As the time for the marriage drew near, Cecily prayed earnestly that her vir-

ginity would somehow be saved. Then she rested in the knowledge that her Savior would protect her.

On her wedding night, Cecily told her new husband about her promise to God, and about her prayer for protection. Then a miracle occurred: an angel appeared and announced to Valerian that he had come to defend Cecily's chastity. [The angel was not—as we might imagine today—a woman with wings, but a heavenly warrior, dressed perhaps like a Crusader, in a white tunic, with a fiery sword.] Valerian was naturally terrified by this apparition, and agreed to leave Cecily alone. In fact, through the persuasion of the angel, he was converted to Christianity that same night. Later, his brother Tibertius was also persuaded to receive baptism, through the ministry of the angel.

Valerian and Tibertius did not keep their new-found faith secret, and before long they were arrested. They were forced by the authorities to decide whether to make an act of worship to the god Jupiter, and denounce the Christian faith, or die. They refused, and so they were martyred—but not before they had convinced one of their captors, an officer of the guard named Maximus, to accept baptism. Maximus, too, received the martyr's crown soon after.

Cecily, being the source of all the trouble, was bound and condemned to die—but not in the ordinary way. In her case a special torture was devised: she was to be boiled to death in her own steam-bath. Miraculously, however, the scheme did not work, and she survived the boiling waters without harm. Her captors were forced to resort to the sword, and a soldier stepped forward to decapitate her. He raised his sword, swung, and—though he used all his might—failed to cut off her head, though he had wounded her grievously. He tried two more times, with the same result. Drenched in blood but still alive, Cecily continued to witness to her tormentors about the love of Jesus Christ.

By law, a soldier could not strike his victim a fourth time. She was left, then, to bleed to death in her bath. During the next three days, she continued to proclaim her faith, and to give away her belongings to the poor. Many soliders were converted by her words and her good deeds; and at last, Cecily received her reward as a martyr. Her three wounds had made her a witness to the bountiful grace of God and the glory of holy Church.

The story of Cecily made a profound impression on our Norfolk girl and inspired her to pray for three "wounds" of her own. She probably did not have in mind a physical martyrdom, which in any case would have been difficult to achieve in Christian England. But she could receive spiritual "wounds" which would allow her to enter as fully as possible into the spirit of martyrdom, and the goal of self-giving and humility which she saw in Cecily. It is possible, too, that she wanted to remain a virgin in service to her Lord, like Cecily, and not marry. This form of self-denial, a "martyrdom" of its own, would not necessarily have been easy for her to accomplish. For economic reasons, the decision to marry or not would not have been her own; and unless she were a woman of some means, she could not have entered into a convent of her choice. Thus she prayed for an interior martyrdom, which would help her to live a chaste and decent life, in God's service.

She came to understand the three "wounds" in terms of three spiritual graces, which had been taught by the theologians in the Church. They were: true contrition, compassion, and a deep longing for God. Obviously, because she was already a faithful Christian who spent much time in prayer (even daring, in her youth, to ask for the two unconventional "gifts" of grace), she already had some knowledge of contrition for her sins, compassion for others, and a longing to know God more intimately. But these prayers had a technical sense of which she was undoubtedly aware, and which made them no longer the prayers of a young girl, but those of a person who was entering spiritual maturity.

The scholastics of the fourteenth century argued about the precise nature of contrition, and—as in the case of many other subtle issues—had reached a kind of theological cul-de-sac. Contrition was said to be of two kinds: ordinary contrition, and so-called "true contrition," or *attrition*.[2] A problem was how to distinguish between the two in the penitent. It had been observed, quite rightly, that there are different psychological conditions which are all thought of as "contrition": for example, one sinner confesses guilt, but repeats the offense;

another continues to experience temptation, but wards it off; still another finds that in time, the temptations are no longer there at all—they have gradually disappeared, or have undergone "attrition." Certainly true contrition meant more than simply "feeling sorry" for sins. It was debated, however, what steps would lead to true contrition as opposed to something less, and what the signs of true contrition would be. In general, it was thought that three steps would be necessary for the purging of a sin, leading to the state of true contrition. These were known as contrition, confession, and absolution (in which a penance would be imposed, and faithfully followed, if the sinner wanted truly to be rid of the vice in question).

The prayer, then, for "true contrition" was a reasonable one which was suggested by the teachings of the Church. It is worth noting that this young woman, who would later be respected as a holy recluse, expected contrition to be a "wound," in imitation of Cecily's wounds and the wounds of Christ. She wanted to lose the desire to sin, but she knew that it would not be easy. Years later, in her visions, she would learn that she would never cease sinning—but that the time would come when she would be taken out of the context of sin; and that until then, even her sins could be redeemed by her Lord, and become useful in the process of fashioning her soul.

The prayer for compassion will be admired by us today, whether we are Christian or not; but it is possible that we do not fully appreciate what it would have meant in medieval times. The Latin words, which give us the English, literally mean "to suffer along with." To the medieval Christian, it was not merely the idea of feeling pity for those who are less fortunate, or even of identifying with their sorrows. It was, rather, *suffering along with Christ*, for his sake. All Christians realized that on the cross, the pains of Christ were redemptive pains which were meant to free us from sin and eternal torment. But they were, furthermore, pains to be shared: Christ invited his disciples to follow him to the cross. To pray for the gift of compassion meant, then, to share in the redeeming passion of Christ. The question was how to go about it: whether through self-denial and asceticism, which was the way of the monks; or through patiently bearing the ills of this life without complaint; or even, perhaps, through illness and physical mortification.

Finally, the desire for compassion went hand-in-hand with the prayer for a "true longing for God." In this time of deep suffering and social misery, it would have been natural to long for the peace of God which is found in heaven alone—departing from a life in which there is, on the face of it, only suffering and disappointment. A deeper insight, however, was to desire God for God's sake: to long for the things of God, and not the things of this life, which soon pass away. This prayer, also inspired no doubt by the teachings of the Church, drew support from the great theologians, including St. Bernard of Clairvaux. St. Bernard had taught that we must love, not merely for our own sakes or because it is commanded by God, but because God is desirable, and because God is God.[3] This was, then, a prayer to long for God alone—to live a truly pure life in the midst of a troubled and immoral time.

The prayers for the three spiritual wounds never really left her—especially the second, for the gift of compassion. As for the earlier prayers, for a vision of the crucifixion and for a mortal illness before she grew too old, she forgot about them altogether—that is, until the spring of 1373, when she was thirty and one-half years old.

2

Revelations to a "Simple Creature"

In the pre-dawn hours of May 8, 1373—the second Sunday after Easter in the Old Calendar—a Norfolk priest was summoned to the house of a young woman who was dying. It was clear that she could not live for more than a few hours: "not until Prime," the women said; that is, not until six o'clock, the first Hour of prayer. The woman's sickness had done its work swiftly. She had taken ill only one week before, and by the fourth night of the fever it had been obvious that she was dying. The family sent for a priest to anoint her with oil. Somehow she survived, however, for two days more. Then on the third night after her anointing—the seventh night of her illness—her condition worsened, and it became apparent that she could not live until morning. As she began to talk of death, her family sent for the priest once more. The woman, who had given herself to God's service and to prayer, was only thirty years old.

The priest arrived while it was still dark. He had brought with him an altar-boy, who was carrying a processional cross bearing a gilded crucifix. They found the woman propped up in bed with pillows, with her eyes already fixed in an upward stare. For a moment it was not at all clear whether she could see or hear anything, for she had not moved for some time. The women related what had happened through the night: During the last few hours they had been standing by her side, wiping her forehead with cool cloths to keep the fever down.

Towards morning the fever began, however, to take an upward turn. She grew delirious and talked continually—about dying too young, too quickly; about having lived a futile life, and about wanting to serve God more faithfully. She seemed to know that she was about to pass away.

In the last hours she told her mother that she was not afraid of death, because she trusted in her Lord. Then she seemed to say that she wanted to go quickly in order to spare the family any more anxiety and also because of her pain. She complained of being "dead" from the waist downwards. Finally she asked to be propped up with pillows to ease her heart. She asked them to fold her hands on her breast; and then, with her eyes fixed on the ceiling, she neither moved nor spoke. She simply stared into the darkness as if she were waiting for her Lord to come.

The priest stooped near the woman's face and motioned to his altar-boy. There he spoke the words which she would remember for many years afterward: "Daughter," he said, "I have brought you the image of your Savior. Look at it and comfort yourself with it . . ."

With that the little boy set the crucifix near her face. We can imagine the scene: the little gold and enamel figure of Jesus on the cross, top-heavy in the child's hands, bowed politely to the pillows. It stationed itself with a jerk next to her bed, and the gilded face glowed softly in the firelight as it looked down on the sick woman. But if she could see it, she gave no indication at all. At first she continued to stare at the rood. Then, very slowly and almost imperceptibly, her eyes moved downwards until they met the face of the image near her bed.

In the next moments several things seemed to her to be happening at once. She found her breathing difficult, with a deep pain in her chest. At the same time, a strange light appeared to rest on the figure of Christ, or to emanate from the cross itself. The room meantime grew very dark and seemed to fill with demons who were waiting for her soul. Her hands fell to her sides and the paralysis which she had felt earlier from the waist downwards now crept up to her throat, making it difficult to breathe. Then she could feel nothing except for a sharp pain in her head.

At this moment she became especially aware of the crown

of thorns on Jesus' head. It looked like a garland of spring flowers; in fact, there were two garlands there, one of thorns and one of clotted blood. Beneath the ring of clotted blood, there was fresh blood trickling down Jesus' brow. It ran down his face and beard, cascaded onto the ribs and mingled with the blood of the wound in his right side. It pooled onto the white cloth around his waist, then ran delicately down his skirt to drip onto his knee. Then suddenly the blood, bright red and warm, was pooling over Jesus' brow and vanishing into midair. The visions had begun.

All at once she felt nothing: no pain, no sensation at all, and all without warning. It was strange, not like the earlier pain and numbness which she took to be the pain of dying. In one way, she felt suddenly "normal" and alive. The headache was certainly gone. It was as if all the pain had been stripped away from her, like a cloth being stripped away in an instant. Her thoughts tumbled from one possibility to another. She had been healed! It was supernatural. On the other hand, something in her did not want to be healed. For several hours now, she had been waiting for death. Oddly, it occurred to her that by being healed, she was being cheated of the chance to share in the passion of Christ—for the pains of dying had begun to seem to her like the pains of the crucifixion. She remembered her prayer for the grace of compassion, St. Cecily's second "wound."

The strange light on the crucifix was still there, together with the blood welling up from beneath the crown of thorns. Bright red blood welled up with each heartbeat and disappeared into midair. Then there was blood everywhere: bright, red blood beneath the crown of thorns, running in rivulets, pooling at the eyebrows, dripping profusely, like spring rain. The droplets came faster and faster until they looked, she thought, like the scales of a herring, one after another, or like rain running down the roof into a barrel. The blood would not stop; it was a torrent that would soak her bed. It seemed that it would fill the whole world.

Benedicite, domine! Benedicite, domine! She was shouting in ungrammatical Church-Latin, "God bless us!" But no one seemed to hear her, and no one evidently could see what she was seeing. She was afraid that the blood would soak her bedsheets. Her mother stepped forward, but instead of speaking to her, reached down to close her eyelids in death. The gesture disturbed her greatly—perhaps because it interfered for a moment with her vision of the crucifix, or because she did not want to believe that she might be dead. But there was no time to reflect on it. The face of Jesus compelled her, and began to absorb her full attention.

As she looked into the face of Jesus, a new presence filled the room. It was not her mother or friends, nor the curate, but something supernatural, a kind of counter to the demonic presence which she had felt earlier. She was being taught something, though there were no voices. Suddenly she realized what it was: the presence of God, not any intermediary, but the Holy Trinity. *This must be the judgment,* she thought; but she felt no fear. Instead she felt herself being encircled by love, like a blanket wrapped around her body. It dawned on her that if this were really the judgment, it had not come as she had expected it. The demons were not taunting her, as expected, but seemed to have fled away. There was only the face of Jesus, smiling at her, with the crown of thorns and the blood; and the sensation of being surrounded entirely by supernatural love...

Altogether the visions were to last for more than thirty hours, including a brief interlude in which she regained consciousness and spoke with a second curate, and those in the room with her. Actually, through all but the last of the visions she remained fully conscious and aware of everything in the room with her—although she appeared to her friends to have died, as she realized even at the time.

Sometime after her recovery she recorded the substance of the visions in her *Revelations.* Although she would not have used chapter divisions (or even paragraphs) in this diary, she did evidently divide the visions into sixteen distinct "showings." Exactly what separated them in her own mind is not clear, since they cannot be neatly divided according to their theological content, type of vision, length, or other immediately obvious criteria. Possibly they had appeared to her in segments, like acts of a play separated by brief intermissions.

Before looking to the meaning of her visions, it is helpful to have in mind the main points of what Julian saw. The following is a brief guide to the showings, although Julian describes so many different phenomena and lessons—some of them quite subtle—that the reader will have to study the *Revelations* carefully to note them all. In each of the visions, however, Julian is aware of certain "lessons" of love which together form a complete "showing." Julian divides her visions into those which she could see with her own eyes (called "corporeal" in Church tradition); and those which were like strong mental impressions. There were also teachings which she called "spiritual," in that she did not actually hear anything, although she was aware of being taught.

The Showings in Outline

The First Showing (Ch. 4-9): A Lesson About Love

A corporeal vision: Of the bleeding head of Jesus, crowned with thorns. (She is shocked at the vision, especially at the cruelty of the wounds. She understands immediately that she is seeing Jesus, not merely a vision; and that the showing is being given by God, and not by an angel or any other intermediary, as was the case in the legend of St. Cecelia. The Trinity fills her heart with joy.) *Two visions—one corporeal, one mental*: Of a little ball, about the size of a hazelnut, in the palm of her hand. (The little ball, probably a corporeal vision, appears at about the same instant as a second "inner" or mental vision.) Of the Virgin Mary, at the time of the annunciation. (Mary is young, only an adolescent, and at first it is not clear what the two visions have to do with one another.)

A lesson: Although it is tiny and insignificant next to God, God loves all creation continually; and this love keeps it from disappearing into nothing. True joy is to know God's love (God's humility) revealed in the birth of Christ to Mary. God relates to all things constantly and intimately, as Maker, Keeper, and Lover. (She wonders: If God is intimately related to us and is in everything, then how—or why—should we pray?)

A lesson: We should not be afraid to pray for things boldly and specifically. There is no need to pray indirectly or to invoke relics, *e.g.* "by the passion," "by the Blessed Virgin," *etc. Another lesson*: God is meek; God is humble ("homely"). God's desire is to make a home with us. We need to experience the love of God, and not merely assent to it intellectually. And this is possible because God has formed a permanent bond with us and with all creatures. *Another lesson on prayer*: We should trust God more completely than we do, knowing that God loves us and wants us to know the depths of divine love. Even though we cannot see God directly in this life, we can have faith apart from sight. We can know God's love through the revelation of Jesus Christ, especially in the crucifixion. For here God has demonstrated love, by bearing all our pain for our sakes. We ought to ask God for all our needs. It is natural for us to need things; in fact, we depend upon God. It is God's pleasure for us to ask. *Another lesson about the Virgin*: Mary thought of herself as "low" and worthless in the face of God's holiness and love. That is why we can say that Mary is "full of grace": because of her humility.

A corporeal vision: Of Jesus' head, still bleeding profusely, impressing her of the suffering which the crucifixion entailed. *A lesson*: God, who is all-mighty and all-holy, has become the lowest and meekest of all, in Jesus' birth and crucifixion. We can scarcely appreciate the humility of God's love.

The Second Showing (ch. 10): On Trust

A corporal vision: Of Jesus' face, which is discolored by severe bruising from the beatings. (She observes in detail the wounds:) dried blood, changes in color of the face, marks from heavy blows. (The vision is "dark" or obscure. She desires to see the face more clearly, but it is too dark.)

An answer: If God had wanted to reveal more, there would have been more light. This stands for something else: in this life, we are spiritually blind, because we are limited in what we can understand. Yet is is good to desire to see God more clearly, even when we cannot.

A translation: (She is carried to the bottom of the sea, finding herself suddenly among the seaweed and gravel on the ocean floor.)

A lesson: Even through the most frightening experiences (such as plunging into the water), we would be comfortable if we could really understand how much God is caring for us, in love. God is continually present, even at the depths of creation, and wants our continual trust.

The Third Showing (Ch. 11): On the Power of God

A lesson: God is in all things, and everything happens by the power of God. (She wonders, "If God does everything, then what is sin?") Silence ... (She concludes: God does not sin; therefore, sin itself must not be the acts we call "sins," but something else. It is "no-deed.")

The Fourth Showing (ch. 12): On the Blood of Christ

A corporeal vision: Of blood running from the scourge-marks on Jesus' body. Blood is running in torrents, completely covering Jesus' body and vanishing into the air. (She observes that if the blood were real, it would soak her bedsheets.)

A lesson: God made water the most abundant element on earth; but it pleases God more for us to "wash" in the blood of Jesus, to be cleansed of sin. The blood of Jesus washes away *all* sin on the earth. It even flows into hell to break the bonds of sin there (for "those that belong to the court of heaven"), and up into heaven itself.

The Fifth Showing (ch. 13): On Overcoming the Devil

A lesson: In the crucifixion, the devil has been overcome. The devil works hard to damn souls, but they can escape anyway because they share in the humility of Christ on the cross. In this way the devil is shamed: the more God allows the devil to work, the more good comes of it in the end. At the same time, God is right to oppose unalterably those souls who constantly try to work evil, even though it is God who allows the devil to work in the first place, yet restrains him. God opposes sinners, but there is no wrath in God for the sinner; only for the sin itself.

A vision: Of the Lord humiliating the devil. (She laughs, but she notices that the Lord is not laughing. She concludes: it does not hurt for us to laugh with joy and in this way to scorn the devil, seeing what God has done to overcome evil for our sakes; however, we are not laughing at evil—which God takes very seriously—but we are enjoying Christ.)

The Sixth Showing (ch. 14): On the Rewards of Obedience

A locution: (Jesus speaks): "Thank you for your service, and for the suffering [travail] of your youth."

A mental vision: Of Jesus in heaven, as Lord of a feast to which all his friends have been invited. A vision of the Lord entertaining his guests at this feast, bringing them great joy.

A lesson: Anyone who has served God for any length of time at all, will experience three degrees of joy in heaven: personal thanks from God; the announcement to all creatures in heaven of the service which was performed; and the gratification of knowing God's appreciation (which lasts eternally).

The Seventh Showing (ch. 15): On Dependence upon Christ

A realization: (She understands that within her soul there resides a place of deep spiritual joy, in which there is certainty of faith, peace, and a complete absence of fear.)

An experience of fear: (Almost immediately, she experiences profound depression and anxiety. This experience alternates with that of comfort and peace for approximately twenty times.)

A lesson: It is good for us sometimes to experience a loss of comfort and peace, so that we learn to trust God whether or not we feel comfortable—because God is always keeping us, regardless of how we feel. Also, we need to realize our dependence upon God—which is why we are sometimes left to ourselves. Therefore, faith is not something to have only when we are comfortable, but particularly when we are troubled.

The Eighth Showing (ch. 16-21): On the Passion

A vision: Of Christ's passion, just before his death. His face is deathly pale, turning blue at the point of death, then darkening. Then, a strange vision of Jesus' flesh drying out in death, especially due to a sharp, dry wind which begins to blow just at the moment of death. The words, "I thirst." (She has the thought that Jesus' thirst is both physical and spiritual.) A closer view of the crown of thorns, with its wounds to the scalp, piercing to the skull.

An experience of pain: (Suddenly she experiences in her own body the physical pains of the crucifixion. Finding this more than she can bear, she regrets ever praying for the gift of compassion, and wonders if she has in fact passed into the pains of hell.)

An answer: "No, because in hell there is the greater pain of despair."

A vision: Of the compassion of Mary for her son. (The realization that all creation suffered in the passion of Christ.)

A temptation: (She desires to look away from the cross, because of its horror. The temptation to look "up to heaven, to his father." She rejects the idea, because she finds her heaven in the crucified Christ, *i.e.* in the incarnate God.)

A vision: (A continued vision of the suffering and mental anguish of the crucifixion.)

A lesson: Jesus' suffering was greater than ours could ever be in this life, because Jesus suffered *as God*. Furthermore, Jesus suffered the actual pains and despair of all human beings, in himself. He still continues to suffer today, even though physically he has risen from the dead and ascended, because of his compassion for us in the pains of our sin.

A vision: (The crucifixion continues; it appears that Jesus is about to die. She prepares herself for this moment, but Jesus does not die, as expected.)

A vision: The face of Jesus is transfigured suddenly from death to life, and from darkness and bruising to an incredible brilliance.

A locution: (*Jesus says*): "Now where is any trace of your pain or of your anguish?"

An experience of healing: (Immediately she loses all her anxiety about the crucifixion and death; and at the same moment, all the pain of the crucifixion which she has been experiencing, ceases.)

A lesson: Passing from this life, with all its suffering, through death into afterlife, is a sudden movement from suffering into untold joy. There is no waiting between the time of death and the moment of glorification. We should not fear death.

The Ninth Showing (Ch. 22-23): On Jesus' Joy

A locution: (*Jesus says*): "Are you really pleased that I suffered for you?" (She answers that she *is* pleased. He responds that it is a joy for him to suffer for her, and if it were possible, he would have suffered more.)

A mental vision: Of three "heavens" or joys experienced by Christ in his suffering. (They are: the Father's pleasure in his Son's obedience; the love of the Son for all humanity; and the joy of having done everything for our sakes.)

The Tenth Showing (ch. 24): The Broken Heart of Jesus

A mental vision: (The Lord directs her to look at the wound in his side. In her mind, she actually passes through the wound, into his heart. The heart is cut in two by the spear, and she sees within it "a fair and delightful place" large enough to contain all human beings who will be saved.)

A locution: "See, how I love you!"

The Eleventh Showing (ch. 25): The Virgin in Glory

A spiritual understanding: (She is thinking about the Virgin Mary, who she saw before. Suddenly, Jesus invites her to see Mary glorified. Mary is revealed to her, but not in a vision as before. This is a spiritual understanding of Mary's heavenly state, sharing the glory of Christ.)

The Twelfth Showing (Ch. 26): On the Lordship of Christ

A vision: (A still more beautiful vision of the glorified Christ.)

A locution: (A series of comforting phrases spoken by Jesus):

> I am he, I am he, I am he who is highest. I am he whom you
> love, I am he who delights you. I am he who serves you. I
> am the one you are longing for. I am the one you desire. I
> am what you mean. I am that which is everything. I *am*
> what holy Church preaches and teaches to you! And I am
> the one who has shown myself to you here.

(These words seem to contain a deeper meaning, which she
cannot explain.)

A lesson: Our soul will never rest until it comes to the fulness
of joy (true life), which is Jesus himself.

The Thirteenth Showing (ch. 27-40): On Sin and Forgiveness

A teaching: (She is reminded how much she had longed for
Jesus earlier, when she desired to be with him in death. Now
she realizes that nothing has hindered her from joining him
except sin—something which is actually true for every human
being. She wonders why sin was ever permitted in the first
place. Jesus answers:)

> Sin is necessary; but all shall be well. All shall be well, and
> all manner of things shall be well!

A lesson: Everything that does not come from God, is sin. Sin
can be seen most clearly in the crucifixion, but everyone suffers
from the effects of sin. The pains which result from sin, however, can also serve to purge us from the inner desires which
are not good.

A teaching: (She asks, "How can everything be 'well,' in view
of all the harm which has come to all creatures, through sin?"
Jesus answers:) On the cross, the greatest possible harm from
sin—the fall of the whole world, in Adam's disobedience—was
reversed. And ultimately it led to a better state than before. So

we must not worry about the power of sin.

Another lesson: There are two kinds of divine truth: the truth which is our salvation in Christ, which we can know in this life; and that truth which is hidden in divine wisdom, and which is not for us to know. We should not occupy ourselves with trying to know things which we cannot understand—for example, how sin has been overcome (or why it was allowed)—and which do not pertain directly to our salvation.

A teaching: (She is continually reassured by Jesus that he has made everything to be all right, on the cross; and that he will continue to make everything all right. He longs for us to be holy, and he continues to "thirst" for all humanity to be one with him. This is his compassion.)

A review:(Two points are repeated): First, God is taking care of everything—not only the great things in creation, but also the minute details and simple things. Nothing will be forgotten. Second, although, from our point of view, there appear to be many evils which God should not have allowed in the first place, we are simply unaware of the power of God to use them. We should trust God, because the more we concentrate on the evidence of sin, and complain about it, the less we are able to receive the joy which God has for us.

A mental vision: At the Last Day, God will accomplish a "great deed" which will effectively reverse the evil effects of sin in creation. However, the nature of this deed is beyond our comprehension; and so it is not revealed to us. It will not even be known in heaven until it occurs.

A lesson (Repeating the Seventh Showing): Faith is grounded in God's promises, in God's word—not in our own feelings. Therefore, we ought to accept that God's promises will stand in all points, and not be afraid. (She desires, nevertheless, to glimpse hell and purgatory. The request is denied. She learns that sin and punishment are never mentioned in the presence of God. Then, she asks to see whether one of her loved ones (perhaps who has died) has received salvation. This request is denied also, and she is told that it is better to trust God's mercy in general, than it is to inquire about individual souls.)

A mental vision: A second "great deed" for the end of time. This "deed" has actually begun already and is understood by those who are "pierced by grace." It will be revealed in full to all who reach heaven. This deed concerns the manner in which God will reverse the effects of sin in us, even though in this life we continue to sin. (She does not at first see further into this "great deed, which is hidden mystically in the lives of Christians.)

A warning: She will continue to sin, even though she does not want to sin. But she should not worry about this unduly.

A lesson: There is a "godly will" in every soul which is undergoing salvation, which does not want to sin. Sin results in pain in this life, but for those who are being saved, who did not assent to sin in their "godly will", even the pains of sin will result in blessing in heaven. Our sin does not diminish God's love for us. On the contrary, God sees us with compassion. Therefore, we should love one another and not look for other's faults. God wills for us to hate sin and to love the soul of the sinner. (This lesson seems to explain in greater detail the "great deed," mentioned above.)

The Fourteenth Showing (Ch. 41-63): On Prayer and Salvation

(In these chapters she reviews all the showings, and comments on prayer at length. The fourteenth showing itself may be summarized as follows:)

A lesson: We should pray diligently and with confidence, because we cannot be separated from God's love in Christ Jesus. Another lesson: There are two "conditions" for prayer: We should pray rightly (*i.e.,* for the right things); and we must trust God completely.

A locution: (Jesus says):

> I am the ground of your asking. First, it is my will for you to have it [what you ask]; and since I made you desire it, and since I made you ask for it and you are asking for it, then how could it be that you should not have what you are asking for? (Ch. 41)

A lesson: We should be confident in prayer, since the Holy Spirit is the one who prompts us to pray. We should pray even when prayer is "dry" and does not seem worthwhile, because this delights God. God has commanded us to pray. All this life is in fact prayer before God. And in prayer, we are made one with God.

An understanding: (She perceives that there are two kinds of judgment.) The "first Doom" is that which she has seen in these showings, in which no blame is assigned for sin. A "lower judgment," however, has been taught to her by the Church, in which we are indeed said to be guilty—and in fact we do deserve blame. (Julian's use of the term "lower" here does not mean "inferior," but that in the second case we are judged guilty.) She desires to see in what sense the first "doom" could be true, since the two kinds of judgment seem to be irreconcilable. There is no answer, except that both seem to be right in spite of the apparent contradiction.)

A visual parable (The parable takes the form of a play): Of a great lord and his servant. The servant falls into a pit and is injured, so that he cannot move. The vision is dark, and she cannot understand it. (At the close of the play she is given to understand that the Lord intends to do something for the servant, but as the showing vanishes she fails to grasp its point.)

A mental vision: God rejoices that he is our Father, our Mother, our true Spouse, and our soul is his beloved wife. Christ rejoices that he is our Mother, our Brother and Savior.

The Fifteenth Showing (ch. 64-65): On Suffering

(She desires to be delivered from this life and its suffering. She is answered as follows:)

A teaching: She will be taken from the context of all pain and sickness into heaven in an instant, when it is the right time for her to die. But that time has not yet arrived. Since pain is due to the absence of God, there can be no pain in heaven. ("Pain" may have the double meaning of suffering, and punishment.)

The Sixteenth Showing (Ch. 66-68): On Evil, and the Reassurance that We Can Overcome It

(After the fifteenth showing the visions cease and she returns to herself, experiencing a terrible headache and the pains which she had when the visions first began. However, she feels now that she will not die, as she has been promised in the previous showing. She is visited by a parson, though not the one who saw her earlier, who asks her how she has felt through the morning. She answers that she has been "raving." But when the parson asks her to describe the "ravings" in detail— including her vision of blood flowing from the crucified Jesus— she is ashamed and refuses to answer. Feeling that she has denied Christ, like Peter on the eve of the crucifixion, she becomes despondent and eventually falls asleep.)

A nightmare: The devil, in the form of a man with red hair and a long freckled face, with hands like the paws of a beast, is assaulting her in bed. (She wakes suddenly, terrified and feeling "more dead than alive.")

A corporeal vision: Smoke seems to be pouring into the room. She screams, "Is this place on fire?" The women in the room answer that they cannot see the smoke.

A mental vision: Her soul in the midst of her heart, like a "large, endless world." Within it is a kingdom, where Jesus is reigning as king.

A locution (Jesus says):

> Now know well that it was not a hallucination which you saw today, but accept it and believe it, and keep yourself in it and comfort yourself with it, and trust yourself to it, and you will not be overcome." [Jesus vanishes from sight.]

A corporeal vision: The fiend returns, accompanied by the sensation of heat and a terrible stench. There is the sound of people whispering, as if they are mocking the saying of prayers by rote. She begins to pray aloud, unsure whether what she is experiencing has actually happened or is taking place only in her mind.

A temptation: The fiends continue to torment her through the night. She begins to recite the faith of the Church aloud (by "faith" is indicated either the Nicene Creed or Apostles' Creed). The fiends do not vanish until daybreak, when they leave behind their bad smell.

An understanding: Whenever we are tested, we can flee to Christ for comfort, and can overcome the devil.

A reminder: (She is reminded of the earlier showing—the thirteenth—in which she was taught that she will continue to sin.) These visions are meant to include all people, not just herself in particular.

A teaching: She should not be concerned with the wrongdoings of other people, but only with her own sins.

Another teaching: She should not be too grieved by the fact that she will still sin, although she should not desire to sin. The love of God is boundless. God recognizes that we will sin in this life, but God desires to teach us not to sin.

A summary of all the showings: In the final paragraphs of the *Revelations*, Julian explains that she has seen three properties of God. These may be described as life, love, and light. By "life" she understands the humble love of God (which leads to life); for God has stooped to humanity, and this humanity is given to us in our nature. It is our own life. By "love" she understands the "endless kindness" of God. Faith is also a kind of light, a gift from God, which serves us in the darkness of this life until the time that we can see God clearly in heaven. But faith and love are, in the final analysis, the same. To love God is true faith. The "light" by which we see God is also love, which is a gift from God to the soul. The purpose of all that God has done for us is to lead us into divine Love: to love as God loves, for God's own sake. In creation we had a beginning, though we were loved by God even from eternity, before we were created. And in love we also have our ending, for we will see divine love in God forever.

3

A Book for God's Lovers

I doubt whether, in the beginning, Julian ever intended to write a theological book. Indeed, for a laywoman of her time it would have seemed impossible. Theology, as everyone knew, was reserved for the men who went to university: the so-called "masters." Women were not teachers of theology because they were not even students. If they went to any kind of school at all, it was an "ABC" school—something like kindergarten to second grade, where they were acquainted with a few basic skills such as reading and counting. The learning of letters, however, was soon set aside for more "suitable" things, including homemaking, sewing, and manners. It is true that for well-to-do girls it was sometimes possible to learn more— French, for example—in the convent schools, when there were enough teachers, and the convents could provide classes. For ordinary girls, however, these things were really out of reach. Later on Julian would, in fact, describe herself as a "simple creature" who was "lewd" and "unlettered"—a rough commoner, in other words, who was comparatively uneducated.[2]

In spite of these limitations, Julian seems to have been well taught. She knows the content of great portions of scripture, whether or not she knew the letter of it; and she is familiar with teachings from the Church Fathers. Besides this, however, she had her "showings." In her mind, they provided her with an education in themselves—although, she thought, it was no more than a beginning. She referred to her lessons as an "ABC." In them she learned in particular about the profound love and compassion of God. The memory of these showings never left her, and she felt a compulsion to tell others about what she had seen. How to go about it, however, was another matter.

We remember that initially, Julian seems not to have told anyone what happened to her. She may have felt that to tell about the showings would only result in some kind of censure, since women were not "theologians," and lay believers were discouraged from dabbling with visions and other supernatural phenomena. On the other hand, not to tell about the visions meant that in time she might forget important details of what she had seen. It is impossible to know today why she changed her mind; but it seems likely, from what we are told, that she began to feel a definite calling to share the content of the visions. Possibly, too, a sympathetic priest or her confessor directed her to write them down, recognizing their spiritual value. The possibility that she could not write need not have proved to be an insurmountable problem. The great Catherine of Siena, who was still alive in 1373, had already gained a reputation for her fiery letters to the Pope—and Catherine, like most women, could not write. Similarly, Margery Kempe, whose *Book* tells of the interview with Julian in later years, could neither read nor write. The problem was to find someone, usually a priest, who would be willing to put everything down from dictation. However Julian went about it, she seems to have done it twice, producing the book in two different forms.

The first draft aimed at setting down, as clearly as she could remember them, the showings themselves. Perhaps they appeared to her as separate vignettes, like acts in a play. In any case, she found that a single "showing" contained more than one vision or supernatural event; while at times a single idea would be repeated through several of the showings. She decided not to outline them according to topic, but simply to present them in the order of the showings themselves. In order to do this, she says, she prayed for a clear memory, and to her surprise the showings came back to her vividly.

A number of questions remained, however, about the meaning of the visions, and their purpose. No doubt at this early stage she did not realize how long it would take her to grasp the depth of what she had seen. Later on she wrote:

And from the time that it was shown to me, I often desired
to understand what was our Lord's meaning. And fifteen
years later, and more, I was answered in a spiritual understanding, saying: "Do you want to know your Lord's
meaning in this thing? Know it well. Love was his meaning.
Who showed it to you? Love. What did he show you? Love.
Why did he show it? For love. Hold yourself in it, and you
shall understand and know more of the same; but you will
never understand or know anything else in it, forever." (ch.
86)

And the puzzling vision of the lord and servant would remain
a puzzle for even longer:

Twenty years after the time of the showing, save three
months, I had an inward teaching, as I shall say: "It is up to
you to pay attention to all the properties and conditions [of
what was] showed to you in that parable, even though you
think that they were murky and indistinct in your vision."
(ch. 51)

At that point she "assented wilfully, with great desire" to recall
all the details of the vision; and then she was able to recall
everything: colors, relationships, meaningful gestures. The details did, in fact, have meaning. In light of them, the whole
parable began to make sense—although there remained at
least three "secrets" which she felt she did not fully understand,
and perhaps never would. (In telling about this parable, she
notes that in fact each of the showings held a number of
secrets which she had not worked out even after years of
reflection.) It was only then, after reflection and "inward
teachings," that she was able to compose the longer, theological
work which became a theology of divine humility.

Wisely, she decided not to fill her book with personal anec-
dotes or autbiographical details which would detract from the
theological content. Some women had done so in their own
"revelations" which had been published and which were well
known. Some of these books, however, seemed to border on
hysterical—tales or emotional outpourings which would never
be taken seriously as theology. A few even confused erotic

feelings with divine revelation or extreme piety. She did not want to allow for any interpretation of this kind. The attention had to be on the teachings from God about divine love, and not on herself.

The range of experiences which she describes in these showings is remarkable. In the first showing, we may recall, she was looking at the crucifix when the showing began. Immediately, she saw the cross begin to glow, and the blood flow from beneath the crown of thorns. Then she saw the bleeding face of Jesus on the cross, in detail; she became aware of the Trinity teaching her and filling with joy, surrounding her with love; she "saw" (mentally) the Virgin Mary; she "held" the universe in her hand, as a tiny ball; and she understood, in all this, a teaching about the love of God.

She took this first revelation, so far, to be on at least three levels at once:

> All of this was showed in three: that is to say, in a *bodily vision*, and by *words formed in my understanding*, and in a *spiritual vision*. But the spiritual vision I cannot—nor may not—show as openly nor as fully as I would like. But I trust in our Lord God Almighty, that he shall of his goodness—and for your love—cause you to understand it more spiritually and more sweetly than I can or may tell about it. (ch. 9; italics added)

It is difficult to tell exactly what kinds of visions and "ghostly" experiences Julian had. Some of them were visions which she saw with her physical eyes, called "corporeal visions" by the Church. Others were spiritual or "ghostly," appearing to an inner eye ("incorporeal visions"). Still others seem to have been strong mental impressions or "inward teachings" as she calls them. These last were sometimes very complex, as detailed explanations or theological concepts. A variety of technical terms exists in the Church for such things; but without sharing Julian's own experience, and lacking much in the way of her own description of it, it is really impossible to tell if we understand her accurately. Much of what she saw, she found later, she simply could not put into words.

As she unfolds the showings, not dividing them into any kind of thematic order, she does not indicate that (for her at least) they could be understood to make a logical argument from one point to another. Each lesson has its own meaning, and is complete in itself. For this reason, it would later be difficult for Julian's editors to outline this Book of Revelations. It does not, in fact, have an "outline."

At the same time, she makes it clear that there were at least three major themes in the showings. She reveals them in the opening sentence of her book, and they are repeated in the closing paragraphs by way of a summary. She begins her description of the showings with an introduction to the three themes of Trinity, Incarnation, and mystical Union with God:

> This is a revelation of love that Jesus Christ, our endless Bliss, made in sixteen showings or individual revelations; of which the first is of his precious crowning with thorns. In it are comprehended and specified the Trinity, with the Incarnation, and the Union between God and man's soul; with many fair showings of endless wisdom, and teachings about love, in which all the showings which follow are grounded and unified. (ch. 1)

Toward the end of the book she describes the three elements of Trinity, Incarnation, and Union again in terms of three kinds of "charity," or love, which she understood to be the substance of all the showings:

> Thus I saw and understood that our faith is our light in our darkness; which light is God, our endless Day. Love is this light . . .

> And in the end, all shall be love. I had three ways of understanding this light, love: the first is uncreated love; the second is created love; the third is given love. Uncreated love is God; created love is our soul in God; given love is [what we call] "virtue." And that is a gracious gift, in which—as it works in us—we love God for himself, and ourselves in God, and all that God loves, for God. (ch. 84)

Although Julian says that all her revelations were shown "in three" (in visions, words, and mental impressions), with three main themes (Trinity, Incarnation, and Union), there are actually many other supernatural events in the showings, and other themes which run through the book. We have already glimpsed some of these events as Julian experienced them even in the first showing; ultimately they broadened to include locutions (words spoken audibly to her), instances in which she seemed to be transported to other places (called "translations"); question-and-answer sessions, in which she spoke with Christ; and so on. Major themes of her book are numerous. They include the relationship between the doctrine of the Trinity and our practice of prayer and of compassion; the feminine side of God's love in Christ, as our Mother; the experience of "falling and rising" in our daily life of faith; the significance of the Transfiguration of Jesus for Christian life; the nature of prayer leading to union with God; the relationship of God to space and time; the psychology of faith and its opposite, which she calls "dread" or fear; the true nature of the Last Judgment; the meaning of sanctification in this life through the experience of compassionate suffering; and the true nature of joy, as it is given through the ministry of the Holy Spirit.

Of these, perhaps the most significant is Julian's understanding of the Holy Trinity—a theme which, she says, runs through all the showings and which has implications for her understanding of prayer and practical Christian life as well as for Christian doctrine generally. But Julian's understanding of the Trinity cannot be separated from the rest of the showings. It defines her understanding of divine Love, of salvation, of compassion, and especially, of joy. For Julian, joy is the chief sign of the presence of the Holy Spirit; and it is a mirror of, or a participation in, the life of the Holy Trinity which is hidden in the transcendent Being of God.

All these themes operate at once and interrelate with one another, so that it is impossible to separate them or to treat them sequentially. Julian's book must be read through again and again, as we find ourselves returning to the same points several times, seeing them from new angles and with new importance. In this sense, we may view the *Revelations* as a kind of spiral, staircase, in which with each "circle" we return to points we have encountered before; meanwhile rising higher and higher in our understanding of what Julian calls her "ghostly showings," and her perception of the mystery of divine love.

Seven "Workings" of Love

While there were sixteen individual revelations or "showings" in Julian's experience, they did not seem to build on one another directly. Even Julian does not seem to have been able to relate them in any kind of theological progression. At the same time, it is possible to see in Julian's book a kind of theological movement which develops alongside the three main themes of Trinity, Incarnation and Union, or of Uncreated Love, Created Love and Given Love. This movement is presented with a mnemonic device, based on counting from one to seven. Each number represents important teachings in the visions, locutions and so forth; and together they help us to organize Julian's theology into a structure which is easy to remember in terms of the following seven categories:

ONE: *One Nature.* God is One, a perfect unity of Father, Son and Spirit. Furthermore, God is "one" with all that exists, insofar as everything which is, has being only because God is immediately present, giving it Being and sustaining it. God's love is continuously creating all things. God desires for us, who have been separated from him through sin, to be "oned" to him, to share the divine nature.

TWO: *Two Secrets.* There are two kinds of "secrets" in God: those mysteries which we are allowed to know, and are capable of knowing in this life; and those which we cannot know, by virtue of our limitation as created beings. These may be thought of in terms of two dimensions of divine being: the external "workings" or "ministries" of God (which we can know, revealed in the incarnation); and the internal mystery of God, the Trinity, which ultimately is beyond our comprehension.

Two Judgments. There are also two kinds of divine judgment, corresponding to the two "secrets." One of these we can understand (revealed in Jesus Christ, and taught in the Church); one of these we cannot grasp now, because it is still to come (though it is also promised in Jesus Christ). These also correspond to *Two Deeds* which God has accomplished in order to unite us to himself: one which was accomplished in Christ, in his birth, death, and resurrection (taught by the Church, and ours by faith); and the other which is known only to God, to be revealed only at the end of time.

THREE:

Three "Heavens." Although God is One, God is also Three: Father, Son, and Holy Spirit. The Trinity always works in three ways at once, through the ministries of the three divine Persons, who are perfectly one. Thus we may call God Creator, Savior, and Sanctifier; Power, Wisdom, and Love, *etc.* The three Persons can never be separated or confused in our creation, recreation (redemption), and keeping (sanctification). Thus, we are brought to heaven in three ways; there are three "heavens."

Three Gifts of Grace correspond to the Persons of the Trinity and the work of salvation. They are Contrition, Compassion, and True Longing (for God), in which we experience divine grace at work in the soul. They also correspond to *Three Longings in God* (to show us divine love; to bring us into heaven; and to fill us with bliss); and *Three Ways to Stand* in this life (*i.e.*, three ways to have a knowledge of what God wills for us: through natural reason, through the teachings of the Church, and through the inner promptings of the Holy Spirit). All these, finally, correspond to the three ways in which God works salvation out in our lives, through *Nature, Mercy, and Grace*, representing God's promise relating to all that exists, that "I made it, I love it, and I keep it."

FOUR:

Four Kinds of Fear ("Dread") are at work in this life, because of our sin or blindness. They are: fear in the face of trouble ("frailty"); fear of pain or punishment; anxiety ("doubtful dread"); and fear of God ("reverent dread"). Only the last can be from God, but it involves a profound change from fear of God in the sense of terror or anxiety, to "fear" in the sense of faith or holy awe. These four kinds of "dread" correspond to *Four Mercies in God*, which draw us to salvation. (God is sustaining us as "Ground of Being;" keeping us in love when we sin; teaching us where we have done wrong; and watching over us patiently while we learn. These "mercies" may be said to operate in all souls who are being saved.)

FIVE:

Five High Joys. As we come to faith, God rejoices in five ways: to be our Father, Mother, Brother, Spouse, and Savior. Experiencing the trails of life, we experience *Five Affections* at work in us at once (rejoicing, sorrow, desire, dread, and hope). In the Spirit, however, and out of obedience, we learn to rejoice in five ways: enjoying God, praising, thanking, loving, and being blessed ("bliss").

SIX:

Six Ways of Prayer are experienced by the soul who is being saved. They are: seeking ("yearning," which is the desire to know God); asking ("beseeching"); thanking; working (which is "dry" or difficult prayer); seeing ("beholding," which is contemplative prayer); and enjoying (the prayer of sur-passing union with God).

SEVEN: There are *Seven Virtues in Christ.* The gift of divine love to the soul makes the soul to be like Christ, who is the image of God and who is true God and true Man. The soul then takes on seven "virtues," which are the life of the Church on earth. They are: Humility, Kindness, Compassion; Peaceful-ness, Faithfulness, Wisdom; and Oneing with God (at-one-ment, or union with God in Christ). These correspond to the *Seven Sacraments* of the Church, by which we are nourished in this life to grow in Christ.

Julian's *Revelations* is a theological expansion of these seven themes, which serve as a kind of framework. (There are, as we have said, many other themes, a simple listing of which would require several pages alone!) Each theme relates to the others, and all together make a whole commentary on the love of God which draws us into God. In the chapters which follow we shall sketch them in, remembering that they form a unity in the "working" of love within the human soul.

4

Maker, Lover, Keeper:
The Mystery of Uncreated Love

Have you ever wondered whether God really cares about you? Whether, for example, it makes sense to pray about something relatively small (a headache, say, or an unpaid bill) to the God who is supposed to have made all that exists, and who controls the vast universe? Have you ever wondered why you have to experience hardships, disappointments, and indignities, if the so-called "God of love" really loves you and intends to give you the things which are best for you? Or have you puzzled whether in fact God *could* be present in tiny things— like microbes and atoms—and in ordinary things, like shopping for shoes and cooking breakfast, if at the same time God is "out there" taking charge of space and time? Or on the other hand, have you reflected, privately and in a moment of fear, that if hell is real—and if there really is an eternal punishment for all our sins—then God might not be a God of love at all, because a merciful God would not have allowed the world to fall into sin in the first place?

If, like most people, you have had these thoughts from time to time (beginning, perhaps, when you were very small), then you are already engaged in theology. Sometimes we are told, especially as children, that there are some questions we should not ask, or which are "improper" for people who respect the holiness of God. Theology, however, seems to begin precisely with questions like these. For it seems right to assume that if indeed there is a God who made everything, and especially if that God is love, then there is an answer for any question we might ask about nature, about ourselves, or even about God. In a sense, these questions could even be said to come from God—simply because God has put us here in the midst of all that exists already, and has given us inquisitive minds. The only limitations would be our own: whether, for example, we are really disposed in love to receive the truth; and the extent to which we are capable of receiving answers, in view of our limitations as created beings.

Julian's theology in the *Revelations of Divine Love* begins and ends with questions like these. It is what might be called a "theological inquiry," that is, an exercise in asking questions. At the same time it is an extended prayer, since Julian's questions are directed to God, and not to her own ability to reason through the questions that she has asked. Perhaps Julian knew the saying attributed to St. Anselm, that "faith seeks understanding."[1] In any case, for her the nature of faith is not so much that we have ready answers for all the deep questions of life, but that we are willing to turn to God to ask what we cannot possibly understand. This turning to God is, in fact, the only way by which we can come to understand ourselves. Julian's discovery, in the process of her sixteen revelations, is that we can know ourselves only by knowing God first: for, paradoxically, it is sometimes easier to know God than it is to know our own soul. In this Julian sees her Lord, Jesus, as a kind of "window" into the unseen mystery of God, and also into our own humanity; and not a window only, but a door through which we can enter and share in the profound mystery and joy of life, which we cannot possibly comprehend.

The starting-point for Julian's theology is the most basic question in any theological inquiry, relating to the being and nature of God: who God is, or what the being of God is "like." At the same time, this question is related to another which always accompanies it, especially in the context of suffering: the question whether God is willing, or even able, to relate to us as finite creatures; to care for us in our limitations and times of need; or (in the Christian understanding) in our unwillingness to hear the answers which God has to give, or to receive the help which God has for us, which unwillingness we call "sin."

The first of Julian's showings therefore addresses the question of the inner being of God, which Julian knew as a Blessed

Trinity; and also the relationship of the Trinity to her personally, and in general to "all that is made." In this showing Julian experienced God as intensely personal, even defining what we call "person:" as intimate and warm, not relating to humanity in some theoretical or abstract way, but in the context of the daily and ordinary affairs of life.

The Blessed Trinity

Julian's first showing began with an experience of God's presence in what she recognized as God "without any intermediary." She understood it to be the presence of the Holy Trinity, and not merely an angel, or a vision, or some kind of emotional reaction. It was a real presence in the room with her, a presence which was unmistakably warm and genuine and which conveyed to her an indescribable love and confidence. She took it to be her Maker.

Before saying more about this first showing, we have to recognize that for some readers Julian's account will already be difficult to accept at face value. The difficulty is not so much that Julian thought she had an experience of God in a vision (which we today would be likely to accept, however we might interpret it) but that the starting-point of her theology and even of her visions is the "undivided Trinity." She says that apart from the Trinity, nothing she saw can be understood, and conversely, that in her vision of the face of Jesus on the cross, she continually "saw" or understood the Trinity:

> And in this same showing, suddenly the Trinity filled my heart full of the highest joy. And I understood that this is how it will be in heaven without end, for all who shall come there. For the Trinity is God, and God is the Trinity. The Trinity is our Maker and Keeper. The Trinity is our ever-Lover, everlasting Joy and Bliss, through our Lord Jesus Christ. And this was shown in the first [showing] and in them all. For wherever Jesus appears, the Blessed Trinity is understood, as I see it. (ch. 4)

Today, many readers—including Christians and even some theologians—will feel that the concept of "Trinity" is simply too difficult to be a starting-point, and is at least irrelevant to everyday life or even to ordinary faith. It is, in fact, a concept which by definition *cannot* be understood. Therefore it would seem better to leave it alone, as a kind of addition to basic Christian belief, or a problem only for the scholastics. But for Julian, as for the Church historically, there is actually no Christian faith apart from the mystery of the Trinity. It is not only basic, but is the starting-point, so to speak, for all Christian faith and practice, the point from which everything else is derived. We will see how this is true for Julian as we learn, with her, about the inner humility of God, the Trinity, as the theological substance of her first revelation. In the meantime we will remember, as basic to all Julian's theology, the principle that "wherever Jesus appears" (both in Julian's visions and in her theology), "the Blessed Trinity is understood, as I see it." In her first showing, Julian *saw* the face of Jesus, who appeared to her on the cross; but she *understood* the whole Trinity, who was at that moment filling her heart with joy.

A Humble God

We recall that in the first showing Julian was looking into the face of Jesus, observing his suffering and the crown of thorns. At the same moment she experienced a bodily healing, and the overwhelming sense of being surrounded by love and the presence of God (ch. 4). The experience was at once wonderful and dreadful. She did not find it unpleasant, but she could not help being afraid in the sudden realization that she was in the presence of Almighty God. It was both something which she did not expect and which she did not feel she deserved. Evidently her expectation at this point was to be plunged into hard testing by fiends, before the time of her judgment. (In her understanding, she explains, she believed that every person is judged at the time of his or her death; and that at that moment, fiends would appear to try to take away, if possible, whatever faith a person had.) She did not, in her opinion, merit any kind of supernatural presence of God because she was a sinner and a common woman, and not a great saint of the Church. So while she could hardly wish to be anywhere else, the first thought which came to her was the question why the vision had been granted to *her*, and not to someone more worthy. This question then led to the speculation how God could, in fact, be present to *any* person, simply because we are creatures and God is God:

> And I said, *Benedicite domine* [Blessed be God]! I said it
> meaning to be reverent, but with a loud voice. For I was
> greatly astonished at the wonder and marvel of it, that he
> who is so holy and dreadful could be so "at home" [homely]
> with a sinful creature still living in wretched flesh. (Ch. 4)

Still unable to comprehend that God really wanted to speak
to her directly, she concluded that the love which she was
experiencing was simply intended to prepare her for the shock
of a confrontation with devils which was still to come:

> Thus I took it at the time, that our Lord Jesus, of his
> courteous love, wanted to show me comfort before the time
> of my temptation. For (I thought) by the permission of God
> I should be tempted by fiends before I died. With this vision
> of the blessed passion, with the Trinity that I saw in my
> understanding, I knew well that it was enough strength for
> me—yes, and to all living creatures—against all the fiends
> of hell, and spiritual temptations. (ch. 4)

Ultimately the point of this revelation proved to be otherwise; it was not just to prepare Julian for the time of temptation
(which did indeed come some hours later) but to teach her
about the humility of God. The showing continued in Julian's
vision of "our Lady, St. Mary." Julian suddenly envisioned
Mary at the moment of the annunciation. At once she understood something profound about Mary which had not been so
obvious to her before.

In this mental vision, Mary appeared in surprising simplicity.
She was not "queen of heaven," but a simple peasant-girl. This
however was the whole point: Mary's greatness lay in her deep
humility and her simplicity. In Julian's vision, Mary simply
said, as scripture records of her, "Behold, God's handmaid."
Apart from the emphasis upon Mary's humility, two other
points were being made here: first, that God (who is almighty,
and the maker of all that exists) desires to make himself known
to simple creatures; second, that he *can* make himself known
to us (specifically now to Julian) because of his own self-
emptiness or humility. The humility of God appears in the
incarnation itself. He deliberately chose to be born of a

common woman, in divine humility; and because God was born of woman, there is now a permanent bond between his own being, and humanity. God is one with us.

Julian's sudden realization that God is humble, and not merely "dreadful," immediately deepened her understanding of how he relates to us in this life. Before, she had been a pious Christian who longed to be with God in heaven. Now, she learned that God—who is all-powerful—is already with us in this life. She learned, furthermore, that he—who is all-holy— wants to be known by us in this life, not merely abstractly (as through doctrines or rules), but intimately and personally. As the first showing developed, including a graphic vision of the blood running down Jesus' face from the thorns in his scalp, Julian began more and more to realize that God is compassionate, entering fully into the suffering and misery of this life; and that he is "courteous," or kind, relating to us as if we were somehow equals:

> This showing [of the crucifixion] was vivid and lifelike, hideous and dreadful, sweet and lovely. And of all the visions it was the most comforting to me, that our God and Lord, who is so holy and dreadful, is so humble and courteous. And this completely filled me with happiness and assurance in my soul. And in order for me to understand this, he showed me this plain example:

> It is the greatest honor that an awesome king or a great lord could do for a poor servant, to be friendly [homely] with him; and specifically, if he shows it himself, sincerely and cheerfully, not only in private but also in public. Then the poor man thinks: 'Ah! What could this noble lord do to honor me more, or to give me more joy, than to show me—simple as I am—this wonderful friendship [homelihood]? Surely it is more joy and pleasure to me than if he had given me great gifts, but he himself had acted like a stranger ... '

> For truly it is the greatest joy that could be, as I see it, that he who is highest and mightiest, noblest and worthiest, is also lowest and gentlest, most humble [homely] and courteous. (ch. 7)

Julian's use of the word "homely" in this passage and else-where is especially significant. It is linguistically related to the word "humble," and may be a variant spelling of the same word (in Julian's English, the two would have been pro-nounced alike). Like the word "kind," which we have already seen to have several meanings, the word "homely" needs to be understood in various ways. We may translate "friendly," "common," "humble," or "personable." It also carries the sense of "hospitable." It includes the word "home," and so suggests something to do with family. It further has the meaning of permanence, that is, of making a "home" and remaining in that place. As Julian uses it here, it means unpretentious friend-ship. In America, where the word appears at all it has taken on a negative aspect: not only "plain," but "unattractive" or even "ugly." In England it still retains the flavor of its original meaning: warm, attractive, comfortable, simple (in the positive sense of being beautiful without being pretentious). In the end, however, there is no real equivalent for "homely" today. Perhaps, in the language of the American South, Julian would have said that God appeared to her in a "down home" fashion, humble, as a family member.

We notice that in this passage Julian describes God both as "homely" and as "courteous." In the fourteenth century, to be "courteous" meant more than it would mean to us today. It had to do with the king's "court," and therefore, with the behavior of people who lived in the palace in the presence of the king. Knights were expected to learn "courtly" manners, which ideally involved many things: a certain way of speech, refinement, self-effacing behavior, fairness, and so on. All these had become the theme of songs and "romances," with which Julian would have been familiar. Modern scholarship would suggest that we should not take the "courtly" ideal very literally as universally true among the knights and nobility in Julian's time. But that would seem to be Julian's point: her experience of Christ was of a *true* lord, a genuine knight. She knew that he would be kind, never rude or proud; that he would listen to her, and that he would give his life—and had given his life—to defend the honor of his own serfs. And there was the promise that one day, she could enter the "court of heaven," where Christ—and no earthly king—would reign eternally.

In the first showing, and in them all, Julian's experience was of a personable, yet holy, God, surrounding her with love. The point of this vision, beginning with the image of Mary at the moment in which she became the Mother of God, was to show that God is both humble and kind: wanting to communicate intimately with his creatures, and also capable of it. Julian was amazed and perplexed, but her soul was overjoyed: "I was greatly astonished ... that he who is so holy and dreadful could be so 'at home' with a sinful creature living in wretched flesh."

God "in a Point"

Then Julian received a second lesson, which relates to the vision of Mary but which carries it still further. It had to do with the conception of Jesus in Mary's womb. Julian calls it "God in a point"—that is, in an infinitely small (or mathematical) point in space and time.

As Julian was looking into the face of Jesus and experiencing the mental vision of Mary, something appeared in her hand "about the size of a hazelnut." At once she understood that it was not merely a ball, but represented the whole universe. Suddenly she was afraid that the ball, which appeared very "frail," would somehow disappear. And then, in the midst of her fear, she felt the reassurance that it would not disappear, simply because of the immediate presence of God: "God made it, God loves it, and God keeps it."

This unspoken reassurance did not have to do with the nature of the tiny point itself, but with the nature of God, the Trinity. Specifically, Julian learned that the God, who is "dreadful" and who made and controls all things, is also "homely" and therefore intimately related to this tiny "point" in the universe. While she did not at first understand this vision, through the showings she began to be comforted by it—eventually calling it the most comforting showing of them all.

In order to grasp the impact of what Julian saw, we can try first to imagine the vision itself. It is possible that in explaining it, Julian had in mind something very common: her "point" may be a stitch of petit-point, something with which any of her friends would have been familiar.[2] In a flash she realized that in the incarnation, God had deliberately been reduced to such a "point" as the embryo in Mary's womb. This thought brought with it the question, how it would be possible for God to be present in such a small space. As Julian looked intently at the "point," her vision expanded.

Now we may accompany her as the tiny ball becomes a "window" into the universe. A voice in our understanding says, "It is all that exists." Suddenly we are traveling beyond the room in which we are sitting, into the night sky and beyond the moon and stars. From our position in space, we are able to observe earth and moon only as tiny bright lights, joining other little lights which make up the universe. As we continue to travel further away, the whole tapestry of tiny lights becomes a single, twinkling ball in the dark sky. The stars—themselves tremendously far apart—are like dust hovering in the air next to an open window. Yet from our distance, they begin to appear as a single, tiny ball of light.

Moving now at an unthinkable speed to fantastic distances, time no longer has any meaning for us and space seems very small indeed. It is as if we had grown to an immense size, so that we are able to look down onto all the galaxies at once. The little ball of light—which we know is actually made up of an infinite number of tiny stars and planets—gives the appearance of being a solid object. Suddenly we realize that it is not so much made up of solid objects or substances, as of *space*— space which in fact is only thinly scattered with lights, many of which themselves are made of nothing solid, but are merely collections of whirling gases and clouds of light.

Immediately the question presents itself: what holds all this together? Why doesn't it fly apart? And if it is chiefly made up of *nothing* (the spaces between the stars and planets), then in what sense can we say that it really exists? It appears to be more "not there," than "there." What is it? Where did it come from? What keeps it from disappearing?

Julian, of course, had no idea of galaxies and outer space as we think of them today; but her description of the vision suggests something like the trip we have just described. It is interesting that her questions about the tiny ball would apply equally well to the universe as to the invisible world of atoms and subatomic particles. Modern science has demonstrated that even the most dense substances, or collections of particles, are more "not there" than they are "there." The relative distances between points of mass in even hard substances, like diamond or iron, are vast. As to what holds things together—whether we mean galaxies, or subatomic particles—it is difficult to say. The invisible "forces" are, in a sense, more important than the substances themselves; yet no one knows what they are. Julian's questions, then, are also modern ones.

Julian recognized that she would not receive final answers to questions like these, but she also realized that she did not have to be afraid. Her initial fear, that the ball would fly apart because of its frailty and insignificance, was suddenly calmed by an overwhelming sense of comfortable love: "It exists only because God loves it." God is at work there, in the "point" itself, constantly re-creating it and keeping it, in love.

While Julian's insight may seem obvious, put in this way, we have to realize that actually it was not obvious in terms of her cultural view of cosmology: that is, of the universe and the way in which God relates to it. Julian's showing, furthermore, is significant for the way in which we tend to look at the same questions today. In Julian's time the popular idea—inherited, really, through Greek philosophy, and making its way through medieval scholasticism—was that God is "in Heaven," outside the reach of ordinary space and time. In this view, things exist without falling apart because they have their own intrinsic order, or "logic." One natural conclusion from this way of thinking is that God set everything in motion long ago (in creation), but that now things run essentially on their own. Another conclusion, perhaps unconscious but nevertheless important, is that God—or our idea of God—is basically irrelevant to the ordinary affairs of daily life. Miracles, in this view, would be a kind of divine interference from "outside." Now, Julian's vision of the "hazelnut" strikes at the heart of this way of thinking; and, interestingly enough, brings her to a concept of God and the universe which is at once modern (in the sense of post-Einsteinian physics) and more in accordance with the historical and traditional teachings of the Church.

It is sometimes shocking to the non-scientist today to discover that, from a purely scientific point of view, what we casually perceive as "natural laws" operating in the universe—such as gravity, for instance—are not really "laws" at all. They are merely hypotheses, or conjectures, on our part. We may "know," for example, that apples always fall towards the earth; but this "knowledge" has to be qualified by the fact that under certain conditions, apples do *not* fall towards the earth; and that we can never be sure apples will fall in that direction tomorrow, just because they did yesterday; and that, in any case, calling this phenomenon "gravity" does not tell us anything about what "gravity" is. *In fact, no one really knows what it is.* This fact need not disturb us, however, because not knowing what "gravity" is does not prevent us from, for example, picking apples. We can live as if things will continue tomorrow much as they are today—even though this is neither a logical nor a scientific certainty. For Julian, our relative certainty about the state of affairs around us (that they will continue, that we can relate to the world in a consistent way and so on) is a matter of faith rather than any kind of certainty. It is trust in the goodness of God, who is the immediate cause of everything that has being. All things continue to exist, and to show predictability, because of the continuous presence of divine love which sustains them.

If God is not *outside* the reference of space/time (and in Julian's visions it is clear that God is not), then "where" is God? In Julian's perception, the humility of God makes God present in every point of space and time—even though we cannot say that God is "in" space/time or subject to dimensions as we are. To understand this concept fully, we will have to see more of Julian's vision. Meanwhile we notice that for Julian it is impossible for God to be a distant Creator, or irrelevant "first cause" of the universe. God is the intimate Love of all that is, and the act of creation—far from taking place in the distant past—is taking place continually, at every point in space and time, in the love of God.

In the third showing, Julian's vision of the tiny ball was repeated, but this time not in a corporeal vision:

> After this, I saw God in a point—that is, in my mind's eye.
> By this vision I saw that he is in all things. (ch. 11)

The idea of God "in a point" was not new with Julian, although her interpretation of it was not what we might expect. In the

Middle Ages, the idea could be illustrated easily in terms of the "center point" of all that exists. This was conceptualized as something like a stone being swung in a circle, on a string. The center of the circle—the middle point—does not move; but the stone itself revolves around the center-point, and the center "makes" it move. Philosophers and theologians compared the idea of the moving stone to that of the universe. God, they said, is like the center of the circle, or a "point" which does not move, but which causes everything else to move by its power.

Put in this way, the idea of the "point" may be traced to the earliest philosophy of Western civilization. It was argued by Plato and Aristotle, as the "unmoved mover" or (in Platonic thought) as the "idea" or *logos* which lay behind all that exists, as its source. We should be careful to notice here that in the Greek idea, this "still point" was not Creator in the Christian sense. The idea of "creation" is essentially dynamic, that of "calling something out of nothing"; whereas for the Greeks, as for much of later philosophy (including, perhaps, our own general world-view today), the idea of the Source of the universe did not have this dynamic quality at all. It was, rather, of something which was unmoved by nature: the Being which may have set things in motion originally, giving order to the primal elements of the universe, but which remains undisturbed and essentially unknowable. It is impossible to know this "prime mover," because "mover" and "moved" do not exist on the same plane; they cannot touch one another. In this view, even if we were to call the center of all things "God" (in a more personal sense), nevertheless we would have to see this "God" as untouched by the world in which we live. Julian's assertion is precisely the opposite.

God, Space and Time

Julian's concept of the divine relationship to space and time deserves to be explored further, because it will help us to understand the rest of what she has to say about the ways in which God works with us in this life, and the way God was revealed to Julian in her visions. It is important to understand Julian carefully here, because on this point she is easily misinterpreted; and because the whole question of God in relation to space/time is critical to Christian theology—certainly in Julian's view—and is, on the other hand, perhaps generally understood very differently in our contemporary culture.

So far, we have said that the most important element of Julian's visions was her awareness of God (the Trinity) as immediately present to her, in "homely" fashion. Now we can see the implications of this experience for the rest of her theology, especially as it relates to her vision of the "point."

Throughout the *Revelations*, as a result of this first showing, Julian assumes that God is present *here and now*. At the same time, she paradoxically assumes that for God, there is no space or time as we know them. God is present in space/time, but God is not bound by the dimensions of space and time.[3] The practical implications for this way of thinking are numerous. For example, if there is no time in God, then "when" was creation? We would have to conclude that the "time" of creation (in our perspective, a long time ago) is actually the same "time" as now. Furthermore, the time of things which have not yet occurred (the Last Judgment, for example) would also have to be *at the same time*. Two people, dying in different years, could enter paradise at the same "time," although at the moment of their own deaths. It becomes obvious that in this scheme, many of the questions which we ask about life, especially with relation to time, no longer make sense. They are not "real questions" any longer, because they become unnecessary in view of the relationship which God has to space and time as we know them.

A survey of the *Revelations* shows that Julian speaks of time indifferently: she can say, for example, that a particular event *will take place*, that it *has already taken place*, and that it *is taking place*—all at the same "time." From the divine perspective (as she learned about it in her showings), it will appear that different events at different times inhere in one another; they are simultaneous, although they are not the same act. There is, in a sense, no past or future, but only "now." On the other hand, this "now" embraces all time, stretching back to creation and forward to the Last Things, which are the end of time as we know it. We cannot say that, in this view, there is so much an *absence* of time (which would imply a cold, immobile "prime mover" outside the universe) but a dynamic "now" in which everything is happening at once: an explosive point, in which God is equally present to all places and all times at once. In the course of her showings Julian seems to have shared this perspective, so that she does not consciously describe it, but assumes it in explaining what she saw.

Having said that Julian's view of space/time is of a single, dynamic "point" which is equally accessible to God, we must immediately remember that Julian's theology, paradoxically, tends to approach the questions of God's interaction with the world in terms of *processes*, rather than as isolated *events*. The effect of Julian's view of time is to "slow down" our way of thinking about creation, for example, or of salvation history. We will see that creation is not merely "once," but continues to the present day. Salvation is not an either/or category, or an instantaneous decision or judgment, but a process of growing into the fulness of humanity, in the image of God. In part, this is because "when" questions must be viewed in a new way. For example, the question "When were you saved?" could be answered, for Julian, equally well by a reference to the past ("On Good Friday, when Christ descended into Hell;" or perhaps, "On Easter morning when he arose from the dead"); to the future ("I am saved in his merciful judgment, which is not yet") or in the present ("I am being saved, by God's grace").

The principle is well illustrated with relation to Julian's view of creation, although we will see it operate through the rest of her theology. Speaking of God's love for us, Julian points out that, in a sense, creation began "before" creation, in the purpose of God to create. Not only this, but our individual creation—as human beings—shares in the original creation of humankind. God is creating now, just as God was always creating, in the sense that God intended to create us out of his eternal love:

> God, the blessed Trinity—who is everlasting Being—just as he is endless, from without-beginning, in the same way had it in his purpose endlessly to make mankind; which fair nature [kind] first was prepared for his own son, the second person. And when he wanted, by full accord of all the Trinity, he made us all at once. And in our making he knit and oned us to himself. (ch. 58)

Julian's language here is open to interpretation. She appears to mean both that it was God's "endless purpose" to make humanity; and that God is "endlessly making" humanity, since creation itself takes place without reference to time. She makes this clear when she says that "he made us all at once," meaning not only that God created us "at once" (in an instant) but also "at once" (all at the same time). Julian's point is not the idea— once found heretical by the Church—that God created all souls, and then gradually released them into bodies at different times; but that for God, the moment of creation is the same moment in which each one of us was conceived.[4] We are all individually created with Adam, the first-man. We are all "at once."

This way of thinking is next extended to include the incarnation (which Julian saw in the visions of Mary, and of the "hazelnut"); and then the judgment, and indeed every divine act. Julian overturns the usual idea that after creation there is a sequence of the "fall" (into sin), the incarnation, and salvation (on the cross), followed in time by our own coming-to-faith. While it is true that these things appear to us to have happened in sequence, separated by time, they are not in fact separate events from God's point of view. In that case, not only do we share in Adam's creation, but when Adam sinned we fell into sin at the same time; and at that same moment, the son of God became incarnate in order to rescue us from sin:

> When Adam fell, God's son fell. . . Adam fell from life to death, into the "hole" of this wretched world; and after that, into hell. God's Son fell with Adam into the "hole" of the maiden's womb—who was the fairest daughter of Adam [i.e., Mary]—in order to excuse him from blame in heaven and in earth. And mightily he fetched him out of hell. (ch. 51)

The moment of Adam's fall, then, is also the moment of his salvation. It is also the same moment as the incarnation of the Son of God and is, coincidentally, the moment of Jesus' descent into hell, by which Adam (representing all humanity) was "saved." All these events took place *in* time and are therefore separated from one another; but from the divine perspective, they were all-at-once. If that were the case, then Julian can conclude—as indeed she does—that in the moment Adam was "fetched" out of hell, we too received salvation. It may be that we were baptized in our own time, but our baptism coincides with the conquering of the "fiend" in hell. And this moment of salvation, finally, corresponds to the moment in which we all are judged—which judgment is not only at the Last Judgment (which finds us all together), but also at the moment in which we die, individually:

> Then I said to those who were with me: "Today is Doomsday for me." And I said this before I went dead [or, "because I knew I was dying"]; for the day that each man or woman dies, he is individually judged as he shall be without end, as to my understanding. (ch. 8; CE)

We need give just one more example of Julian's perception of the divine relationship to space/time. It is in the promise, which she received from Jesus on several occasions, that "all shall be well, and all manner of things shall be well." This passage is often quoted in literature about Julian—always in the future tense. However, Julian actually heard the promise in past, present, and future tenses. It is something which God has already accomplished, will accomplish, and is accomplishing, all at the same time.

In the thirteenth showing, Julian reflects that if sin had never been allowed to exist in the first place, then all things *would have been* "well" (ch. 27). In response, Jesus tells her than sin is "behovable" (i.e., "just as well," or necessary and useful) but nevertheless all *shall be* well:

> But Jesus, who in this vision informed me of all that I needed to know, answered in these words and said: 'Sin is necessary, but all shall be well, and all shall be well, and all manner of things shall be well.' (ch. 27)

Later, when Julian repeats her doubt that all could be "well" in view of the damage which has been caused by sin, she is told for the second time that God *has already* provided a solution for the sin of Adam (ch. 29). Still later, she is told that

> I may make all things well, and I can make all things well,

and I shall make all things well, and I will make all things well; and you shall see for yourself that all manner of things shall be well. (ch. 31)

The promise here includes what is possible by virtue of divine authority ("I may"), what is possible by virtue of divine wisdom ("I can"), by divine intention ("I will"), and finally, in the promise ("I shall"). Julian concludes from this that *all is well already:*

> ... for in the third showing, when I saw that God does all that is done, I did not see sin. And then I saw that all is well. But when God was showing me about sin, then he said, 'All shall be well.' (ch. 34)

Thus, what God *will* do, God has *already accomplished* in his purpose and in the incarnation of the Son of God. It is the inner nature of God to act freely, without respect to time or space as we understand them. To have said all this, however, is to run ahead of ourselves slightly; for we are here concerned first of all not with the interaction between God and the world (the "workings" of the Trinity), but with the Being of God the Trinity as God is in himself.

Three 'Heavens': The Mystery of Indwelling

Earlier we saw that the principle of revelation which Julian experienced in her showings was that Jesus, appearing on the cross, acted as a kind of "window" into the unseen Being of God. Wherever Jesus appeared, the whole Trinity was to be understood, as she saw it. Julian was unable to make a separation between the incarnate God whom she could see, and the "hidden" nature of God, whom she could not see.

We note that Julian nowhere says that she could see into the essence of God, the Trinity—something which, she would have regarded as impossible. Instead, she experienced the presence of God in his "workings," which revealed the unseen nature of God to a certain extent. This revelation was never separated from the flesh of Christ, and she did not experience it in any other form. The principle at work here may be called "indwelling"; that is, that the Son of God lives in flesh and so has become visible to us; and that the whole Trinity lives in the Son of God, and so—through him—has become known. Julian describes her understanding of the principle in terms of a strange vision of three "heavens." They do not seem to have been literal "heavens" in the sense of places, but rather three kinds of joy, or three ways by which we come into heaven:

> Experiencing this [the voice of Jesus], my understanding was lifted up into heaven. And I saw three heavens, and greatly wondered at the sight. And I thought: 'I see three heavens, and all are in the blessed humanity of Christ; and none of them is greater, and none of them is less; none is higher, and none is lower; but all are equal in blessedness.' (ch. 22)

The three "heavens" were all "in the humanity of Christ," that is, visible to Julian in (or through) Jesus' humanity. By "heavens" she means three kinds of "blessedness" in God. She continues,

> As for the first heaven, Christ showed me his Father—not in bodily form, but in his Fatherhood and in his way of working; that is to say, I saw in Christ *what the Father is*. (Ch. 22, emphasis added)

Further along in this same passage Julian says that she saw in the "second heaven" an eternal love, which she identified with the ministry of the Holy Spirit. She is careful, then, to point out that she did not *see* the Father and the Holy Spirit, but only their "working." In Christ, she could see what the Father does, and what the Spirit does; and she could see that the Father and the Spirit are "at work" in the incarnate Son. Therefore, the Son revealed to her the nature of God, the Trinity. In a vision of Jesus speaking to her from the cross, she sees the Father's love expressed in the Son. Similarly, the Creator of all that is, is the Father—who nevertheless has created through the Son. In this sense, although the Father is not incarnate, nevertheless because the Father works or lives "in" the Son, we can say that the Father himself has come down into the place of suffering and humiliation on the cross, in the Son:

> For truly it is the greatest joy that could be, as I see it, that
> he who is highest and mightiest, noblest and worthiest, is
> the lowest and meekest, homeliest and most courteous. . . .
> For the perfect fulness of joy that we shall have, as I see it, is
> this marvellous courtesy and homeliness from our Father,
> who is our Maker in our Lord Jesus Christ—who is our
> Brother and Savior. (ch. 7)

Here we see that the Father is at work in the Son and is
present in the Son, and the Son in the Father; but only the
Son is "visible," because only the Son took flesh from Mary
and became fully identified with the created world. Julian
concludes from this that we will be unable to see God in any
other way, because the nature of God is otherwise too far
above our own nature to be comprehended:

> Man is blinded in this life, and so we may not see our
> Father, God, as he is. And whenever he, in his goodness,
> shows himself to man, he shows himself humbly [homely],
> as man. Nevertheless, I saw truly that we ought to know
> and believe that the Father is not a man. (ch. 51)

This insight leads us to the central visual parable of the
showings, the vision of the lord and the servant (the fourteenth
showing). This particular showing seemed to hold within it the
key to all the rest, but it remained a puzzle to Julian for nearly
twenty years. One reason is that in the beginning, Julian's
interpretation of the vision amounted to a case of mistaken
identity.

In the vision, Julian saw two men who looked just alike,
except that they obviously occupied different stations in life.
One of them was a great lord, and the other was a poor
servant. Julian naturally took the great lord to be Christ and
assumed that it was Christ seated in judgment. The servant, on
the other hand, stood for Adam, insofar as she could tell, and
therefore represented "all men." It was some time, before she
realized that the servant also represented Jesus, the incarnate
Son—who himself represents, or comprehends, all humanity:

In the servant is comprehended the second person of the Trinity. And in the servant is comprehended Adam; that is to say, every-man. Thus when I say "the Son" it means the Godhead which is equal to the Father. And when I say "the servant," it means Christ's humanity, which is the true Adam. (ch. 51)

If the servant also stood for the Son of God, embracing all humanity, then who was the great lord on the throne? Julian suddenly realized that the lord on the throne was indeed the Father, but the Father represented to her *in the form of the Son.* Her conclusion was therefore that, while it is impossible for any mortal to see God, it is nevertheless possible to "see" God in the incarnate Son; for God shows himself "in homely fashion, as man," through the Son who suffered and died on the cross.

We have said that Julian's concept, which is basic to Christian faith, is called "indwelling," that is, that the Father and the Holy Spirit live "in" the Son, and the Son "in" the Father and the Spirit. Through the Son it is therefore possible to "see" the unseen God. Julian relates this principle especially to Christ on the cross, whom she continually sees in her visions:

The whole Trinity was at work in the Passion of Christ, bringing overflowing virtue and grace to us through him. But it was the Virgin's son alone who suffered. And so the whole Trinity is filled with endless joy through this. (ch. 28)

The Trinity, then, is "three kinds of joy," or "three heavens," all of them present in the incarnate Son, and all perfectly One.

A Circle of Love

The "indwelling" principle which Julian develops here is linked directly to her understanding that God is "homely." Because of the inner humility of God, two things are true: first, the Father chooses to be known only in the Son, in "homely" fashion (and in a like way, the Spirit is known only in the Son, and the Son in the Father, *etc.*); second, the Son has become flesh through the Virgin Mary, in "homely" fashion, taking to himself humanity and human suffering and humiliation. Now Julian shows that his "homely" relationship within the being of God actually defines what we mean by "love." It is an existence of absolute self-giving, so that each Person only lives "in" the others. Julian calls this mutual indwelling "uncreated charity."

Extending the principle that through the "workings" of the Trinity we become aware of the inner being of God (which cannot be seen), Julian learns all the various ways in which the Trinity is at work in us and in the world around us. Using the traditional language of the Church, she sees the work of the Trinity in terms of the different attributes or "virtues" of the three divine Persons. At the same time, these individual dimensions of the divine Being—who are really distinct Persons—can never be separated. It is characteristic of Julian's theology here that she resists a tendency, found especially in Western scholasticism, to divide the Trinity on the one hand; or to depersonalize the Persons, by seeing them merely in terms of "virtues" or attributes, on the other hand.

In the early Church, St. Augustine had referred to the Persons of the Trinity in terms of three primary virtues, or ways in which the Persons are seen in the scriptures to work. They are: Power (the Father, who is "source" and creator of all things); Wisdom (the Son, who has saved us in the "wisdom" of God); and Love (the Holy Spirit, who is the bond of love between the Father and the Son, and who sheds love into the hearts of the faithful).[5] While using Augustine's basic language, Julian stresses that all three Persons are always at work in every "work" of God, always at the same time; so that no lines of separation can really be drawn between the divine Persons. Furthermore, the Spirit cannot be seen as merely the "love" between the Father and the Son, because Love itself is defined by the relationship of indwelling—the humility, or "homeliness," of God—which is within God as the Father, Son, and Spirit live within one another and work in one another. In her view, Father, Son, and Spirit all share in creation; all are present in the crucifixion, even though only the Son of God is incarnate; all participate in the work of our sanctification. All three, together, are "love:" for love is to live and work in another, in absolute humility.

Julian says that in her vision of Jesus on the cross, she also "saw" the Father, "inwardly." She sees, too, that both the

Father and the Son participate in creation (ch. 7). Finally, all three Persons work together in a necessary relationship of Maker, Keeper, and Lover—creating, saving, and loving as One:

> The Trinity is our Maker, and Keeper. The Trinity is our everlasting Lover, everlasting joy and bliss, through our Lord Jesus Christ. And this was showed in the first [showing] and in them all. For wherever Jesus appears, the Blessed Trinity is understood, as I see it. (ch. 4)

The Trinity, then, is a circle of love, in which all three Persons are constantly present in and with the others, and the work of the Trinity (in creating, saving and sanctifying) is all one work, creating love in us.

Since the "workings" of the Persons of the Trinity cannot be separated, Julian always speaks of the Persons of the Trinity together. She refers to God in a variety of ways, following the conventional language of her time, but she always emphasizes that the Persons of the Trinity do not work separately. God is "Maker," "Lover," and "Keeper" (ch. 4); "Truth," "Wisdom," and "Love" (ch. 44); "Fatherhood," "Motherhood," and "Lordship" (ch. 58). The Father creates us, the Son re-creates us, the Holy Spirit perfects us (ch. 58). The Father creates, the Son saves, the Holy Spirit moves us to repentance (ch. 39). "Our Father wills, our Mother [the incarnate Son] works, our good Lord the Holy Spirit confirms" (ch. 59). "The high might of the Trinity is our Father, and the deep wisdom of the Trinity is our Mother, and the great love of the Trinity is our Lord" (ch. 58). "God Almighty is our kindly [natural] Father: and God All-Wisdom is our kindly Mother; with the love and the goodness of the Holy Spirit; which is all one God, one Lord" (ch. 58). The work of each Person would be incomplete without the others.

The "workings" of the Trinity, therefore, lead naturally into one another. There is a kind of continual motion within the Being of God, such that each Person is directed "outward," so to speak, to the others both with relation to God's work among us, and within the Being of God itself. Thus, our creation leads to our "re-creation" (in the Son of God) and our perfection (in the Spirit). Creation is followed by salvation, and by our own repentance and faith; the Fatherhood of God is complemented by God's act of Motherhood (in our salvation) and the Lordship of God (in our life of faith). The Being of God as Truth leads naturally to the expression of truth, which is true Wisdom (the Son); but true Wisdom is also divine Love (the Spirit). The will of God (the Father) is expressed in the outward work of God (in the Son), which is made sure in creation by the Spirit of God. The Father cannot be seen except in the Son, who is incarnate; and we cannot recognize the Son except by the Holy Spirit. The love of God, then, is like a circle: the Love which is the Father leads naturally to the Love which is the Son, and this love is expressed in Love which is the Holy Spirit.

The Divine Paradox

If the Trinity represents to Julian a kind of "circle" or movement of divine Love from one Person to another, at the same time we have to say that for Julian there is within the Trinity a perfect peace, or rest, in which there is not any "motion" in the sense of change at all. Julian sees in the Trinity a paradox of motion and stillness. The medievals referred to this paradox in terms of two states, or qualities, within God: the state of "procession" (the movement of one Person into the others, and vice versa); and the state of "session" (the divine peace of the Persons, in which they are sitting still). Both are true of God at the same time.

In speaking of the "workings" of God, or any kind of acts of God or "motion" within God, the medievals did not understand that there is literally any movement or change within the Being of God. "Procession" and "Session"were used by way of analogy, to point to the relationship of the divine Persons to one another. Julian therefore makes it very clear that change itself is excluded from God, in the sense of earthly motion in which there is always a change in the state of affairs. In the picture of the stone swinging in the circle, which we saw earlier, the stone is always changing position—something which the center point cannot do, because "God does not change."[6] Julian emphasizes the teaching of the Church on this point, assuming that it would be impossible for God to age, decay, to be consumed—or even to change his mind. She points out that while humanity is always changing in certain respects, God cannot change:

> I understood that man is changeable in this life, and falls into sin through weakness and by being overcome. On his own, he is weak and unwise, and also his will is led astray. And in this life he is storm-tossed, and in sorrow and woe. And the cause of this is blindness, because he does not see God. (ch. 47)

or again,

> And when I saw him scorn the devil's malice, it was to lead my understanding into our Lord—that is to say, it was an inward understanding of his steadfastness, that he does not change his mood. For this, as I see it, is a fact of God that must call for praise—*that he does not change*. (ch. 13, emphasis added)

She therefore conceives the Trinity to be at perfect rest or peace:

> Now the Son no longer stands before the Father on the left-hand side like a laborer, but he sits at his Father's right hand in everlasting rest and peace. But it does not mean that the Son sits on the right hand, side by side, as one man sits by another in this life; for there is no such sitting, as I see it, in the Trinity... Now is the spouse, God's Son, in peace with his beloved wife... Now the Son, true God and man sits in his city in rest and peace, which his Father has prepared for him by his will, which has no end and no beginning. And the Father is in the Son, and the Holy Spirit is in the Father and in the Son. (ch. 51)

The paradox of motion and stillness in God is summarized by the phrase "homely love." On the one hand, "homely" means a movement away from the self—making a home with someone else, visiting, being "friendly." On the other hand, it implies peace and rest, as someone who finds a dwelling-place and remains there. Julian may have been familiar with the teaching of the Church that we have mentioned, in which there was expressed a play on words in Latin: God is in constant (or incessant) motion, which is a "process" of love. At the same time, in God there is a steady peace, or "session." Like the circle, which may be thought of at once as a point which is constantly moving in a circle around the center, and also as a constant perimeter which does not deviate or change in position with regard to the center-point, God has the quality of *circum-incessio* ("constantly running in a circle"), and *circum-insessio* ("constantly sitting in peace").

Interestingly, Julian's explanation of the paradox exactly parallels the development of this idea in the historical theology of the Church. When the image of the "circle" was first applied to the Trinity in Christian theology in the Greek idea of *perichoresis* ("running the circle"), it was applied to the revelation of the Father in the Son: the idea, as Julian puts it, that "I saw in Christ what the Father is." Later on, it was applied to the self-giving relationship of the Persons of the Trinity, such that all three Persons are always present whenever one is present: or again, as Julian has it, "Whenever Jesus appears, the whole Trinity is understood."[7]

Finally, Julian seems here to anticipate by some six centuries the development of an idea in theology known as "process theology." Put simply, Process Theology—taking its cue from contemporary science and philosophy—proposed that God is dynamically involved with all that exists.[8] If in the past Western philosophy and theology had assumed that God is more or less "outside" the realm of space and time as an unchanging "unmoved Mover," the recent idea of relativity in science has seemed to imply that God, too, is related to every thing. As against the rather boring picture of God—that God does not change or move—process-thinking has attempted to see God within the world of change as we know it. The reasoning is that if God is related to everything which takes place in the "system" of space/time—all that is —then God, too, must be "dynamic" and must undergo change, for change is an integral part of the universe as we know it. In fact, if anything in the universe were to change at all, everything else (according to this theory) would have been altered to some degree, however slight; God, too, would have "changed."

Julian would accept the idea that God is dynamically involved with all that is. This is, as we have seen, the meaning of her vision of God "in a point." On the other hand, it is fundamental to her theology that God does not change; for if God could change in anything, the universe itself would not be predictable, and our salvation would be impossible. Julian will argue, as we shall see, that God's mercy lies precisely in the fact that God's judgment is not changed by our actions. There is a paradox, then, in Julian's theology of divine interaction with all that exists, on the one hand, and divine peace and unchangeableness on the other. God is compassionately involved with all that happens in this world, including (and perhaps especially) our suffering; but at the same time, God does not "suffer" in the sense that we know it. Thus, we will see that, for Julian, whenever there is change in the universe, however slight, there is corresponding compassion in God; and conversely, that the whole universe suffered when God (in Christ) suffered on the cross. At the same time, the fact that God does not change but remains infinitely humble and self-giving, enables us to be healed from the effects of change in this world which cause pain to us in this life.

The unchanging humility of God is what we call "love." It is built into the nature of God. If this is so, then it is impossible for God not to love:

> I saw truly that our Lord was never wrathful, nor ever shall be. For he is God: he is Good; he is Truth; he is Love; he is Peace. His might, his wisdom, his charity and his unity do not allow him to be wrathful. For I saw truly that it is against the nature of his goodness. God is the Goodness than can never be wrathful; because God is nothing but Goodness. (ch. 46)

The love of God is identical with the Being of God, his "substance:"

> For as soon as he [God] made us, he loved us. . . This is the love [which is] made of the divine substantial love of the Holy Spirit, powerful because of the power of the Father, wise in the consciousness of the wisdom of the Son. (ch. 53)

God's love is constant and does not exclude anything:

> God is all that is good, as I see it. And God has made all that is made, and God loves all that he has made. (ch. 9)

Or most simply,

> Love which is unmade is God. (ch. 85)

5

Two Secrets:
The Mysterious Gardener

(A Vision of Doom)

It may be very comforting to say that "God is all goodness" and that God is present and at work in everything; but it also raises serious questions about what we can see with our own eyes in this life. In this world not everything is "good" as we see it, and even a moment's reflection will reveal to us (if we are at all honest) that we ourselves are hardly infallible or even wholly desirable. Now, if God does everything and is in everything, then it seems clear that God is at fault for all the wrongs in the universe. To state the problem in another way: If God has allowed evil to come into the world (whatever evil may be), then God has caused—or at least allowed for —every kind of suffering and depravity, including death. It is clear that we are at the mercy of God, but it is not clear that this God is really "love."

These questions occupied Julian very early in her experience of the showings. To blame God for all the evil in the world seemed, on the face of it, to be unthinkable; on the other hand, she could not escape the unavoidable questions raised by the first showing:

> After this, I saw God in a "point." (This vision, as I saw it, was in my understanding.) I paid close attention to this, seeing and learning in it that he does everything which is done. As I saw it, I wondered quietly, with a feeling of dread, and I thought: "What is sin?" (ch. 11)

Other questions soon came to mind, relating to the vision of God in the "point." How, for example, can we hope to avoid sin and to do what is right, if ultimately God is responsible for everything which happens? Are we pawns in God's hands, and therefore cannot help doing either good or evil—depending upon what God has decided for us in advance—or are we somehow responsible for what we do? But if we are held responsible, isn't it unfair, since God does everything? And is there ultimately any difference between good and evil, if God has permitted both? In view of this dilemma, how can we pray? For surely God will do whatever God has already determined to do; and it remains that some of what God wills appears "evil," in that God has allowed suffering to enter into the world. In the thirteenth showing Julian expressed her doubts along these lines:

> After this our Lord brought to mind the longing that I had for him before; and I saw that nothing prevented me but sin, and I saw this generally in us all. And I thought that if sin had never existed, we would all have been as clean and like our Lord as when he made us. And so, in my folly, before this time I often wondered why, in the great foreseeing wisdom of God, the beginning of sin was not prevented. For then, I thought, everything would have been all right. (ch. 27)

Later, as she is taught that there is no wrath in God, she once again puzzles how we can possibly understand sin:

> But yet here I wondered and marveled, with all the diligence of my soul, thinking like this: 'Good Lord, I see you, who are Truth itself; and I know surely that we sin grievously all day long, and are worthy of much blame. Now, I can neither leave off knowing this truth, nor can I see you showing to us any manner of blame. How can this be?' (ch. 51)

Julian goes on to say that so far, in her visions, she has seen no more blame for us than if we had been holy angels in heaven.

But this did not square with her understanding of the teaching of the Church. Moments after thinking these things, however, an answer appeared in the form of a parable.

Julian seems to have understood that this parable occupied a central place in her showings, but she does not seem to have realized, initially, that it had anything to do with the questions at hand. It was a story acted out rather like the "miracle" and "morality" plays which were commonly presented at the city market. In this case, it was a "mystery" play of a special kind, having to do with Doomsday, or the Last Judgment. This kind of play, always popular with children, was acted out on a "hell-cart"—a special type of wagon which served as a portable stage. In the wagon floor was a secret trapdoor. At the right moment, the antagonist in the play would fall through this door into "hell."

From Julian's narration, it appears that her play was in this case a mime, in which the actors say nothing until the end. Then the principal actor makes a short speech to the audience to explain, with some wit, what has just taken place. The audience is expected to guess, meantime, the meaning of all the actors' gestures, and the answer to the riddle or "mystery" which has been presented. In Julian's particular play there were only two actors, who could be recognized by their costumes: a nobleman, or lord; and a simple laborer, who appeared to be a gardener. The object of the play was for the audience to guess its meaning, and at the same time to enjoy the inevitable jokes which would take place on stage. The whole play, however, took only moments to perform. We can imagine that in Julian's vision, it may have lasted for only a few seconds. In chapter 51 Julian tells us exactly what she saw.

The Play...

The scene is a large, barren stage. There are no props, except for a single chair which resembles a throne. Around it everything is deserted; in fact, the scene reminds us of a vast desert. Two actors enter from either side. One of them appears, with his ample robes, to be a man of high rank. The other is a workman in a muddy kilt. The gardener waits until the nobleman is seated on the throne, and then takes his stand, back to the audience, a little to the nobleman's lefthand side.

As we watch in silence, the gardener receives his instructions for the day's work. There is a treasure hidden in the earth, he learns, which belongs to the nobleman. The gardener is to find it. With pick and shovel, he begins to dig a deep hole. (The audience claps with delight.) The hole which the serf has dug now appears to be an irrigation canal, or a farmer's dike.

The play continues: What grows in the ground that is a "treasure?" Food, of course! (Laughter ensues; the peasants immediately recognize the reference to recent famines, and the fact that food is always being requisitioned for the land-owning nobility.) Now the serf is given instructions to perform a new task, which this time is truly impossible. He has to plant fruit trees in the master's garden, and when the trees have grown and have borne fruit, he must harvest it all and prepare a meal for the master. All this must be done swiftly, of course, because the master is hungry and thirsty. The gardener sets out with a tiny appleseed in his hand. (The audience is delighted with the obvious political implications of the scene.)

We watch now to see how the servant will perform this "great deed," but it is not to be. As he turns to do his master's bidding, he carelessly falls backward into the pit which he has just dug—down through the trapdoor! After one or two hapless attempts to pull himself out of the hole, he slides to the bottom and lies unconscious. (The audience gets to its feet and roars with laughter.)

At the same moment, something is happening on stage. The lord has risen from his seat and is approaching the trapdoor. Bending down, he extends his hand into the hole. We expect him to lecture the poor servant for his carelessness, but instead the master simply looks at him with pity and concern. Then the nobleman turns to the audience and begins his soliloquy, gesturing dramatically:

> [Shaking his head:] "Look, now. Look at my beloved servant! [Laughter.] What harm and injury he has taken, and all in my service and for love of me! Yes, and all out of his own good will, too. Is it not reasonable that I should reward him because of this dreadful fright—his injury and all his unhappiness? [Members of the audience shout, "yes, yes!"]

"And not only that, but doesn't it fall to me to give him a
gift which would be better for him—not to mention more
... ahem! ... honorable, that this [gesturing to the trap-
door] *hole* of his could ever be? Otherwise, I think, I've
done him no favors at all! [The audience signals its approval
by clapping.]

The master extends his arm into the hole, and the curtain falls.
For Julian, the two actors on stage have vanished, and the
play—and the vision—have ended.

An Unsolved Riddle
    Who was this mysterious gardener, and what was the mean-
ing of the play? Apart from the fact that Julian could not link
it with the serious theological questions which she had just
raised about sin, the nature of prayer, the divine judgment,
and so on, she found herself unable to solve the riddle of the
play itself. At first it seemed that the characters, however, were
simple enough to guess. The nobleman in his beautiful blue
robe, seated on the throne, was obviously intended to be Christ
in judgment. (Manuscript paintings, called "illuminations,"
inevitably depict Christ in judgment in this way.)[1] The gardener, on the other hand, digging in the soil, must represent
Adam; for Adam was the "gardener" of Eden, and he had
gotten into trouble over a fruit tree. His punishment was to till
the soil forever, and for committing the sin of bringing evil
into the world Adam had surely been cast into hell. This
interpretation, however, did not satisfy Julian. It seemed too
simplistic, as she thought about it; and anyway there were
several difficulties with it in view of the traditional elements in
any morality play.
    The chief puzzle in this play was its outcome. Adam, as
everyone knew, ought to have been scolded by the Lord because of his carelessness. In one sense, "Adam" represented a
comic figure—a kind of clown, who tumbled into hell through
his own stupidity. On the other hand, the symbol of his "fall"
had to be taken seriously. He had committed the greatest sin
in the world; equal, perhaps, only to the sin of those who
crucified Jesus (ch. 29). However, at the moment that the
Lord should have rebuked him, he did not. In the closing

soliloquy the Lord spoke rather of rewarding him. As Julian contemplated the gardener's misery, she found that she, too, was unable to find any fault in him:

> I wondered how this servant could suffer all this woe so meekly. And I looked with attention to see if I could perceive in him any fault, or if the Lord should assign to him any blame; and truly, there was none to be seen. For only his good will and his great desire was the cause of his falling; and he was as likeable and as good inwardly, as when he stood before his lord, ready to do his will. (ch. 51)

In fact she had become fascinated with the gardener, and found herself pitying him for his plight, instead of laughing at it. When he fell headlong into the ditch, she was suddenly struck by the notion that this might not be a comedy after all; for the gardener really had been wounded, in more ways than one. She later recalled seven different kinds of wounds:

> The first was the sore bruising that he took in his falling, which was to him a "feelable" pain [*i.e.* a serious injury; he wasn't acting]. The second was due to the heaviness of his body. The third was his weakness, following on these two. The fourth was that he was blinded in his reason, and stunned in his mind, so much that he nearly forgot who he was [*or*, "whom he loved"]. The fifth was that he could not rise. The sixth was the most significant to me, and that was that he lay alone. I looked around to see, and far or near, high or low, I saw no help for him. The seventh was that the place where he lay was narrow, hard and grievous. (ch 51)

Finally, in the closing soliloquy she had the impression that the servant would be elevated to a higher state than that which he had occupied before the fall; higher, in fact, than he could have occupied if he had not fallen:

> And in this an inward spiritual showing of the lord's meaning descended into my soul, in which I saw that it is necessarily so—and worthwhile, in view of his great goodness and his own glory—that his most valuable servant

whom he loved so much should be truly and blissfully
rewarded without end, above what he would have been if
he had not fallen; yes, and furthermore that his falling, and
all his suffering that he had taken from it, shall be turned
into high and surpassing glory and endless bliss. (ch. 51)

At this point, however, the showing itself ended. Although in
the next moments a new showing began, Julian found that she
could not follow it. The play was still in her mind, and the
riddle was still unsolved.

A Further Explanation
Julian explains in her *Revelations* that the parable remained
in her thoughts for the next several years. At the time of the
showing she felt that she had some measure of insight, that the
wounds of "Adam" were significant, although she was not sure
why. Afterwards she continued to gain insight into the meaning
of the play, which she found herself visualizing constantly. In
the passage of time, she was unable to separate in her mind
those things which she had understood from the beginning,
and those which came to her only later on. In any case, she
relates that she had further explanations of the parable from
time to time, the last being nearly twenty years ("save three
months") from the time of the showing.
In her supernatural teaching, twenty years afterward, Julian
was instructed to notice the details of the play itself, some of
which she must have overlooked initially. An inner voice said
to her,

> It is up to you to pay attention to all the properties and
> conditions [of what was] showed to you in that parable,
> even though you think that they were murky ["misty"] and
> indistinct in your vision." (ch. 51)

Julian's words here could mean either that she found the vision
difficult to understand (it was "misty," *i.e.* mysterious), or else
that in the actual vision itself there had not been very much
light, so that things appeared indistinct to her. However, she
found at this point that she could, indeed, recall many details
which before had not meant very much to her. She reflected

especially upon the way the lord had taken his seat; the place where he sat; his face, and the color of his robes; the position of the gardener before his fall; the condition of the gardener's clothes, and so on. These things helped to give her a new interpretation to the vision, which she saw as having been given on several levels at once. Although she felt that these details helped her to have a deeper insight into the meaning of the vision, she never felt that she understood it fully—nor, indeed, the rest of the visions either.

In the parable of the lord and servant, Julian had already noticed that the lord's blue robe was "very ample," like the sky. She recalled that his face was very handsome and young, with dark, sincere eyes. The servant's clothes were muddy and worn, as if they had been used for many years; on the other hand, the servant himself appeared to be clean and pure, like a novice who had not soiled himself in the mud. Julian also noticed for the first time that the throne really was situated in a desert, outside of which it was very dark; and that the servant had been standing at the lord's left-hand side before turning and falling into the ditch. It seems to have been during this later reflection, too, that she noticed the several ways in which the servant was injured in his fall.

We have already seen that the blue robe of the lord identified him, to Julian, as Christ seated in judgment. In some paintings, artists also attempted to depict God the Father; and they clad this figure in blue too, although he was depicted as an old man with white hair and beard. However, in the case of Julian's vision the lord did not have a white beard, but a youthful face—like the face of the servant.

The servant, she thought, could not represent simply Adam but would have to stand for All-men in the fall into sin. It was vexing, however, that this person did not seem to incur any guilt or blame when falling into the ditch. If this figure were to represent the fall into sin, surely he should have been guilty of a great sin! There was an additional clue in his clothing, which was worn and muddy even though he himself seemed to be pure; however, she was not sure what the clue meant. One thing was sure: the vision was intended to answer her questions about sin and blame. From the play, it was clear that God did not blame "Adam" in his fall but pitied him because of his

injury. Julian especially noticed that Adam fell because of
weakness, and not because of ill will. After the fall, he was
unable to see his lord clearly and so had fallen into darkness
and despair. The lord, then, judged him with pity and not with
blame:

> And this was the beginning of the teaching, which I saw at
> that moment—whereby I might come to know in what
> manner he views our sin. And then I saw that only pain [in
> the "fall"] blames and punishes, whereas our courteous Lord
> comforts and succors. He is always of good cheer to the
> soul, loving and longing to bring us to bliss. (ch. 51)

Now Julian reflected on the kindness and compassion of the
lord. It was as if, she thought, Christ judges Adam—and all
humanity—with the same compassion which the Father has
for his own Son, on the cross. This interpretation seemed very
beautiful, but the problem of our guilt remained. Also, what
was the meaning of the desert? And why were the gardener's
clothes so worn? Meantime she realized that the "treasure"
hidden in the earth represented more than literal food. It meant
that the great lord, who represented Christ, was hungering and
thirsting for something on the Earth. The desert meant that in
the place where Christ had taken his seat, this spiritual "food"
was missing. He would have to depend upon the humble
servant to bring it to him.

The Final Solution

The solution to the riddle lay in finally identifying the mysterious figure of the gardener, whom Julian first took to be
Adam and then All-men. Suddenly she realized that he represented not only Adam (and all humanity), but also the Son of
God. He was true man, and also true God. The purity of the
servant was the purity of the Son of God, who does not soil
himself with our sin. On the other hand, the mud on his kilt
represented the "travail"—the suffering and the pains—of all
the sins in the world. The kilt was, indeed, the same as that
which Jesus wore on the cross. Furthermore, in this vision the
white loincloth represented humanity itself, which the son of
God "wore" in order to serve the Father. It had been soiled

and stained by sin and by the "sweat" of our own hard labor in the condition of sin. Adam's hard work in digging the dyke was not merely a punishment for disobeying God but represented the hard "work" of living in the place of sin. And it was also the work of Christ in bringing us out, by descending into the place of hell.

In the moment that Julian realized the servant was also Jesus—the servant of the Father—she had to rethink the meaning of the great lord. She realized then that the lord was not merely Christ in judgment, but also a vision of the Father, in the Son. The Father was not to be depicted as an old man (because God does not have attributes of age, a literal right and left hand, and so on), but the Father had made himself known on earth in the form of the Son. Just as the Son of God had come to live in the flesh, so the Father lives in Son. Therefore, in order for the Father to appear in Julian's parable, he appeared in the form of the Son. Julian then had the solution to her riddle:

> In the servant is comprehended the second person of the Trinity; and in the servant is comprehended Adam, that is to say, all-men. And therefore when I say "the Son," it means the Godhead which is equal to the Father; and when I say "the servant," it means Christ's humanity, which is the true Adam. By the nearness of the servant [to the Lord], is understood the Son; and by standing on the left side is understood Adam. The lord is our Father, God. The servant is the Son, Christ Jesus. The Holy Spirit is the equal love which is in them both. (ch. 51)

In the last chapter we examined the theological concept of revelation which Julian derived from this parable; and also the concept of indwelling which was illustrated here. Now a new principle is revealed concerning the nature of the Last Judgment. Three points are made: first, the Father has given over all judgment into the hands of the Son; nevertheless, it is the Father who judges, "in" the Son. Second, the Father judges humanity in light of the Son: when he looks upon Adam, he sees not only Adam, but also the "second Adam," who is Christ. Third, in the judgment of God, the pains which we suffer from sin are the pains of the incarnate Son of God on the cross. The cross comprehends all the sin of the world; therefore, when the Father looks upon the suffering of his Son he sees the suffering of the world, and when he sees the suffering of the world, he looks upon it with pity, as the suffering of his only Son.

We remember that Julian saw seven ways in which "Adam" suffered in his fall. She could now see these in a new light, in terms of Jesus' suffering on the cross. They are, at the same time, the chief ways in which all human beings suffer in this life. She interpreted them as follows: 1) physical pains; 2) a sense of "heaviness" in this mortal life (our corporeal nature, which leads us into sins of the flesh); 3) human weakness (a spiritual inability to overcome temptation); 4) spiritual blindness (in which we forget that we are children of God and cannot see that God looks upon us with love and pity); 5) our inability to help ourselves (we cannot rescue ourselves from the misery of sin and the fear of death); 6) anxiety, especially the sense that we are utterly alone, and have no one to help us as we face the reality of death; and finally, 7) the harsh confines of this life, including its shortness and its pain, because the fall into sin is also a fall into death.

The "fall" of Adam into the deep chasm therefore represented two things: the fall of humanity into sin and death, and also the fall of the Son of God into the human condition—even into hell, where Christ went in his desire to serve the Father. From God's point of view, these events could not be separated, not only (as we have seen) because there is no time in God, but also because in the will of God, there was provision to heal the sin of Adam (all-men) in the moment that it occurred. Humanity, so to speak, did not "lose time," because God had already made provision for our fall. Julian concludes, then, that for God, there is no separation between our individual "falls" into temptation, and the "fall" of Christ into the place of suffering and death on the cross. From the beginning, God has had compassion on us in our suffering:

> ...in all this, our good Lord showed his own Son and
> Adam to be but one man. The virtue and goodness that we
> have is from Jesus Christ, and the feebleness and blindness

that we have is from Adam (which two things were symbolized in the servant). And thus our good Lord Jesus has
taken upon himself all our blame; and therefore our Father
cannot, nor will not, assign any more blame to us than to
his own son, the beloved Christ.

For he too was a "servant" before his coming into the earth,
standing ready before the Father with this purpose—that at
the right time he would send him to do that glorious deed
by which mankind was brought again into heaven. That is
to say, even though he is God, equal to the Father with
regard to his godhead, nevertheless in his foreseeing purpose—
that he would be man, to save men by fulfilling his Father's
will—he stood before his Father as a servant, willfully taking
upon himself all our charge. (ch. 51)

A Vision of the Transfiguration

A final lesson in all this came in the "touching" of grace
which Julian received many years after the initial vision. In a
new flash of understanding, Julian saw the servant lifted out
of the "hole" and clothed in a new robe more beautiful than
the blue one of the Father. It was the color of the rainbow,
more glorious than anything she could have imagined. This
inward teaching was, she realized, a glimpse into the glory
which Christ now has at the right hand of the Father and also
a symbol of the resurrection of Christ from the dead. His
suffering was greater than ours might ever be because he suffered *as God*: blameless, from eternity. The Father did not
make any effort to spare his Son this pain, because it was his
purpose from the beginning to share with us in every way, and
more. But in death, the Son descended into hell and "fetched"
Adam out. Rising on the third day, he was glorified by the
Father. In so doing, he raised our own human nature out of
suffering and death (the "narrow" and "straight" place) into a
vast kingdom, the place of God's own nature. This glorification
corresponds to Jesus' own glorification:[2]

The body lay in the grave until Easter morning, and from
that time on, he never lay down again. For then was right-
fully ended the wallowing and writhing, the groaning and

the moaning. And our foul, deathly flesh that God's Son took onto himself, which was Adam's old skirt—straight, threadbare and short—then by our Savior was now made fair, white and bright and of endless cleanness, wide and ample: fairer and richer than the clothing which I saw on the Father. For that clothing was blue; but Christ's clothing is now of a fair, becoming mixture which is so marvelous I cannot describe it, for it is all truly glorified. (ch. 51)

Julian notes that in her vision of Christ in glory, he was no longer standing on the Father's left-hand side, but was seated on his right, clothed in the rainbow, with a crown of precious jewels on his head. These jewels, she learned, are the faithful:

> For it was showed that we are his crown, which crown is the Father's joy, the Son's glory, the Holy Spirit's pleasure, and endless marvelous bliss to all who are in heaven. (ch. 51)

The desert, which represented our soul in the place of sin, has now turned into a fair city where the Son rests in eternal peace and joy. All this she understood to be a parable of the reality of heaven; for, she is careful to point out, Christ is not sitting at a literal "right hand" of the Father, but in "the highest nobility of the Father's joy. . . . " And where he sits, we sit—for we are one in him; and his throne is in our own soul:

> And then our Lord opened my spiritual eye, and showed me my soul in the midst of my heart. I saw the soul so large, as it were an endless world; and as it were, a blissful kingdom. And from the circumstances that I saw in it, I understood that it is a glorious city. In the midst of that city sits our Lord Jesus, God and man, a fair person and of large stature; highest bishop, most solemn king, most worshipful lord. And I saw him dressed solemnly and gloriously. He sits in the soul, established in peace and rest . . . The place that Jesus takes in our soul—he shall never be removed from it, without end, as I see it. For in us is his "homeliest home," and his endless dwelling [or, "endless union,"—*wonying*]. (ch. 68)

The Compassion of God: "I Thirst"

So far, we have seen in the parable something about the nature of divine judgment. We have seen that there is compassion in God, in that the Son of God (in whom the Father lives, has taken humanity upon himself, so that when the Father looks upon the suffering of the world, he sees the suffering of the Son of God on the cross. Now this lesson can be explored further in light of Julian's vision of the hunger and thirst of the great lord—the original riddle in the "play" which she saw in her vision.

The hunger and thirst of the nobleman represent, for Julian, the "thirst" of God to draw all humanity to himself. This is something which could not be accomplished except through the Son (depicted in the servant); and it could not be done except with hard work, the "travail" of falling into the place of sin and death. At the same time, it comprehends the thirst of Christ on the cross, a graphic vision of which Julian had earlier, in the eighth showing. She understood it spiritually:

> And thus our good Lord answered all the questions and doubts that I could make, saying most comfortingly: 'I may make all things well; I can make all things well; I will make all things well; and I shall make all things well. And you shall see for yourself that all manner of things shall be well.'
>
> ... And in these five words God will be enclosed in rest and peace; and thus shall the spiritual thirst of Christ come to an end. For this is the spiritual thirst of Christ: the love-longing that lasts, and always will, until we see that sight on Judgment Day...
>
> Therefore this is his thirst: a love-longing to have us all together, whole in him, for his bliss, as I see it. (ch. 31)

The "thirst" of God, which was enacted by Christ on the cross, defines what Julian means by divine compassion. It is God suffering with us, and also God being compassionate in the sense of looking upon us with pity and understanding. It is made possible by the incarnation itself—because by taking flesh to himself, it became possible for God (who is Spirit) to share in our suffering. God does not suffer in his own divine nature; but God has taken our suffering into his own nature, through the fact of the incarnation:

> And so I saw Jesus lingering for a long time; for its union with the godhead gave strength to his human nature to suffer, out of love, more than all men might suffer. I mean not only more pain than any man might suffer, but also that he suffered more pain than all the saved men who ever existed, from the very beginning to the last day, might tell or even imagine...

> ...and for every man's sin that shall be saved, he suffered. And every man's sorrow and desolation, he saw; and he grieved out of kindness and love. For as much as our Lady sorrowed for his pains, so much did he suffer sorrow for her sorrow—and more, inasmuch as his sweet humanity was more worthy by its nature. For as long as he was passible, he suffered for us and sorrowed for us. And now that he is risen and no longer passible, still he suffers with us. (ch. 20)

The compassion of God is a "thirsting" for all humanity to be holy. In a common medieval motif, Julian sees this as God's desire for all humanity to be saved. This thirst continues to the present time:

> ...for the same thirst and longing that he had upon the cross—which desire, longing and thirst, as I see it, was in him from without-beginning—he still has, and shall have until the time that the last soul that shall be saved has come up to his bliss. For as truly as there is in God a property of compassion and pity, as truly there is in God a property of thirst and longing. By virtue of this longing in Christ, we are able to long for him in response. Without it no soul comes to heaven. And this property of longing and thirst comes from the endless goodness of God, just as the property of pity comes from his endless goodness—although longing and pity are two different properties, as I see it.

> In this, the point of spiritual thirst is established—which will last in him as long as we need it, drawing us up to bliss.

All this was seen in the showing about compassion (which itself will cease with the Judgment Day). Thus he has pity and compassion on us, and he has a longing to have us; but his wisdom and his love do not allow the end to come until the best time. (ch. 31)

It is a lovely point of Julian's theology that God, who longs for us to be "in bliss," nevertheless does not allow it until the "best time."

The Servant's Fall

The nature of God is compassion, and God—who is in all things—suffers with us, on our account. But the question remains, "What is sin?" Does God sin? Julian is sure that God himself does not sin; at the same time, God is responsible for everything that happens:

I paid close attention to this, seeing and learning in it that he does everything which is done. As I saw it, I wondered quietly, with a feeling of dread, and I thought: "What is sin?"

For I saw truly that God does everything, however small. And I saw truly that nothing happens by accident or by chance, but everything is in the foreseeing wisdom of God...

Therefore I found it necessary to grant that everything that is done, is done well—for our Lord God does everything (for in all this time, the work of creatures was not showed, but the work of our Lord God in the creature). For he is the mid-point of everything, and he does everything; but I was certain that he does not sin. And here I saw surely that sin is not anything which is done; for in all this, sin itself was not showed. (ch. 11)

Pursuing this question later, in the thirteenth showing, she learns that it is impossible to see sin itself; what we see, rather, is the pain which sin causes in this life:

In this naked word, "sin," our Lord brought to my mind in general all that is not good, and the shameful despising and

utter humiliation [*or*, "nothingness"] that he bore for us in
this life, and his dying, and all the pains and passions of all
his creatures, spiritual and physical . . .
But I did not see sin. For I believe that it has no substance
of any kind, not even a particle of being. Nor could it even
be known, except by the pain that it causes. (ch. 27)

In the fourteenth revelation, the nature of sin is however
shown clearly for Julian in the parable of the lord and servant.
Sin is like the ditch, or "hole," into which the servant fell. Its
power is that it "is not," for a "hole" is actually a spot of
nothing, in the midst of something. In this case, it is the
absence of God's work and God's will. There appear, then, to
be two reasons why Julian could not see sin: first, it cannot be
seen at all, insofar as it is the absence of something rather than
a positive sustance or activity; second, it is so destructive in
itself, that God will not allow us to see it directly. The nature
of sin is revealed by what is good; otherwise we would not
know of it at all:

Our Lord, in his mercy, shows us our sin and our weakness
by the sweet gracious light of himself; for our sin is so vile
and so horrible that he, out of courtesy, will not show it to
us except in the light of his grace and mercy . . . [for] we
could not endure to see it as it is. (ch. 78)

In light of the divine compassion, which reaches into hell to
rescue Adam, Julian begins to understand sin in terms of an
injury to humanity—or a "weakness" or incapacity, which
must be overcome. It is not merely the things we do, but the
context in which we live our lives. We have already seen the
various pains which result from sin, as Julian saw them in the
gardener's fall. Now we may sketch the nature of sin itself as
she sees it illustrated in the parable:
1) Sin is weakness ("frailty" or "feebleness"). While Julian sees
God in terms of "Might," "Wisdom," and "Love," sin is our
inability to do, to know, to love. It is immaturity; it is power-
lessness (like the gardener at the bottom of the ditch).
2) Sin is blindness. In light of God's love, we should know all
things. But sin is a kind of darkness, in which we do not

understand even ourselves. (Julian will elsewhere link this "blindness" to our attempts to judge others.) Chiefly, it prevents us from seeing and understanding the compassionate love of God. Therefore, we blame God for our suffering in this life. The blindness leads to doubt and despair, and is evident in our unreliability and changing moods:

> I understood that man in changeable in this life, and falls into sin through weakness, and by being overcome. On his own, he is weak and unwise, and also his will is led astray. And in this life he is storm-tossed, and in sorrow and woe. And the cause of this is blindness, because he does not see God. For if he saw God continually, he would not have any feelings of mischief, nor any kind of stirrings and desires that serve sin. (ch. 47)

3) Sin is double-mindedness. It is "two contraries" struggling constantly in us, especially in those souls who are being saved. For on the one hand, we choose to do the right things, and on the other hand we find ourselves to be doing what we know is wrong. Then we find ourselves having to repent for something we knew not to do in the first place. Julian relates the experience in the showings, when she was tempted to look away from Jesus to find "heaven:"

> Repenting, and deliberately choosing [Jesus] are like two contraries which I felt both at the same time, and they are like two different "parts:" one is outward, the other is inward. The outward part is our mortal flesh, which is now in pain and woe, and shall be in this life (in which I have indeed suffered much); and that is the part that repented. The inward part is a high, blissful life which is always in peace and in love ... and it is in this part that mightily, wisely and deliberately I chose Jesus to be my "heaven." (ch. 19)

4) Sin is wrath on our part. It is the source of blame; for God does not blame us for sin, but we do—and we also blame God. It is "contrariness:"

For I saw no wrath except on man's part; and he forgives that in us, for wrath is nothing else than a perversity, and a contrariness to peace and love. And it comes either from a lack of power, or a lack of wisdom, or a lack of goodness. These failures are not in God, but are on our part. For we, because of sin and wretchedness, have in ourselves a wretched and continuous contrariness to peace and to love. (ch. 48)

5) Sin is a "sickness" in the human soul. It is not merely a state of mind, in which case it would not be so deadly, but is something which is lacking in our being itself. The most common "symptoms" of this illness are anxiety and despair:

God showed me two kinds of sickness that we have: One of them is our impatience, as we drag along—for we are weighed down by all our troubles and our pains. The other is despair or anxiety [doubtful dread], as I will explain later. He showed sin in general, which includes all our individual "sins"—he did not show any in particular, except these two. But these are the two which most trouble and disturb us, as our Lord showed me; of which it is his will that we be healed. (I am speaking of those men and women who, for the love of God, hate sin and dispose themselves to do God's will) . . . (ch. 73)

6) Sin is a mortal wound. The full effect of sin is death, because it is a separation from life itself, who is God. It renders us insensible, like the servant who fell into the ditch; for he could neither help himself, nor see the source of his help, and he died. Although he was not really far from God (who was drawing near to him), he could do nothing on his own to regain his life.

Two Great Deeds: a "Double" Vision

Julian says that the vision of the lord and the servant was showed to her "double," and "in two." It appeared, in other words, on at least two levels at once. Adam, for example, represented both Adam (and all humanity) as well as Christ, the "new Adam." Similarly, she understood human nature to be "in two," that is, torn in two by sin itself. God, too, looks at us "in two," as symbolized by the great lord in the last scene of the play: for he looked upon his servant both with love and pity, though not with blame. Now Julian sees two ways in which God seeks to heal the pain of sin. She refers to these as two "deeds" which God does, to remedy the "non-deed" of sin which is at work in our lives. These two deeds correspond to two ways in which God judges us, both now and at the time of the Last Judgment.

We have already seen that for Julian, the Last Judgment is not only the last event "in time" (the end of time), but is also something which takes place for each individual person at the moment of death. With regard to the judgment itself, she found her visions to be a puzzle. On the one hand she wanted to believe the teaching of the Church, that the guilt of sin incurs the wrath of God; on the other hand, she had no vision of this wrath at all in her showings. Nevertheless, she makes it clear that she did not waver from the accepted faith:

> Our faith is grounded in God's word, and it is necessary for faith to believe that God's word stands at all points. This point of our faith is that many creatures shall be damned: for instance, the angels who fell from heaven because of their pride, and now are devils; and those human beings on earth who die out of the faith of Holy Church (that is to say, the heathen). And also those who have been baptized, maybe, but who live an unchristian life and so die out of charity; all these will be damned to hell without end, as Holy Church teaches me to believe. (ch 32)

At the same time, in the vision of the mysterious gardener she could not conclude that the gardener himself stood for only *some* human beings, upon whom God looks with pity. He represented Adam, who is all-men. It seemed to her that, just as the fall affects all human beings, so also the work of God affects all humanity. And in God, there is no blame. There appear, therefore, to be two kinds of judgments: that which is in the teaching of the Church, and which seems necessary if we are to avoid sin and to understand the perfect nature of God; and another, which Julian sees illustrated in the play, in which there is no blame.

Although it appears at first that these two kinds of judgment are opposites, Julian comes to understand them as complementary. Whereas from the human point of view, we tend to judge ourselves based upon what we *do* (which changes from day to day), God judges us, rather, upon who we *are*. In the parable, who we are was illustrated in the fallen servant: here, Adam is incorporated into the Son of God. When the Son of God was rescued from the "hole," we were also rescued. Julian concludes from this that, at least for those souls who are being saved, there are two kinds of judgment which are both right. One is related to what we can see in ourselves, which is the pain of sin. The other relates to the way in which God sees us, in light of his own Son. The judgment of God, then, is radically different from what we may imagine it to be:

> All his doings are comforting and sweet, and bring great comfort to the soul who is turned from contemplating the blind judgments of man, to the fair, sweet judgment of our Lord God. For a man sees some deeds as well done, and others as evil; but our Lord does not see them this way. (ch. 11)

If this is true, then even the presence of sin in this world could be seen, from the divine point of view, as somehow useful or even beneficial. This is the other "judgment," the one which we cannot, from our point of view, appreciate. In God's sight, even sin itself has a purpose:

> . . . Jesus, who informed me in this vision of all that I needed to know, answered in these words and said: 'Sin is necessary; but all shall be well, and all shall be well, and all manner of things shall be well.' (ch. 27)

The idea that sin might somehow be "necessary" or "beneficial" (Julian's word "behovely" includes both meanings) is an ancient one in the Church. The liturgy for Easter Eve taught it in its phrase, *O felix culpa*—literally, "O fortunate fault."[3] Here the Church expressed the idea that if Adam had never sinned, we might never have been saved in Christ. We would not, furthermore, have been raised into the position to which we will be raised, in Christ's glorification. Julian saw this illustrated in the final "spiritual" vision at the end of her parable. The servant, wearing only a muddy kilt, fell into the ditch; but when he was raised up, he wore a robe of many colors, shining like a rainbow and more beautful, even, than that of the great lord. Julian's earlier idea (in ch. 27)—that if sin had never been, things would have been all right—is now gently overturned, as she sees that indeed things are better in view of the fall itself. The rescuing of Adam involves a great "deed" on the part of the lord, which ordinarily we cannot see. It had been explained to her earlier, in this way:

> 'It is true that sin is the cause of all this pain, but all shall be well, and all shall be well, and all manner of things shall be well.' These words were said very tenderly, showing no manner of blame to me nor to any that shall be saved. Therefore it would be a great unkindness to blame God, or to wonder at him, because of my sin, seeing that he does not blame me for sin. And in these same words I saw a marvelous high secret, hidden in God; which secret he shall openly make known to us in heaven. In knowing it, we shall truly see the reason why he allowed sin to come, in the sight of which we shall endlessly have joy in God. (ch. 27)

This "deed" is partly secret, and partly revealed to the Church in this life. In that sense, there are two "deeds:" one which has already been accomplished, and one which is still to come: The latter cannot be seen:[4]

> There is a deed which the Trinity shall do on the last day, as I see it; and when that deed shall be, and how it shall be done, is unknown to all creatures that are beneath Christ, and shall be until it is done. The goodness and the love of our Lord God wills that we know it shall be; but the power and the wisdom of him, by the same love, will hide it and conceal from us *what* it shall be, and how it shall be done. And the reason he wishes for us to know it is, that he wills for us to be more comforted in our soul, and peaceful in love, leaving aside contemplating all the troubles that might

keep us from the truth, enjoying him. This is the great deed ordained of our Lord God from without-beginning, treasured and hidden in his blessed breast, and known only to himself, by which deed he shall make all things well. (ch. 32)

The other deed, on the other hand, is already known to the Church, that is, to those who trust in the grace of God—that is, his healing love:

> Our Lord showed that something will be done, and he himself will do it ... This deed will be begun here, and it will glorify God and will be abundantly profitable to those who love him on earth ... And the reason why he showed it is to make us enjoy him and all his works ...
>
> But this deed and the other one (mentioned before) are not both the same, but are two different ones. This deed, however, will be done sooner; and that one will be done when we come to heaven. And it may be understood partially by those to whom the Lord gives it; but the "great deed" mentioned before will neither be known in heaven or in earth, until it is done. (ch. 36)

Julian does not explain the enigmatic "secret" of the two mighty acts of God any further, but we can understand something about it in light of her parable. The "hidden" deed is the one which will take place at the end of time, and it has to do with the glorification of humanity in the Servant who is himself glorified. It is secret, because it transcends time and space as the end of all time, and it is impossible for us to imagine in this life. (Similarly, Julian could not describe the color of the Lord's coat when he was glorified.) It is, furthermore, beyond our understanding in this life, because it will render all things— including suffering and sin itself— "well." The other deed, however, is at least partially revealed in this life. It is made known in the mystery of the gardener/servant, who tilled the soil to bring forth fruit for the great lord. This is the mystery of Christ, who is at work in this life drawing us into union with God. It is the act of the death and resurrection of Jesus, which is also beyond our understanding, but which forgives sin, and reconciles us to God in this life.

Now we have seen that humanity is "two" through its frailty, in sin; and that God's vision is also "two," in pity and compassion; and that there are two mighty acts of God which will raise us out of the situation of sin and death. One of these has begun already, and the other is still to come—which no human being may yet know.

6

Three Wounds: Created Love which is Our Soul in God

There is a famous painting by the French Impressionist, Paul Gauguin, which is entitled, "Who Are We? Where Are We Going? Where Did We Come From?" The large canvas depicts Gauguin's daughter running through darkened streets and aimlessly playing with a child's hoop. The black background of this canvas illustrates the darkness in our own minds when we attempt to answer these basic questions of life; for, although they are the most simple of all questions, they are also life's most difficult riddle.

Julian's second showing addresses itself to the question of human nature, our origin and our destiny, and—like Gauguin's painting—begins with a darkened image. The showing itself began with a corporeal vision of Jesus' face as he hung on the cross. Julian noticed in particular the marks of beating on his face, along with signs of deep humiliation, scorn and spitting. At first, blood running from his scalp covered the upper portion of the face ("from the ears upward"), but later made its way downward, obscuring the rest of the features. The color of the skin changed from a fair brown color (Julian's vision of Jesus' face depicts an olive-skinned man with black eyes) to blue and green, from the bruising; and then to purple and brown, and finally, black.

During the time of this showing, everything was quite dark and indistinct—so much so, that Julian complained aloud of the need for more light, so that she could see clearly what was being shown to her. She was sharply rebuked in her own thoughts:

> "If God wants to show you anything else, he will be your light. You do not need any other light but him." (ch. 10)

She was not sure, at first, whether this vision ought to be taken as a genuine "showing," or not. Its darkness made it more like a nightmare. The face of Christ itself was horrible to see, and Julian found herself uncomfortable. But then it was revealed to her that the vision of Jesus' face was, indeed, a second revelation about the nature of divine love. If the first had been about love which is uncreated—the love which is in God—the second would be about love which is created. This "created love," Julian was given to understand, is our own human nature.

The realization that this vision had to do with human nature and the human condition, was shocking. Julian found the vision "mixed": that is, it seemed to contain opposites at the same time. Jesus' face in itself was handsome, and looking at him delighted her. At the same time, the deep cuts and bruises on his face were disfiguring and horrible, and depicted the worst side of human nature; she did not want to continue looking at it. She indicates that for some time afterward, she continued to doubt whether this part of her vision could be as real as the one which had just gone before, in which she experienced deep, abiding love. However, she gradually came to understand that the picture which she had seen—of a bruised and battered likeness of Christ—accurately depicts the human condition itself. Humanity is a portrait of Christ; but the portrait has been darkened by sin. Jesus' flesh, with its bruising and wounds, is like a robe which our Lord put on. It has become dark and filthy, stained and battered. Julian would see it again in her vision of the lord and the servant:

> This second showing was so poor and so small and so simple that my spirits were in great distress as I looked at it—mourning, full of dread and longing. And I sometimes doubted whether it was a showing. And then, at various times, our good Lord gave me more insight, by which I

understood that indeed it was a showing.

It was a portrait and a likeness of the dirty, mortal "veil" of ours that our fair, bright, blessed Lord wore for our sins. (ch. 10)

But is humanity itself really so foul and horrible? Julian began to understand that, actually, it is not. What we see in this life, however, is not the fulness of humanity, but a dark image. We do not see true human nature clearly when we look at the shameful deeds of ourselves and of humanity in general. Immediately Julian thought of another way to understand her vision in a famous portrait of Christ known as the portrait "not made by hands."

A "Dark" Portrait

A popular legend in the Middle Ages was the story of the Holy Vernicle, or Veronica's Veil, in Rome. This was a cloth on which was imprinted an indistinct portrait of Jesus. The veil, which was supposed to have belonged to a St. Veronica (who is not identified in our calendar of saints today) was an object of pilgrimage and a favorite subject for pilgrim's conversation. According to the legend, St. Veronica had stepped forward to wipe the bloody sweat from Jesus' face as he walked with the cross towards Golgotha.[1] Later she discovered that a miraculous portrait of Christ was imprinted on the cloth—a portrait "not made by hands." Since no artist had painted it, but it had appeared through an imprint of Jesus' own face, it was taken to be a true and accurate image of our Lord. The portrait, furthermore, had strange properties. It was said, for example, to change color from time to time, being usually a dark brown with smudges, but sometimes exhibiting marvelous colors to those who had seen it. This part of the legend was reminiscent of Julian's vision, in which Jesus' face changed color from its original brown to blue and green, to purple and black, from the bruising of the face.

A question which pilgrims sometimes asked about Veronica's Veil now came to Julian's mind. It was the kind of "theological" question which might occupy laypersons, gathered at a tavern, for hours of argument and speculation. The question seems to have been this: If Christ was perfect, and if he could work great miracles, then why was the "portrait not made by hands" not more beautiful? Faith taught the pilgrim to believe that Jesus' own face, as that of the True Man, would be the fairest and most handsome on earth. But this portrait was anything but fair. Some pilgrims even reported that they could not see a real portrait at all; the cloth held only a few dark, indistinct smudges which, with considerable imagination, might resemble a face—but certainly not the face of the "fairest of the sons of men."[2] If the portrait on the cloth were genuine, then why would the Lord have allowed it to be so unattractive?

One answer to the question seems to have been that sceptics did not see more because they did not have enough faith. The cloth appeared in different ways to different people. Those who looked at it with faith saw it as a lovely and colorful portrait of Jesus, whose appearance was fair. Others, however, saw only smudges, which were a reflection of their own sinful lives. Julian tells us, then, that

> Because of the brownness and blackness of this image, and its pitiful and emaciated look, many wondered how it could be—seeing that he imprinted it with his own blessed face, which is the fairest in heaven, the flower of the earth and the fruit of the Virgin's womb. (ch. 10)

But the image did not always appear so unattractive:

> . . . I dare say (and we ought to acknowledge it) that there was never such a fair man as he, until the time that his fair color was changed, through his hard suffering, and sorrow and passion and dying.
>
> . . . And it is said of the Veil in Rome that it is almost alive, in its changing to different colors and appearances, sometimes more comforting and life-like, and sometimes more pitiful and death-like. (ch. 10)

These observations seemed to hold in them a lesson about human nature itself. While Julian admitted that the face of Jesus ought to be the most fair on earth, nevertheless it had been disfigured by the crucifixion—which was really the product of our own sin. In the same way, human nature itself might be truly beautiful; but in this life, it has been disfigured by sin. Our own humanity, then, is a "dark portrait" of Christ. Nevertheless, it is also a portrait "not made by hands." We were created by God, to resemble Christ in our flesh.

Human Capacity and Incapacity

Julian begins with the assumption that human nature was created in the image and likeness of God:[3]

> We know in our faith, and believe—through the teaching and preaching of holy Church—that the blessed Trinity made mankind according to his image and to his likeness. (ch. 10)

This is our true nature, or what Julian will call our "natural substance." Our capacity, then, is to resemble the Trinity. We are not, of course, uncreated beings or spirits, and in that sense we cannot be "like" God. On the other hand, God (who is uncreated Love) has created us to be created love. This may be understood very simply by thinking about what human beings are normally capable of doing in this life.

Earlier we saw that in the Trinity there is a perfect co-operation of Persons, such that Three are only One. The three Persons, we said, may be thought of in terms of their own divine works or attributes—so long as we realize that these attributes are not only "properties" of God, but are really divine Persons. Julian listed some of these attributes for us, in terms of traditional theology: God is "Power," "Wisdom," "Love;" and so on. Now Julian points out that human beings share all these attributes to some extent, by nature. We have the ability to do things ("power"); we have the reasoning capacity which animals do not share ("wisdom"); and we can love. Love especially is a reflection of the Being of God at work in us. Our capacity, then, is to live in the image and likeness of God.

At the same time, Julian is aware of human *incapacity*. We saw that Adam has fallen into a hole, and has become incapacitated. This incapacitation, or injury, is obvious to us in everyday life. We fail and are weak; we cannot do the things that we want to do, and sometimes we seem to do the opposite. We may be clever, but it is obvious that our knowledge is limited and that often our "wisdom" only results in trouble for ourselves and others. Scripture teaches that our "wisdom" appears to God, in fact, as foolishness. Finally, while it is obvious that human beings are capable of love and need love, we cannot deny the reality of hatred and indifference in every human life.

We can see a difference, therefore, between what human nature is, in its original creation and purpose, and what human nature is in its present condition. That does not mean that human nature is "evil" in itself, because human nature belongs to God and was created in the divine image. Julian learns that human nature, itself, has never been lost; it is preserved in Christ, for whom it was first prepared:

> God ... had it in his purpose endlessly to make mankind; which fair nature first was prepared for his own Son, of the second Person. And when he wanted, by full accord of all the Trinity, he made us all at once. (ch. 58)

At the same time, human nature as we see it in this life is incomplete and disfigured.

Julian concludes that, just as God desired from eternity to create human beings, so it was in God's purpose to restore humanity to its full capacity after the great injury done to us by sin. This restoration could only be done by God; for we, like the gardener who had fallen down, are too incapacitated to help ourselves:

> ... the blessed Trinity made mankind according to his image and to his likeness. In the same way, we know that when man fell so deeply and so pitifully into sin, there was no other way to help restore him but through the one who made man. And the one who made mankind out of love, would by the same love restore mankind to the original state of bliss, and much more. (ch. 10)

Julian's thoughts here are traditional in the Church, echoing the teachings of early theologians such as St. Augustine (that

we are a "created trinity" in the image and likeness of God) or
St. Irenaeus (that Christ is the "second Adam" in whom humanity was restored and re-created).[4] However, Julian has
added her own emphases rather than merely quoting from the
Doctors of the Church. While she does not mention Augustine's famous teaching about "memory, reason and will" as the
"made" Trinity, she does acknowledge it in passing:

> ...our soul is a created trinity, like the uncreated blessed
> Trinity—known and loved from without-beginning. (ch. 55)

But then she goes on to speak of the restoration which is
necessary because of sin. Her point is not merely that God
wishes to restore humanity to its *original* capacity, but that
God wishes to raise us to a *higher* condition than we had
before. If Christ is the "second Adam," he does not merely
replace Adam but glorifies the humanity which in Adam was
incomplete:

> And just as we were made like the Trinity in our original
> creation, our Maker wanted us to be like Jesus Christ, our
> Savior, in heaven forever, by virtue of our re-creation. (ch.
> 10)

The glorification or completion of humanity is possible because we share in the humanity of Christ, who was glorified.
In order to accomplish this, the Son of God "hid" himself in
the "veil" or "robe" of human nature. Julian compares Jesus'
seamless robe to our own humanity. In sin, it is torn and
soiled:

> Then, between these two creations, he wished to make him-
> self, out of love for man and to honor him, as much like
> man in this mortal life—in our foulness and pitiful con-
> dition—as a man could be, without any guilt. That is the
> meaning of what was said before: it was in the image and
> likeness of our foul, black mortal "veil" that our fair, bright,
> blessed Lord God is hidden. (ch. 10)

We remember that when the gardener fell into the "hole" of

sin, the cloth he wore was muddy and torn. When he was raised up, however, his robe became transfigured. It was not only made bright and clean, but became more fair than the heavenly robe which was worn by the great lord, who represented the Father. This vision represented the glorification of the Son of God in human flesh. The "robe" of humanity was glorified with him, containing all the colors of the rainbow. In the same way, we shall see that for Julian, humanity is the highest point of creation—summing up the virtues of all the various animals and natures that God has created—and that the highest point of humanity, is Christ.

Growing into Maturity

We may now turn our attention to the way in which God has brought about our restoration in Christ. We note here that in Julian's thinking, salvation is basically the healing of human nature itself. When we are "saved" we are "made whole." For Julian, there are three different ideas which go together to make up "salvation:" 1) healing, or restoration, of the nature which we have had since creation (which Julian calls our "remaking"); 2) completion of maturity in human nature, so that we grow into the fullness of humanity which we were meant to have, and which we can see in Christ (which Julian calls "forth-bringing"); and 3) union with God, who is un-created Love and who has created us in order to be created love, in the image of God.

These three dimensions of salvation represent the work of the whole Trinity, in creation, re-creation and "keeping" in the Holy Spirit. However, they are also all summarized in the work of the Son of God, who "hid" himself in our mortal flesh, and whose portrait we are. Perhaps the most compelling image which Julian uses here is the second one, of growing into maturity.

Normally, when Christians think of Adam in the Garden of Eden, they think of him as "perfect." Julian, too, says that Adam was created in the image and likeness of God. However, it is not clear in this scheme how it would be possible for Christ to restore Adam to something more than Adam had been in the first place. We saw that for Julian, God wished to "restore mankind to the original state of bliss, *and much more*" (ch. 10). What is the "more"?

The implication of this way of thinking is that God's purpose, in Christ, is to re-create Adam as a kind of supernatural being. In Christ, Adam is to be "more" than he was in the first creation; therefore, he would have to be more than human nature itself. Many Christians, correspondingly, think of Christ's own humanity as "more" than that of Adam (or of ourselves). Jesus worked miracles and walked on water; hence, his human nature must be different from ours. Julian suggests, however, that this approach is basically mistaken. The humanity which was created in Adam is the same as ours today, and it is the same which is shared by Christ. Adam, however, did not grow into the fullness of humanity because of his fall into sin. In Christ, we are given the fullness of humanity: what we were meant to be, and what we can become in the Spirit of God.

To understand Julian's idea here, we may think of a simple illustration. When a baby is born it may be either complete or incomplete. If it has all its organs, fingers and toes and so on, we would say that it is a "perfect" child, and in that sense is "complete." At the same time, the infant is still an infant. It has not reached maturity—it has only begun to live, in fact—and in that sense, it is really "incomplete." While there is nothing missing, nevertheless it is the child's whole life which is still to come. In the same way, Adam was created in the image and likeness of God; and in that sense, Adam was perfect. At the same time, Adam had yet to grow into the fullness of humanity, as it was meant for him. It was prevented by his fall into sin, but has now been made possible again through Christ. This is accomplished through the ministry of Christ our Mother, who gives us life and who nourishes us into adulthood, the fullness of life in him.

Christ Our Mother

In Julian's visions, she sees humanity as mystically incorporated into Christ: "mystically," because Christ has hidden himself in human nature, or—in the vision of the lord and servant—has "clothed" himself in the "veil" which is our human nature. Because Christ has done this, we can also say that all human beings participate in the humanity which is his. We are children of God, created to look like God—which is to say, like Christ. If the nature of the Trinity is to be uncreated love, then the human nature is intended to be created love: the love of the Trinity, shared in created human nature.

Julian's showings illustrate these theological concepts in a simple way. Julian learns that Christ is our divine "Mother," who has given our human nature to us and who sustains us, drawing us to the maturity which is his. Sometimes she understands Christ to be the Mother who has given us birth into the kingdom of God as well as into this world and who nurses us at his "breast" in the sacrament of the Church. At other times, she sees Christ as our Mother who is carrying us still in the womb: for we are not yet "born" into the eternal life which is promised to us, although we are destined for it and we belong to it already. Just as the womb protects and nourishes an unborn child, so Christ protects and nourishes us in this life.

It was natural for Julian to see Christ in terms of motherhood. While fathers may pride themselves that the first words of their infant children are "daddy" or "papa," nature has insured that infants rely less upon their fathers than upon their mothers. The mother carries her baby for nine months, giving it nourishment and life, often at a great cost to her own body. She gives birth to the child in "travail"—that is, with hard labor and much pain. She nurses the child when it is born, with milk produced by her own body. And from the beginning, she cares for the child day and night, with hardly a moment's peace, until the child is old enough to be self-sufficient. Even then—in the teenage years, for example—a mother frets about her child and offers consolation and advice, a helping hand, and her healing knowledge and love when there is sickness and pain. What loving mother has not often said to her child, "I wish that I could take all your pain away from you by going through it myself—for I hate to see you suffer, and I could bear it better than you"? In the Middle Ages, then, it made sense to think of the saving work of Jesus in terms of a mother's work: in giving us birth, in his sacrifice for us, in guiding us to maturity, and in giving us the gift of life itself.

The idea of Christ as "mother" was not new in the Middle Ages. Jesus himself used the image on his way to Jerusalem, when he was facing the crucifixion:[5]

Jerusalem, Jerusalem, killing the prophets and stoning all those who are sent to you! How often I would have gathered your children together, just as a mother hen gathers her brood together under her wings, but you would not let me do it. Now look. Your house is forsaken and empty.

The image of motherhood is echoed by St. Paul, who compares himself to a "nursemaid" taking care of her children; and who several times uses language which reminds us of childbirth, in his epistles. Paul speaks of his own birth in Christ (and of his "untimely birth," that is, that he was "aborted" and destined to die, until he had been saved in Christ); of Jerusalem, who was barren, rejoicing in the birth of her offspirng; or the "travail" which this world is undergoing before the birth of the Kingdom of God in power.[6] In all this, Paul simply recalls language of the Old Testament in which God relates to Israel not only as Father and Husband, but also as divine Mother and nursemaid.

St. Anselm, whose works were still popular in Julian's day after three centuries, recalled the imagery of Christ as mother in one of his meditations which he addressed to St. Paul:[7]

> And you, Jesus, are you not also a mother?
> Are you not the mother who, like a hen,
> gathers her chickens under her wings?
> Truly, Lord, you are a mother!
> For both those who are in labor
> and those who are brought forth
> are accepted by you.

In her later life as an anchoress Julian would have encountered the idea again in the *Ancrene Riwle*. This time, the image was not that of Jesus comforting his children, but of the opposite. The *Riwle* takes up the question of spiritual dryness and of our "falling" into sin, and asks why God would permit the Christian to experience these times of difficulty. The author concludes that in these times we feel that God has abandoned us; and indeed he has, at least in a sense. It is like a game which a mother might play with her little child, to teach it to value her presence. The mother plays "hide-and-seek," gently letting her child know that alone, it is not safe; but that the mother's will is for the child to come whenever it is afraid:[8]

> ...our Lord, when he allows us to be tempted, is playing with us as a mother with her darling child. She runs away from him and hides, and leaves him on his own, and he looks around for her, calling "Mama! Mama!" and crying a little, and then she runs out to him quickly, her arms outspread, and she puts them around him, and kisses him, and wipes his eyes. In the same way our Lord sometimes leaves us alone for a while and withdraws his grace, his comfort and consolation, so that we find no pleasure in doing things well, and our heart's savior is gone. And yet, at that very moment our Lord is not loving us any less, but is doing this out of his great love for us.

The idea of Christ playing with us like a mother is discussed by other authors, and recent research would indicate that in fact the image of Christ as mother was not uncommon in Julian's day.[9] There were popular associations which were well known but which would not seem obvious to us. It was thought, for example, that in the sacrament of Holy Communion, Christ "nurses" us at his side: the wine, which is mystically the blood of Christ which flowed from his side on the cross, is also heavenly "milk" from our Mother's breast. This image seemed more natural in a time which supposed that mother's milk was processed blood, and in which it was evident that without the milk of a nursemaid, every child would die.

While the idea of Jesus as our divine Mother was not, then, unique with Julian, she develops the image into a consistent theology of salvation and sanctification. Julian sees essentially three ways in which Christ may be seen as our Mother. First, she makes the observation that ordinary "motherhood" is a reflection of the motherhood which belongs to Jesus:

> And so Jesus is our true mother by nature, in our first creation; and he is our true mother by grace, by taking our nature upon himself. All the good work and all the sweet,

kind care of beloved motherhood are given to the Second Person. (ch. 59)

She then summarizes the three kinds of motherhood in this way:

> I saw three ways to understand the motherhood of God. The first lies in our natural creation; the second is in Christ taking that nature—and here begins the motherhood of grace; the third is the work of motherhood—and in this begins an outpouring, by the same grace, of an endless length and breadth and height and depth, of all his love. (ch. 59)

Christ himself cares for us in everything:

> Our natural Mother, our gracious Mother—for he wanted wholly to become our mother in all things—humbly and gently found the place to begin his work in the Maiden's womb.

> That is to say, it was in this humble place that our high God, who is the sovereign wisdom of all, set himself to grow, and clothed himself willingly in our poor flesh so that he himself could undertake the work and care of motherhood in all things. A mother's care is the closest, nearest and surest, for it is the truest. This care never would, nor could, nor should be fully done except by him alone. (ch. 60)

Unlike our natural mothers, however, Jesus' motherhood is to a life without pain and death:

> We know that our own mother bore us only into pain and death. But our true Mother, Jesus, who is only love, bears us into joy and endless life. Blessed may he be! (ch. 60)

And in that sense, he is our true Mother, who feeds us:

> ... He nourishes us with himself, out of love; and he labored until the full term, because he wanted to suffer the sharpest

pangs and deepest pains that ever were, or ever shall be. And at the end he died ...

He could not die any more, but he did not stop working. And so, out of our need, he fed us. For the dear love of motherhood has given him a duty to us. A mother may gave her child to suck her milk, but our precious Mother, Jesus, feeds us with himself. He feeds us courteously and tenderly with the Blessed Sacrament which is the precious food of life itself. (ch. 60)

While our natural mothers give birth to us into this world, Christ keeps us within his "womb"—always keeping us safe:

A mother may hold her child tenderly to her breast, but our tender mother Jesus can easily lead us *into* his blessed breast, through his dear wounded side. (ch. 60)

And our Savior is our true Mother, in whom we are end-lessly born; and we shall never come out of him. (ch. 57)

Finally, all mothers in this life participate in the "motherhood" which belongs to Christ alone:

This fair lovely word, "mother," is so sweet and so natural [kind] in itself, that it cannot truly be said of any but him, or to her [*i.e.*, Mary] who is the true mother of him, and of all. (ch. 60)

In this last passage, Julian identifies the Virgin with Eve, the "mother of all."[10] Her meaning is that Christ was born of Mary: but Christ himself is the Mother of all, in nature and also in the Church. Julian will see Mary as a "type" of the Church, that is, representing the Church and all the faithful; for, as we have said, Christ is at once our Mother, and also born in us—because we "carry" him within us in faith. Thus, Julian can say that

She who is mother of our Savior, is mother of all who are saved in our Savior. And our Savior is our true Mother ... (ch. 57)

We will investigate this theme later, as we look at the nature of the Church. First, however, we need to understand the natural working of "motherhood" in God, our creation.

Kindness in God
The first step of divine "motherhood" towards us is in our creation. Julian does not see creation as an event which God has worked out, so to speak, "over our heads," by divine *fiat*. Rather, it is a process in which God is involved with us, just as a mother is involved with her child from the moment of its conception. For this reason, Julian can say that our nature as human beings is *located in God*: it was there from the beginning, in God's purpose to create; it exists in the image of God (just as a child resembles its mother), and it is sustained only because of our divine Mother's sustaining love.

Julian's assertion that our nature is found in God follows her reflection that God is at work in everything. Recalling that Julian's use of the word "kind" is also a play on words, in which "kind" and "nature" use the same term, we read that

> God is "kind" in his being. That is to say, the goodness which we call "kindness" is God. He is the ground; he is the substance; he is the very thing called "kindness." And he is also the true Father and Mother of "kinds."
>
> All the various "kinds" [i.e., animals, etc.] that he has made to flow forth from him, to work his will, shall be restored and brought back to him through the salvation of man, by the work of grace. For all the different kinds that he has set out in the various creatures, are only partial. But in humanity is the whole, the fulness: in virtue, in fairness [beauty], in goodness, in royalty and nobility, and in every kind of solemnity, or preciousness, or glory. (ch. 62)

If we substitute the word "nature" for every occurrence of "kind" in this passage, then we see that God is also "nature." Human nature, made in the image of the Trinity, is the summation of all creation. Humanity contains within it all the virtues of all the other creatures, which they in turn have only in part, individually; we are the whole. In that sense we are images of the divine nature, who has created all the animals and also humanity so that we might mirror God. Human nature, then, is located in God:

> I saw and understood that the supernatural power of the Trinity is our Father, and the deep wisdom of the Trinity is our Mother, and the great love of the Trinity is our Lord. And all these we have in our nature, and in our actual creation. (ch. 58)

As we have already seen, Julian extends this idea to say that human nature itself was created not first of all for us, but for God's Son. We share his nature; not he ours:

> God, the blessed Trinity . . . had it in his purpose endlessly to make mankind; which fair nature first was prepared for his own Son, the second Person. (ch. 58)

We can also say that Christ is the high point of human existence, the completion of what we are intended to become:

> And so he wishes for us to know that the noblest thing he ever made is mankind, and that the fullest substance and the highest point of mankind is Christ. (ch. 53)

Substance and Sensuality

If we take seriously the idea that God is our Creator, and even our "Mother" who gave us flesh and blood, out of love, then we also have to consider seriously the place of human flesh in what we call "human nature." We believe for example, that "God is Spirit."[11] But in that case, how would it be possible for human nature—which includes our bodily existence—to be located within God? Or is our bodily existence (our "flesh") really part of our "nature?" For some forms of spirituality, at least, it has appeared that to know God at all we would have to leave our bodily existence behind—to deny it even in this life—because it weighs us down, and prevents us from knowing the spiritual existence which is our true "self."

As against the idea that the body is somehow opposed to the Being of God, Julian advances her theory of what medievals called "substance" and "sensuality." To understand Julian here, we will have to try to shed our own suppositions about "body, soul, and spirit"—not only because they are not entirely consistent with what medievals would have thought, but because they are arguably not part of the Christian scheme as it is depicted in the New Testament. Julian, in any case, rejects the notion that we are a spirit inhabiting a body, which body would have to be left behind if we were to grow spiritually. This concept—always strong wherever Neoplatonism gained a foothold in the worldview of the culture—undoubtedly lay behind much of what lay-Christians in Julian's time thought about the human relationship to God. Julian challenges this notion strongly, to say that our whole human life, including our bodily existence, is created by God, loved by God, and somehow located in God in the mystery of divine love. It is, in fact, the key to what we mean by "love which has been created."

In general, we can say that in the spirituality of Julian's day the body occupied only a negative position: its role in spiritual development is to be punished, disciplined, ignored, or overcome. Asceticism is necessary to the spiritual life, although (as we have seen) English spirituality did not elevate asceticism to the role which it received in other parts of the Christian world. Nevertheless, fasting, abstinence, wearing hair-shirts, and the like were part of the normal trappings of the Christian life. The body, then, is seen as subservient to the soul; and the soul, in turn, is divided into a "lower part," which has to do with the body itself (our nervous system, so to speak, relating to sensations and motion and the affairs of the body), and a "higher part" which concerns itself with abstract reason, with moral questions, love and finally, with the soul's relationship to God.

Walter Hilton, writing exactly during Julian's lifetime, illustrates this scheme very clearly in his analysis of the soul.[12] Hilton describes the "lower part" of the soul as that part which we have in common with the animals, called "sensuality;" and the "higher part" has that part which is uniquely human, and which is therefore the "substance" of human nature. These two parts of the soul are also designated in popular literature as the "external," and the "internal" parts of humanity. The "external" is "animal," and relates to appearances; while the "internal," which is "human" or "spiritual," has to do with ideas and therefore (in a Neoplatonic scheme) with realities.

Interestingly—and not too happily for women readers today—Hilton further divides the higher, or reasoning faculty of the soul, into its own "higher part" which is identified as the *male* side of human nature; and a "lower part" which is essentially female. The "female" half, it was reasoned, is closer to the (animal) faculty of the body itself, being preoccupied with cognition (our awareness of the world around us) and therefore with bodily functions, including such things as the menstrual cycle (woman's changeability), passions, childbirth, and so on. The "male" portion of the soul or mind, on the other hand, was free to aspire to know God. It is here, in the "male" part of the soul, that knowledge of God is possible, and that spiritual development really takes place. It is also here that we are *truly* human, and therefore "substantial." The body and soul together, therefore, may be understood like this:

SUBSTANCE

—Higher (Internal) = Reason —

SOUL

—Lower (External) = Sense —

SENSUALITY

BODY

= MORTAL FLESH

"higher part" which aspires
toward God (affection) = MALE

"lower part" which knows
the world (cognition) = FEMALE

in which we experience
bodily sensations and
control body motion = ANIMAL

corruptible; made of
matter = EARTH

In this model, it is natural to think of "substance" and "sensuality" as opposites. Our "substance" as human beings is rational and spiritual; while our "sensuality" is always being distracted by the things of this earth. Medievals reflected that sin might somehow originate in the body itself, since it is in the body that gross sins occur and it is the body which, it seems, tempts the soul into sin—in lechery, fornication, greed, gluttony, drunkenness, avarice, sloth, and the like. Carried to an extreme, this scheme would imply that the body, with its "earthy" desires, is unloved by God and is a burden for the soul who would desire to lead a spiritual life in communion with God.

Students of Julian have assumed that she shares this basic approach to human nature and especially of the soul, with its two divisions of "sensuality" and "substance." Certainly Julian uses these terms, as for example where she says that

> God judges us upon our natural substance, which is always kept whole and safe in him, to eternity; and this judgment is of his righteousness. But man judges upon our changeable sensuality, which seems now one thing and now another, depending upon what it takes from the different parts [i.e., "higher" or "lower"]; and on what shows outwardly. (ch. 45)

It would therefore appear that when Julian says that "our substance is kept in God," she is referring only to the male part of the soul, which aspires toward God. Julian would even give the impression that the higher part of the soul *is* God, or at least that there is very little difference between this highest part of the soul and the Being of God:

> We ought to highly rejoice that God dwells in our soul, and much more highly rejoice that our soul dwells in God. Our soul is created to be God's dwelling-place, and the dwelling-place of the soul is God, who is uncreated. And it is a lofty understanding to inwardly see and to know that God, who is our Maker, dwells in our soul; and a still higher understanding to see inwardly and to know that our soul, which is created, dwells in God's substance (of which substance— God—we are what we are). And *I saw no difference between*

> *God and our substance, but as it were, all God.* And yet my
> understanding took it that our substance is in God: that is
> to say, that God is God, and our substance is a creature *in*
> God. (ch. 54; emphasis added)

On the basis of these passages, the conclusion has sometimes
been drawn that Julian shares with others writers a Neoplatonic view of the soul in which, for example, there is a "spark"
of the divine nature in the innermost or "highest" part of our
soul. Julian seems to bear this out when she says that there is a
part of the soul which does not will to sin, because it is kept
safe in God:

> In this showing I saw and understood most clearly that in
> every soul that shall be saved, there is a godly will that never
> assents to sin, and never shall. This will is so good, that it
> can never will evil, but always continually wills good and
> performs it, in the sight of God. (ch. 53)

There is, however, another way to understand Julian's point
in these passages, and in her treatment of the soul generally.
We note, first of all, that in the passage above—which is
essentially a commentary on Romans 7—Julian refers only to
those souls "who are being saved," that is, to the Church on
earth.[13] The problem which is under discussion for her is the
way in which Christ, our Mother, has permanently bonded
the "saved" soul to himself, through nature, mercy and grace;
she does not take up the argument with relation to those souls
who are *not* being saved. Second, Julian relates "substance" to
the person of Christ himself. Our "substantial self" is what we
are when we are truly human, that is, complete. It is the
humanity of Christ. On the other hand, our "sensual" nature is
what we appear to be in this life, in the context of continual
change and of sin. We shall see that the "godly will" is actually
Christ in us (that is, in the person of faith); and that, on the
other hand, even our sensual nature is taken up into the being
of God, in Christ, and is therefore important in our salvation
ultimately, and even in our spiritual life today.

For Julian, spiritual fulfillment does not mean leaving sensuality behind. In a passage somewhat reminiscent of Richard

Rolle's description of "heat," "sweetness," and "song" in his experience of the outpouring of the Holy Spirit, Julian says clearly that the *lower* faculties of the soul—which are necessarily tied to our body—will be completely satisfied and fulfilled in heaven. God wishes to fulfill our capacity as sentient beings, not destroy it:

> Then we shall all come into our Lord, knowing ourselves very clearly and possessing God fully. We shall also be completely possessed by God, forever, seeing him in truth; and fully touching him, spiritually hearing him, delectably tasting him. And there we shall see God face to face. (ch. 43)

We have already seen, in analyzing Julian's use of middle-English dialect, that Julian understands the lowest bodily functions to be the work of God:

> A man walks upright, but the food in his body is safely enclosed, as if in a purse. And when it is the time of his necessity, it is opened and closed again, very neatly. That it is he [God] who does this is shown there, where he says that he comes down to us to the lowest part of our need; for he has no contempt of what he has made ... (ch. 6, P)

Julian concludes, then, that God has joined himself to us— that is, to every aspect of humanity, body and soul, "substance" and "sensuality"—through the working of Christ our Mother; and he has done this in three different ways, so that we need not doubt it: in our creation (body and soul); in the incarnation; and in the shared life of the Holy Spirit, in the Church.

Knit Together in Love
The image which Julian uses to describe the way in which we are joined to God, making us complete human beings in Christ, is "knitting." The image is reminiscent of a biblical one, and also one which is used by other authors of her time.[14] Julian, however, also seems to write about "knitting" out of personal experience rather than merely scholarly reflection. In the *Revelations* she frequently uses images which recall scenes,

as we may imagine them, from the Norfolk countryside. Norfolk, as we have seen, was a center for woolen trade and for the textile industry. Julian would have seen rows of freshly-dyed skeins of yarn, colored from natural dyes produced in the area, drying outdoors on sunny days. She refers to cloth drying in the wind, in her description of the appearance of Christ experiencing dehydration on the cross; and she would have known how to knit, in any case, simply because it was a practical necessity for any woman if she were to have something to wear.[15]

Julian's point is that God has "knit" us to himself in our natural creation; and also in our re-creation in Christ, as well as in the life of the Church. Because of this, no soul who loves God should doubt whether salvation is possible or whether she is acceptable to God. There are three kinds of "knitting":

1. *Knitting in creation*: On the simplest level, this means our natural formation in our mother's womb. In the womb, bones and muscles, nerves and connective tissues are all "knit" together by the unseen hand of God. Julian reminds us that this "knitting" is done by the Son of God, through whom the Father has created all things. The making of our physical "self" cannot be separated from the making of our soul, however, which is "knit" to the body at the time it is created. We are in fact just one "self," which is body and soul together.

Julian reminds us, then, that in a sense we were "knit" to God in creation long before we were individually created in our mother's womb. In part this is because, as we have seen, there is no time in God; we were, therefore, created at the same time as Adam. It also has to do with the will of God, in which God purposed to create us (as individuals, as well as sharers in humanity-in-general) from eternity.

In order to knit anything, it is necessary first to have in mind what we are going to make. We knit according to a pattern. In the same way, Julian observes, God has created us according to the divine purpose, having clearly in mind who we are to be, and how we are to be made. We were, therefore, loved before we were made, in the timeless love of God—just as a woman knits a pattern because it is her favorite, or loves her child before it is born:

For I saw that God never began to love mankind; for just as mankind shall be, in endless bliss , fulfilling the joy of God according to God's plan, in the same way mankind has always been, in the foresight of God, known and loved from without-beginning, in his righteous purpose. (ch. 53)

And again,

Before he made us, he loved us. And when we were made, we loved him. And this is a love made of the natural, substantial goodness of the Holy Spirit: powerful, by reason of the power of the Father, and wise in the wisdom of the Son. And thus man's soul is made by God, and at the same time knit to God. (ch. 53)

Julian now turns her attention to the soul itself, which she says is intended to be the dwelling-place of God. Thinking first only of that part of the soul which is called "substantial," or the "higher part," Julian argues that this is indeed the seat of God she saw in her vision of the lord and servant, in which the lord took his seat in a throne in the middle of a vast desert, which she took to be her own soul; later this same dwelling-place appeared glorified, as a delightful city. She argues that in this first "knitting," we can say that God is *spiritually* "knit" to the soul-being-saved, and this because the soul itself is capable of receiving the spiritual Being of God. It is not that the human soul *is* God, nor that it is an emanation of God, nor that there is a part of all human beings which is of itself holy. Rather, the soul is created by God out of nothing, so that it might receive the Spirit of God in purity:

And so I understand that man's soul is made from nothing; in other words, it is created, but created out of nothing that was itself created. It is like this: When God created man's body, he used the mud of the earth, which is all the elements of the earth, mingled and mixed together; and he made man's body from that. But when he wanted to make man's soul, he took no ingredients, but simply made it. And so created nature is closely joined to its Maker, whose substance and nature is uncreated—that is, to God. And from this, it follows that there is nothing—and never shall be anything—to stand between God and man's soul. (ch. 53)

Julian has in mind here the biblical account of creation, in which God "breathed into Adam the breath of life."[16] In saying this, she speaks first to the notion that God perhaps could not dwell with us, because we are physical beings, whereas God is Spirit. She answers that God can dwell with us because we were made in the image of the Trinity:

> And so my understanding was led, by God, to see in him and to understand, to recognize and to know, that our soul is a created trinity, like the uncreated blessed Trinity—known and loved from without-beginning; and in the making, joined to the Maker, as I said above. (ch. 55)

In the original creation of humanity, then, a dwelling-place was established for God in the human soul. A second kind of "knitting," however, joins God to the sensual side of human nature, including our body, in Christ.

2. *Knitting in the Incarnation.* The second "knitting" is that which we have in the humanity of the Son of God, who has taken our flesh upon himself. This is the fulfillment of human nature, because it is the point at which our sensual nature is joined to God. Julian observes that sometimes, we may be fearful that we cannot be "one" with God because of our bodies. However, God has overcome this objection by joining soul to body, and himself to the soul and body, in the incarnation:

> And because of the glorious union that was made by God between the soul and the body, it necessarily follows that man's nature would be restored from a double death— which restoration could never be until the time that the second Person of the Trinity had taken the lower part of humanity, to whom the higher part was already joined in the first creation. And these two parts were in Christ, the higher and the lower, which are but one soul. The higher part was one in peace with God, in full joy and bliss; the lower part, which is sensuality, suffered for the salvation of mankind. (ch 53)

In this passage, Julian points out that in Christ there were two natures, human and divine, which were absolutely united; however, it cannot be argued that the eternal divine nature of Christ suffered on the cross, because the Being of God within himself is "impassible," that is, incapable of suffering. Nevertheless, God *has* suffered, by taking our sensual nature into himself. In Christ, the divine and human became perfectly one, and at the same time, the "higher" and the "lower" aspects of human nature also became perfectly one. They were "knit" together, so that they cannot be separated. Julian puts this another way when she says that

> ... our nature, which is the higher part, is knit to God in its creation; and God is knit to our nature which is the lower part, in taking flesh. Thus in Christ our two natures are joined. For the Trinity is comprehended in Christ, in whom our higher part is grounded and rooted; and the second Person has taken our lower part, which nature was first prepared for him. (ch. 57)

Thus it is impossible that the body, or the so-called "sensual" side of human nature (or the "female" aspect of the soul, with its "lower" inclinations), could separate us from the love of God. God loves us wholly, body and soul, as one living being created by God.

3. *Knitting in the gift of faith.* If the first kind of knitting is seen primarily as the work of the Father (in preparing a dwelling-place in our soul), and the second is the work of the Son (in taking our whole nature to himself), the third kind of knitting which our Mother does is the work of the Holy Spirit. It is ours in the gift of faith. In the passage just quoted above, Julian goes on to say that

> ... the next good thing that we receive is faith, which increases to our profit. (ch. 57)

Her concern here is not merely with faith in general—as an abstract possibility for any human being—but also with our individual faith, that is, faith in each soul who is being saved. It is the third way in which, as individuals, we are knit to God.

Julian begins with an analysis of faith in general:

> ...It comes from the high riches of our natural substance,
> into our sensual soul; and it is grounded in us, and we in it,
> through the kind goodness of God, by the working of mercy
> and grace. From this working may come all the good things
> by which we are guided and saved. (ch. 57)

In other words, faith is a possibility for every human being
because our nature, created in God according to God's plan,
provides for it. It becomes real in our lives, however, only as
God's grace works to make it so. And Julian notes that "faith"
is not genuine unless it descends from our "substantial self"
(which is intellectual), into our "sensual soul" (which includes
our feelings and thoughts towards others). Faith must be of
the heart as well as of the mind.

If faith is due to the operation of God in the soul, however,
then the nature of faith is radically different from what many
of us would suppose it to be. Faith is not something which we
do ourselves; it is not a feeling or even a decision on our part.
Faith, rather, is something which God creates in us, to "knit"
us to himself. In one sense (as Julian uses the word "faith") it is
from God, because the love of God itself creates faith in us: we
trust those whom we love, and we know who loves us by the
love which is shown towards us. Hence Julian echoes the
argument found in the New Testament, that we love God
because God first loved us.[16] In another sense, faith comes
from God, because faith means seeing God clearly in this light
of divine love:

> Our faith is a light, which shines naturally from our endless
> Day, who is our Father, God. In this light our Mother,
> Christ, and our good Lord, the Holy Spirit, lead us in this
> passing life... This light is love. (ch. 83-84)

In this sense, faith itself is Christ. The Son of God has
perfect faith in the Father and in the incarnation, has lived in
the light of faith, in human nature. Through the work of the
Holy Spirit, Christ himself comes to live in us, and his faith
becomes ours. For those souls who love God and who are

therefore being saved, it can be said that from the beginning, it was the purpose of God to dwell in them and to will what is good. This is the will which never wills to sin; and it is kept eternally in God:

> ...in each soul that shall be saved, there is a godly will that never assents to sin, and never shall. This will is so good that it can never will evil, but always continually wills good and performs it, in the sight of God ...

> Therefore our Lord wills for us to know this, both trusting it and believing it—to realize, specifically and truly—that we have all of this blessed will whole and safe in our Lord Jesus Christ. This is so because each kind of nature which will help to make heaven complete and full must be (and ought to be, in view of God's righteousness) so knitted to, and made one with, him that in each kind of nature there is preserved something which can, and never will, be separated from him. This is accomplished through his good will, and his endless foreseeing purpose, of which I have spoken before. (ch. 53)

We may conclude from this all that in Christ, we are "knit" to God. Christ himself is our divine Mother who has done this "knitting," and in so doing has prepared for himself the spotless garment of humanity which he will wear eternally.

Three Wounds of the Spirit

Every kind mother wishes that she could suffer in place of her child, and every kind mother teaches her child to be contrite when it has done wrong and to desire to do what is right. A good mother, too, creates love in her child by loving it so that the child longs for its mother, in love. Each of these dimensions of a mother's love involves pain; and each of these is part of the work which our divine Mother does in the soul who loves God. Julian prayed for the three wounds of the spirit long before she understood them. In her experience of the passion of Christ , in the sixteen divine revelations, she began to know what it means to be wounded by contrition, compassion and true longing for God. The three wounds are:

1. *Contrition.* We recall that Julian prayed, in her youth, for the gift of "true contrition;" and that her contemporaries made a distinction between genuine contrition, in which a particular sin and even the temptations to commit it were driven out (or underwent "attrition"), and false contrition in which the sinner confessed to sin but did so with a false heart. For the latter, there would be no real desire to change, and the sin would recur. Julian did not wish to be hypocritical in her hatred for sin and so early on prayed for the spiritual gift of feeling true compunction for her sins, so that they might gradually be overcome. She wished to be genuinely "contrite."

Contrition, as Julian learned about it in the showings, was however somewhat different from what she expected it to be. It is interesting, for example, that Julian does not mention it until she tells about the thirteenth showing (in ch. 39), almost at the end of her book. This is significant because as it was generally understood, contrition is the *first* step of spiritual life (in contrition, confession, and absolution). Theologically, it was taught that we must first feel contrition for our sins before we are ready to receive the grace and mercy of God. Although Julian will say that the soul has to recognize its sinfulness in order to grow into the humility of divine love, at the same time the recognition of our sin cannot come first in the order of salvation. Actually, apart from the revelation of what humanity is supposed to be in Christ, we would not even know what sin is; nor would we know that we were supposed to be anything besides what we already are. We can say, then, that it is the revealed love of God which gives us a concept of sin. In the same way, contrition is not ours until we have received a measure of divine love ourselves; for contrition is, first of all, something which is in the heart of God, and which is shared with us in the Motherhood of Christ.

But how would it be possible for contrition to be a divine property? For we know that God does not sin, and even in the incarnation the Son of God was "as much like man in this mortal life...as a man could be, without any guilt"(ch. 10). If Jesus was not guilty of any sin, it would seem obvious that Jesus did not experience contrition—since contrition is the proper response of a sinful soul to the revelation of its own sin.

For Julian, however, genuine contrition is much deeper

than simply feeling sorry for our own misdeeds. It is the means by which we are brought into heaven, along with compassion and true longing:

> By contrition we are made clean, by compassion we are made ready, and by true longing for God we are made worthy. These are the three means by which, as I understand it, all souls come to heaven...for it is by these medicines that every soul is healed. (ch. 39)

In this sense contrition (and also compassion and true longing) is the result of the work of divine love in us. We can say that it is engendered in us by our divine Mother; and that, therefore, contrition originates in our Mother, who is Christ.

To understand how this is possible, we may first reflect on what is *not* true contrition, as Julian has already seen it in her showings. We have seen that in God there is no blame: God reveals our sin gently, in the clear light of his own love. Blame, on the other hand, is the essence of sin itself and is the natural result of evil at work in us. Contrition, as we ordinarily think of it, is also a product of blame—although perhaps in a very subtle way, which often masquerades for religious piety or moral uprightness. Usually, we think of "contrition" as the emotion of remorse when we have done something wrong. If so, it is the product of self-blame. Its natural results are the feelings of guilt and despair and hopelessness which end in a kind of terror of God (because we are afraid of punishment), and the fear that we cannot remedy the mistakes which we have made.

While it might appear at first that "contrition" as we have just described it is what contrition ought to be—the deep sense of guilt and remorse of the sinner—Julian learns that this is actually what is false "contrition" and that it does not benefit the sinner at all. In themselves, feelings of guilt and hopelessness do nothing to restore us to a fuller or richer life, nor to bring us into communion with God. They are more likely to drive us *away* from God, and even from ourselves: for the end-result of utter despair of this kind would be suicide. It is shocking to Julian to discover that what she has thought of as contrition is therefore actually worthless as a spiritual remedy.

True contrition, on the other hand, is experienced by Christ on the cross. Julian witnesses it in the thirteenth showing, when she sees that God does not desire for the sinner to fall into despair over sin. (We will examine this showing in more detail in the next chapter, as we see how our Mother works with us in our falling into sin.) For the moment our interest is in the nature of contrition itself, as a holy response to the presence of evil. We can say that for Julian, contrition is the deep sorrow which is felt by Christ to see the presence of evil at work in humanity: bearing the burdens of guilt and anxiety which others bear for their sake and out of love. When the soul-to-be-saved experiences contrition, it is sharing in the remorse which is in God for the sins of the world—even though God did not bring about that sin, and even though the Son of God did not commit sin. Christ has taken sin into himself, which is the nature of true contrition.

The principle of contrition is evident when we think about the humility and kindness of God, which we have already seen in Julian's showings. It is God's nature to share the divine nature with us—to make us created love, in the likeness of uncreated love. In the same way, it is natural for God to enter into the place of evil (the "hole") in order to share it and to rescue us from it. The deepest point of sin is the experience of despair over our own failure. The divine humility means, then, that God also enters into the experience of hopelessness in order to bring about its healing. True contrition is to repent on behalf of others for their sake; and, at the same time to turn to God for the remedy—as an injured child turns to its mother—on behalf of those who do not know where to turn.

True contrition absolutely excludes blame, or it could not be contrition. There is no sorrow in blame, but only a kind of self-exaltation and pride. It is to exult in another's humiliation. For the soul who loves God, this would be impossible; for God knows only humility, and cannot rejoice over our sin. Julian learns therefore that the nature of true contrition is silence: that is, in God there is no mention of our sins, and God does not desire for us to inquire into the sins of others. The sorrow of contrition is so deep a wound that the soul who suffers it is unable to speak about it at all. Thus, Julian sees first that sin is so hateful in the sight of God that neither it—nor those who are slaves to it—are discussed in God's presence:

> And still I desired, if I dared, to have had a full vision of hell and purgatory. It was not my intention to find proof of anything that belongs to our faith—for I steadfastly believed that hell and purgatory are for the purpose that holy Church teaches they are—but my intention was to see for my own edification all the things that belong to my faith, so that I could live more to God's glory and for my own profit. But for all my desire, I could [see] absolutely nothing of this...
>
> In this vision I understood that of all the creatures who are in the devil's condition in this life, and so come to their end, there is no more mention of them before God and his holy ones than there is of the devil—even though they may be human beings, and whether they have been baptized or not. (ch. 33)

The reason these souls are not mentioned is that they bring deep sorrow to God, so that we ourselves must not inquire into their fate—lest we fall into blaming them for their sins. We should simply look to Christ:

> As long as we are in this life, whenever we in our folly turn to look at those who are being reproved, our Lord tenderly touches us and blissfully holds us to himself and says, "Let it go, my love, my dear child, and listen to me. I am enough for you. Rejoice in your savior and in your salvation." (ch. 36)

The true penitent, then, is not only sorrowful for sins as an individual, but for the sins of the world; and this contrition comes from the Holy Spirit, and is his:

> But when we see ourselves so foul, then we think that God is angry with us for our sin; and then we are stirred by the Holy Spirit to contrition...(ch. 40)

This is the response of a child to its mother:

...our courteous Mother does not want us to run away;
for him there would be nothing more horrible. Rather, he
desires for us to behave as a little child: for when it is
injured or afraid it runs hastily to the mother for help, with
all its might...saying, like a meek child, "My kind mother
... have mercy on me..." (ch. 61)

2. *Compassion.* The next step of love, after contrition, is compassion. Julian's whole theology is in effect a "theology of
compassion," because it is centered in the crucifixion and the
passion of Christ. The passion of the Son of God is always
compassion, because it is the suffering of God with us and in
our nature (we recall that "compassion" means "to suffer along
with"). The gift of compassion may be thought of, in Julian's
theology, as operating in two directions. It is, on the one hand,
the suffering which Christ has done with us and on our behalf:
when we suffer in sin, Christ also suffers on the cross. At the
same time, compassion becomes *our* gift when we begin to
suffer with Christ on the cross, on behalf of others. In Christ,
our own suffering becomes compassionate suffering, and we
share in the redemptive work of Christ.

In her showings, Julian learns that the chief suffering of
Christ on the cross was not the nails or the crown of thorns or
the beating, but the spiritual suffering which he felt on behalf
of humanity. As Christ suffered in contrition—the deep sorrow
for our sins which he knew as the Son of God—he also suffered
with us, *in* our sins, as the true human being. We can say that
in Julian's idea, Christ suffered more because of his divine
nature than he might otherwise have suffered—because he
suffered as God, who does not know sin—and also that he
suffered more in his human nature than we might ever suffer,
because as the true human being the sin which he felt in us was
unnatural to him. Because of the "knitting" which had already
taken place in the creation of humanity and in the incarnation
(one "act" on the part of God), it was necessary that whenever
we suffered in sin, Christ also suffered.

Julian sees compassion first in the great "thirst" of Christ on
the cross (in the eighth revelation, ch. 16-17). The physical
thirst which Julian saw represented the deeper "thirst" which
God has for all souls to be one with him. In her visions Julian

next saw Mary, who stood at the foot of the cross, concerned for her Son and suffering with him (ch. 18). This compassion extended, then, to the whole world. It is not that the world knew or cared about Christ dying on the cross, but that a bond had been formed between him and the world long ago in creation. Therefore when the world suffered in sin, the Son of God suffered; and when he suffered on the cross, the world was in pain also:

> Here I saw, in my understanding, the great union between Christ and ourselves. For when he was in pain, we were also in pain; and all the creatures who could suffer pain suffered with him—in other words, all the creatures that God made to serve us. The firmament and the earth failed, in their own natures, for sorrow at the time of Christ's death—for it belongs to their nature too to know him as their God, in whom all their virtue was established. When he failed, it was inevitable that they too would naturally fail with him as much as they could, for sorrow for his pains. And thus all who were his friends suffered pain, for love. (ch. 18)

Recalling the Gospel accounts of the passion, Julian goes on to describe the earthquakes, the eclipse of the sun, and so on.[17] This relationship of compassion, or shared pain, did not end with the crucifixion. We have seen that in God, there is a continuous sorrow for our sin. In the same way,

> Thus our Lord suffered for us; and we also all stand in this pain with him, and we shall do until we come to his bliss. (ch. 18)

The pain which we suffer with Christ in particular is the thirst which is in God for all souls to be one with him. At the same time, Julian points out that the soul who loves God will actually be persecuted in this life on account of her love, for Christ's sake. Just as the world attacked him, it will also attack all those who are "in" him. Martyrdom in various forms is to be expected by every soul-to-be saved. It is compassion with Christ.

3. *True Longing for God.* The experiences of contrition (on behalf of the world) and of compassion (in the sins of the world and its suffering) now lead to a deep longing for God. In the fourteenth showing, Julian begins to experience a deep desire to be "one" with God (ch. 54). This deep longing comes from God's own love, rather than from a contemplation of our own sinfulness. The soul sees the joy which is in God, and desires it. As before, however, a true longing for God is not one which is limited to the soul as an individual. It is the longing to see the whole world at peace with God, and in love.

Julian's longing for God is deepened through her experience, in the fifteenth revelation, of the apparent "absence" of God. Like the child who cannot see its mother, she desires to see her savior clearly and to be with him. True longing, however, is not the "longing" which some souls feel, which again masquerades for genuine love at work in the soul. At times we desire to leave this world, with its sin and sorrow, to be one with God. Julian is taught that this desire is wrong; it is selfish, a desire to escape responsibility rather than love which desires to see healing in others. Gradually, Julian's experience of personal frustration with this life (and with her illness itself, with its pain) is replaced in the showings by a genuine longing to see humanity restored to God. Once again, it is a genuine wound. To look at the loneliness and suffering in the world due to sin produces a deep sorrow in the heart of the soul-to-be-saved, which sorrow grows out of the heart of God.

These are the ways in which Christ, our Mother, has "knit" us to himself, in nature, in mercy and in grace. Now we are ready to see how this "knitting" occurs in daily life.

7

Four Dreads:
Falling and Rising in
Ordinary Life

Everyone knows that ordinary life is a series of "ups" and "downs." In every life there are good experiences and bad, successes and failures, joys and sorrows. Our moods, correspondingly, swing from one end of the scale to the other, often depending upon simple adjustments to our surroundings or upon our estimate of how others see us, or upon the measure of success or failure which we have in our own eyes. And regardless how we might like to think of ourselves, the truth is that even the soul who loves God knows what it is like to experience ecstatic prayer one moment and depression the next; or periods of great spiritual "blessing" followed by periods of inner dryness and joylessness in prayer.

All too often, however, we expect spiritual progress to involve only a constant succession of "ups." However unrealistic it may be, we think that if our faith were strong enough, or if we were really among the "saved," we would not fall down any more. And we look upon periods of "backsliding" as more grave, it may be, than the sins of those "who did not know better." The twin results of this attitude towards spiritual growth are, first of all, that we experience a great burden of guilt whenever we fail, which prevents us from rising up again; and second, we experience discouragement and even more failure. First we expect more of ourselves and of others than proves to be possible; and when we fall down, the discouragement which results weighs us down and brings about even greater mistakes, because we lose faith in God and in ourselves.

This is, in summary, Julian's analysis of the popular approach to spiritual growth in her time. The effect of her showings is to lend a positive note to this somewhat dismal scene by—paradoxically—promising that no matter how hard we might try, we are bound to fail. Spiritual growth, Julian learns, takes place not so much in spite of the mistakes we make, but because of them. It would be impossible to grow spiritually by deliberately falling into sin; but on the other hand, the moments when we learn about our frailties in sin are the moments when we most recognize our dependence upon God, and so draw near to God in faith. Faith is not our own strength, but the recognition of our weakness, in which we depend upon the grace of God.

The Ladder of Perfection

There is much evidence to suggest that Julian's analysis of how spiritual growth was understood in her time is essentially correct. (Indeed, it has much to say to pious Christians in our own time as well.) Medieval tradition implied that spiritual growth should take place in a steady climb towards heaven— or, at least, toward a purified life here on earth, insofar as it were thought possible. The climb was conceptualized as nearly vertical: like Jacob's ladder, it was thought to be a stairway leading upward from earth to heaven, and stretching downward from earth to hell.[1] An interesting theme in fourteenth-century art, therefore, is the "ladder of perfection." It is a frail ladder crowded with climbers of all kinds: serfs, rich men, pilgrims, nuns, monks and priests. Poor sinners—some of them ironically dressed in the gowns of bishops or cardinals— are plunging off the ladder into perdition far below, while other climbers push their way past to new spiritual heights.

The idea of a "ladder" of prayer and spiritual growth is an old one in the Church, and by the Middle Ages it had gained general acceptance through the writings of a number of spiritual masters. One writer who early described the "ladder" from a monastic point of view was even named after the image which he used in his writings: Johannes Climacus, "John of the Ladder," whose book, the *Ladder of Divine Ascent*, became a spiritual classic. Another important writer to use this image was our old acquaintance, Pseudo-Dionysius, who proved to be responsible for the whole framework in which spiritual growth came to be understood by Julian's time. St. Denys suggested that spiritual growth could be understood, for the sake of argument, as taking place in three stages, or levels of maturity: the stage of purification; the stage of illumination; and the state of perfection, or union with God. There is some evidence that the idea of these three "stages" of spiritual life was discussed even before the advent of Christianity, but whatever their origin, they came to be firmly implanted in the conscience of the Church by the early Middle Ages.

The first stage, which is also less delicately referred to as "purgation," is that of the "beginner." Here the soul attempts to rid itself of gross sins, temptations, and distractions to prayer. At this level, contrition plays a major role, with penances and acts of mortification or self-discipline, designed to rid the penitent of the lusts of the flesh. In the second stage, for "proficients," spiritual instruction has become possible and there is even a certain amount of wisdom given by God (called "illumination"). At this point the darkness of former sins has begun to be swept away, so that one might see the things of God more clearly. In the final stage (that of the "perfect"), active learning has been replaced more and more by passive rest in the experience of peace, joy, and love infused by the Holy Spirit. Then, meditation—an activity of the mind, focussing on the scriptures, the crucifixion and so on—begins to be replaced by contemplation, in which the mind ceases from activity and simply beholds the surpassing wonder of God's grace and divine nature.

It is against this background that the *Revelations* has to be understood. Julian appears, for example, to have the three stages of spiritual growth in mind when she speaks of the three "wounds" of contrition, compassion, and true longing for God. On the other hand, it is curious that in her book Julian nowhere mentions the spiritual "ladder," nor the stages of spiritual growth which were universally accepted as necessary. Some writers have felt that Julian simply assumed the "ladder" image for spiritual growth, and so did not find it necessary to mention it in her book. A closer look at the *Revelations*, however, suggests that in fact Julian intended to paint a very different picture. We cannot say flatly that she rejected the idea of the "ladder" altogether; for there is much truth in it (as anyone who has entered deliberately into a discipline of prayer will know). Nevertheless Julian did want to say that the whole idea had been misapplied. It no longer encouraged lay persons to faith, but seemed, rather, to discourage believers from prayer altogether.

Julian's showings seem to point to a more flexible picture of spiritual growth for the soul who loves God, a picture in which God is seen to work *in* the circumstances of ordinary life, rather than in spite of them. The soul who wishes to grow in grace does not need to feel guilty, for example, about "secular" work, but rather discovers the work of God in everything and at all times. The vertical ladder, meanwhile, has been replaced by a kind of roundabout journey, up and down, in times of blessing and times of dryness, falling and rising. Julian's picture is based upon the assumptioin that God is working out his love in us even in those times when we least believe it, and least acknowledge it. God can make all things to be "well." This picture, then, implies that we can rest from our hard spiritual labors from the beginning, seeking rather to enjoy the grace of God even in simple things. The soul *will* be "travailed," but it is not always up to us to decide when or how. Instead of attempting to master the soul through hard effort, then, we should look to the grace of God and allow ourselves to be changed by it, in divine mercy. It is the kindness of God at work in us in all things.

"You Will Sin Again"

It is a tradition in much of the Church that whenever a penitent goes to confession, the penitent's last words always include the promise, "I will not sin again." Obviously to make such a promise it is not merely enough to have good intention. We would have to believe that something will soon change in us in order to allow the promise to come true. The fact is that we do commit wrongs, and furthermore that often our sins are habitual ones, part of a pattern which we tend to repeat whether we want to or not. Perhaps originally, this confessional formula was not meant to sound like a denial of any sin at all in our future, so much as a matter of volition: "I *will* not sin again" really means, "I do not *want* to sin again," or more specifically, "I do not want to commit *this* sin again in the future." However, the question remains how we would work a change in our lives so that sins would not occur again. The "ladder" seems to imply that at some point, a true Christian would indeed cease to sin; or at least that temptations to sin in certain ways would no longer occur. The fact that we continue to experience "ups" and "downs," however, seems to show that we have fallen off the ladder, or at least that we have been unable to climb past the first one or two rungs.

We must not think that in Julian's day the idea of rising up the ladder, even beyond the experiences of temptations to sin, seemed to be absurd or impossible, even to the average believer. It made sense that, with effort, one could eventually kill desires for many of the things of this world which tempt the soul away from spotlessness: lechery, for example, or drunkenness, gluttony, laziness, avarice, arrogance, and so forth. The scriptures make plain what are the "works of the flesh." In addition, the Church had drawn a distinction between those sins which are more easily overcome through mortification and penance ("venial sins") and sins which cut the soul off from the grace of God ("mortal sins"). Julian is aware of the distinction:[2]

> But now I must tell in what way I saw mortal sin in those creatures who will not die because of sin, but who live in the joy of God without end. (ch. 72)

Julian is shown, however, that we cannot avoid sin. It is a condition of this life; and even though we may not desire it, and even if we attempt to overcome it, we will fall and we will fail. At the same time she is shown that God can use our experience of failure in order to purify us. Sin can become, so to speak, its own worst enemy. Julian will say that it produces pain, and in that sense—for the soul who loves God—it becomes its own "scourge." Harsh penances are not necessary, because the consequences of our actions become their own "penance." The work of grace, then, is to teach us to turn towards our Mother, Christ, when we fall and are in need. At these times the wounds which we have received from sin, heal; and although they leave scars behind, even these scars can become reminders of God's healing love. "Honorable scars," she calls them, which point to the kindness of God and to our own spiritual growth.

Julian's insights into "falling and rising" began somewhat unexpectedly, in the blunt revelation that she would not be able to overcome certain sins in her own life. At the time when her showings began, Julian seems to have shared the general picture of spiritual growth on the "ladder," as we have sketched it above. She regretted, in any case, that she had not served God more fully with her life, and perhaps felt that she had not risen very far on the ladder of perfection. The Shorter Version of her book especially contains this negative reflection in her description of her feelings at the time of her illness. It is possible that at this point, Julian regretted not having been a nun in the "years of her youth," which years she evidently filled up with hard work, very likely the work of motherhood which she describes so well.

As the showings progressed, Julian's desire to be "oned" to God, in the wound of true longing, increased. She saw, then that nothing would prevent her from this spiritual union with God, except her own sin. This revelation in itself should not have been startling, except that it seems to have been given *specifically*. Julian mentions her own "sloth" (laziness and depression), and anxiety—as if these were the specific kinds sin she hoped to overcome.[3] She was hoping, too, that her experience of suffering in the visions themselves (in which she experienced the pains of the cross) would have the effect of "purging" her from her own impurity. It came as a shock, then, when the Lord revealed to her that, in spite of her good intentions and her suffering, she would sin again:

> After this the Lord brought to my mind the longing that I had for him before; and I saw that nothing prevented me but sin. And I saw this generally in us all ... for we are all partly brought to nothing, and we shall be brought to nothing, following our Master Jesus, until we are fully purged: that is to say, until we are fully brought to nothing in our mortal flesh, and are purged of all our inward desires which are not very good. (ch. 27)

But later Julian is forced to confess,

> God brought to mind that I would sin; but because of the delight that I had in looking at him, I did not really pay attention to that showing at the time. So our Lord very kindly waited, and gave me the grace to pay attention. At first I took this showing to apply individually to me; but because of all the gracious comfort which follows, as you shall see, I was taught to apply it to all my fellow Christians in general, rather than individually. Although our Lord showed me that I would sin, by "me" alone is understood everybody.
>
> And in this, I conceived a gentle fear; but our Lord answered it saying, "I am keeping you completely safe." (ch. 37)

The lessons which followed may be summarized as follows. God showed Julian that:

—Sin and suffering are inevitable in this life, even in those souls who are being saved. However, we should look at them as opportunities for victory, rather than as defeats.

—God is always fully in control of what happens to us. There are not two gods, but only one—who is Love. God does not allow us to fall too far.

—God himself undergoes whatever suffering God permits.

—In every life, there are unhappy things which God has permitted, in order to draw us to himself and to teach us compassionate love, which is the love of God. If there were no suffering, evil would be able to overwhelm us with pride. But for those who love God, even the experience of "falling" in sin and in suffering is turned into good, and becomes the occasion of great rejoicing in heaven because of our healing, in God's love.

In these four points, Julian learns that the experience of sin and suffering is essentially different for the soul who loves God, as opposed to the soul who believes that God is only wrath and condemnation. For the soul who trusts in divine love, suffering begins to be wedded to the suffering of Christ on the cross. Whereas sin naturally leads to death and to despair (the pains of hell), in faith the experience of forgiveness and healing lead to great joy. The soul begins to suffer, not because of what it perceives as hurts to itself, but because of the pain of others. *Passion* becomes *compassion*; contrition becomes sorrow for the sins of the whole world; longing becomes the longing that the whole world might be saved. Suffering ceases to be something which happens *to* us, and begins to be something which we have deliberately taken into ourselves, where it can be healed and turned into joy by the indwelling Spirit of God.

Rejoicing in Tribulation

We have already seen that in Julian's analysis, human nature is firmly grounded in God's own nature. It is, therefore, steady and consistent in charity. However, in the context of sin humanity has become notoriously fickle and changeable. Julian did not reach this conclusion merely through abstract reflection on human frailty, however. It was actually a description of herself, as she learned about her own soul in one of the more interesting events in her showings.

At one point in the sixteen revelations, God permitted Julian to see for herself how "unsteady" she really was. In this showing, Julian found herself being alternately cheered and encouraged by what she had seen, so that she felt her faith was unshakeable; and then plunged into an experience of deep depression and fear, bordering on hopelessness. In the seventh revelation, Julian had just grown confident that her own spiritual insights were very deep indeed. She felt that her faith was stronger than it had ever been, and that she would probably never fall into fear again:

> After this he showed me an abundant spiritual joy in my soul. I was filled full of absolute certainty, firmly established, without any more painful fear. This experience was so happy and so spiritual, that I was quite at peace thinking that there was nothing on earth that could bother me. (ch. 15)

An unpleasant surprise, however, was soon to follow:[4]

> This lasted only for a while. Then I was returned to myself, and left to my own depression—weary with my life and

irritated with myself—so that I hardly had the patience to go on living. There was no comfort or ease for me except for faith, hope and charity. These three things had never really abandoned me, though I hardly felt them.

And suddenly, after this, our blessed Lord gave me once again the experience of comfort and rest in my soul, in delight and with a certainty so blessed and so strong that no fear or sorrow, nor any physical pain that could be suffered would have bothered me.

Then the pain showed up again in my feelings, and then the joy and delight: now one, and now the other, several times; I suppose about twenty times. And during the times of joy and delight I could have said with St. Paul, "Nothing shall separate me from the love of Christ." And in the pain, I might have said with Peter, "Lord save me, I perish." (ch. 15)

The reason for this unsettling experience was to show Julian that it is good for us to recognize our dependence upon God's grace:

The reason that this vision was showed to me, as I understand it, is that it is helpful for some souls to feel this way: sometimes to be comforted, and sometimes to fail and to be left to themselves. God wants us to know that he keeps us equally safe, whether we are experiencing sorrow, or well-being. (ch. 15)

In the experience of suffering and disappointment, the temptation is to believe that God is punishing us. However, Julian is shown that how we fare is not so much a question of our personal merit or guilt before God (who is not punishing us), as a reality of life in which God is teaching us to depend upon him alone:

For the good of man's soul, he is sometimes left to himself, even though sin was never the reason for it. (During this time, I had not myself committed any sin that should have caused me to be abandoned—because it all happened too suddenly; and besides, I did not deserve the good feelings either.) But our Lord gives freely when he wills, and he allows us to suffer in woe sometimes. Both of these come from the same love. For it is God's will that we hold onto comfort with all our might, because joy will last forever, without end; whereas pain passes away, and will come to nothing in those who are being saved. Therefore it is not God's will for us to follow up the feelings of pain by feeling sorry and by mourning over them, but to pass over them quickly and to keep ourselves in endless delight. (ch. 15)

All experiences of suffering and fear are potentially opportunities to learn the grace of God. They are in fact necessary if we are to know God in this life; and in this life, suffering and sin are inevitable. In that sense, we might consider "travail" part of the birth-pangs of life in this world. Faith, then, is to look to God and to trust at the moments in which we are in the most pain. Faith is, therefore, not so much a strength as the recognition of our own weakness and dependence upon God. Faith is established most in the times of our frailty.

In light of all this, Julian is able to say that in one sense God is indeed responsible for at least some of our suffering, in that God puts it there. It is not that evil comes from God, nor that God is punishing us in these times. Rather, God permits us to function on our own sometimes—not giving us the sense of his immediate presence—because he wishes for us to know him better. These times have the effect of drawing us closer. We should bear them, then, not with complaint and irritation, but with rejoicing and anticipation—because ultimately they will lead us to a deeper experience of divine grace and joy:

Thus I saw how Christ has compassion on us because of our sin. . .

Yes, and I saw that our Lord rejoices at the tribulations of his servants—though with pity and compassion—to the extent that in order to bring each person whom he loves to bliss, he lays on him something that is not a failing in his sight, but by which the person will be brought down in the eyes of the world, or scorned, or beaten and outcast. And he does this to lessen the harm that he might take from the pomposity and vainglory of this wretched life, to make their way ready to come to heaven, and raising them up in bliss forever without end. And he says, "I shall completely break you of you vain affections and vicious pride, and after that I shall gather you together and make you meek and mild, clean and holy, making you one with me." (ch. 28)

The work of grace in these times is to turn our experiences of falling down in sin and suffering and despair, into joy:

> Mercy works to keep us, and mercy works to turn everything into good. In love, mercy allows us to fall in a measure, and insofar as we fall we also die—for we necessarily die inasmuch as we fail to see and feel that God is our life. Our failing is dreadful, and our falling is shameful and our dying is sorrowful. But in all of this, the sweet eye of pity and love never is taken off of us, and the operation of mercy never ceases. For I saw the property of mercy, and I also saw the property of grace ...
>
> For grace turns our dreadful failing into abundant, endless solace; and grace turns our shameful falling into a high, glorious rising; and grace turns our sorrowful dying into holy, blessed life. (ch. 48)

We might still ask, however, why it is *necessary* for us to have the experience of falling. Would it not be equally easy for God to comfort us all the time? Julian concludes that if God gave us continuous comfort, we would not grow. It would be like a mother who carried her baby all the time: we would never learn to "walk"—that is, to overcome sin and to live in the image of God. The worst dimension of evil, in fact, is pride. Our pride would be insufferable if we were allowed never to have the experience of being "put down." However, Julian reckons that God does not show us our sin directly, as it really is, or otherwise we would be too depressed to go on. He reveals it, rather, indirectly, in light of his own gracious love:

> Our Lord, of his sweet mercy, shows us our sin and our
> weakness by the sweet gracious light of himself... And so,
> in this gracious knowledge, we may see our sin for our own
> good, without despairing. For certainly we do need to see it;
> and by seeing it we are made ashamed of ourselves, and
> broken down as against our pride and presumption. For it
> truly does us good to see that in ourselves, we are absolutely
> nothing but sin and wretchedness. (ch. 78)

In this passage we can see that Julian does not share the
Neoplatonic view of humanity which implies that each one of
us is, in our innermost being, basically "good" or perfect.
However, the key to Julian's understanding is that "*in ourselves
we are nothing;*" for in Christ, we are everything, because
Christ is our true nature, which is always kept safe, even when
we fall. Julian learns from all this that we may expect to sin;
but that, on the other hand, we can expect the Lord to comfort
us afterwards, and to heal the effects of our sin and even to
glorify us afterwards:

> In this I also had another insight, in his showing me that I
> would sin. I took it simply to apply to myself, as an in-
> dividual, because at the time I was not moved otherwise.
> But in the high, gracious comfort of our Lord which fol-
> lowed afterwards, I saw that this was meant for mankind in
> general. That is to say, all men are sinful, and will be until
> the last day; of which "men" I am included (I hope!) by the
> mercy of God, because the blessed comfort that I saw was
> large enough for us all. (ch. 79)

And,

> Also God showed that sin will not be to the shame, but
> rather to the glory, of man: for just as it is true that for
> every sin there is an answering pain [or, "punishment"], it is
> also true that for every sin there is given a blessing to the
> same soul, by love. Just as different sins are punished with
> different pains ["punishments"] according to how serious
> they are, in the same way they will be rewarded with dif-
> ferent joys in heaven according to the measure in which

they have been painful and sorrowful to the soul on earth.
For the soul that will come to heaven is precious to God,
and the place is so glorious that the goodness of God never
allows a soul that is coming there to sin, unless that sin is
rewarded...(ch. 38)

In the remainder of the chapter just quoted, Julian goes on
to speak of the way in which God used great sinners to serve
him:

> ...in this vision my understanding was lifted up to heaven,
> and then God brought merrily to my mind David, and
> others in the Old Testament beyond number; and in the
> New Testament he brought to my mind first Mary Mag-
> dalene, Peter and Paul, and those in India [*Padds*: Thomas
> and Jude]; and St. John of Beverley, and also others beyond
> number: how they are known in the Church on earth for all
> their sins, but it is no shame to them because everything has
> been turned to glory for them. (ch. 38)

In a delightful passage, she digresses to elaborate on the local
saint, John of Beverley, who was known as a great sinner
before the time of his conversion.[5] Julian assures her readers
that Jesus

> called him "St. John of Beverley," just as we do

and that although St. John had served God in his youth, God
had permitted him to fall. However, all turned out well in the
end, so that St. John did not die in his sins—and his wasted
time was not really lost. He was raised up to a greater grace,
because of his greater repentance, having received such great
mercy. And this vision, she concludes, was given in order to
make us glad and merry. We should not lose heart, but rejoice
in the forgiveness that we have, pick ourselves up, and go with
life.

"I Am Keeping You Safe."

Earlier we saw Jesus' promise to Julian that in spite of her
sin, he was keeping her completely safe. In chapter 61 she

summarizes the argument that God keeps us even when we sin:

> And when we fall, he quickly raises us up by his lovely embrace and his gracious touch. And when we are strengthened by his sweet working, then we deliberately choose him by his grace, to be his servants and lovers, forever. (ch. 61)

It may be, however, that we have already chosen to serve him; nevertheless, he will sometimes leave us to ourselves in order to strengthen our faith through the experience:

> And yet after this he allows some of us to fall even harder and more seriously than we ever did before, as we think. And then we think that we have not been at all wise, and that everything we have begun has come to nothing. But it is not true; for we needed to fall, and we needed to see it. For if we did not fall, we would not know how weak and how wretched we are in ourselves, nor would we fully understand the marvelous love of our Maker. For we shall see in heaven, without end, that we have grievously sinned in this life; and notwithstanding this, we shall also see that we were never damaged by it, in his love, and were never less precious in his sight because of it. (ch. 61)

Julian compares the experience of falling to that of a child who has injured itself. A mother will sometimes allow her child to fall, so that it might learn the necessity of obedience; and so that it might learn to turn to her in times of need:

> A mother will sometimes allow her child to fall, and to be more distressed sometimes for his own profit; but she would never allow any kind of real danger to come to her child, because of love. (ch. 61)

At these times, God does not want for us to become depressed over our own failures, but to turn to him in love:

We have soiled ourselves in sin, like a child who has soiled its diaper or spoiled its clothes. Then we should say,

> "... I have made myself dirty, and unlike you; and I cannot
> nor may not clean it up except with your special help and
> grace." (ch. 61)

When the soul has learned to recognize sin, so that sin no
longer seems desirable, it becomes possible to understand for
the first time what human nature really is. Sin is not natural
to the soul, although in our fallen state we fail to realize what
true human nature is, in Christ. Once we have learned of the
grace of our Mother, we do not want to go back to sinning.
Sin becomes its own "scourge." Now sin itself turns us to our
Mother, and no other punishment is necessary for us to realize
that we do not want to sin again:

> Sin is the sharpest scourge that any chosen soul could be
> smitten with—a scourge which does nothing but beat a
> man or woman, breaking him in pieces in his own sight so
> much that sometimes he thinks himself unworthy of any-
> thing but to sink into hell—until the time that contrition
> takes over, and by the touching of the Holy Spirit turns the
> bitterness into hopes for God's mercy. And then his wounds
> begin to be healed, and his soul revives, and he is turned to
> the life of Holy Church. (ch. 39)

The experience of falling thus leads us to penitence, and a
deeper compassion for the failures of others. In all this God
does not allow us to fall too far, but reassures the soul that
loves God, that it will not be overcome. In Julian's final experience of the "fiend" in her last showing, she hears the promise that for the soul that loves God there is a sure keeping in
his love:

> "... you shall not be overcome."

> These last words were said in order to teach me that true
> security, which is in our Lord Jesus, who showed me every-
> thing. And just as in the first word that our good Lord
> showed me—"With this the devil is overcome" (meaning his
> blessed passion)—in the same way in the last word he said
> with true, full conviction, "You shall not be overcome"
> (indicating us all).

...He did not say, "You shall not be storm-tossed, you shall not be troubled, you shall not be diseased"; but he said, "You shall not be overcome." God wants us to pay attention to these words, so that we would be equally strong in faithful trust, both in good times and in bad. (ch. 68)

Four Kinds of Fear

The final showing which Julian experiences was truly dreadful, in the original meaning of that word: full of fear. We recall that Julian encountered a demon, who attempted to assault her in her bed. As she describes these events (in chapters 74-76 of the *Revelations*), she pauses to analyze four kinds of fear which all people experience in life. Her point is that even though we cannot say that all these fears are holy or God-sent, nevertheless God can use them to turn us to faith. Actually, within the Being of God there is no fear at all, because God never has a "failing of might." However, God works in absence as much as in presence, to draw us to himself. It is possible for God, then, to work in the midst of our own failings and resultant fears. The four kinds of fear which Julian especially notes are:

1) anxiety, due to our own failings or weaknesses
2) the fear of punishment or pain (or, the fear that believes all our pains are punishments from God)
3) doubts and faithlessness
4) holy fear, or awe of God.

The first kind of fear comes over us when we realize that we are helpless:

One is that kind of fear which comes upon a man suddenly, in his weakness. This fear does good, because it helps to purge a man, just like a physical illness or some other kind of pain which is not sin. For all such pains help a man, if they are patiently borne. (ch. 74)

The realization that we cannot help ourselves is good, insofar as it can have the effect of turning us to God. Even those who do not believe in God at all will begin to pray in the face of this kind of fear. Julian also notes that in weakness, we can be helped not to sin ("purged"); for example, in a weakened condition—as through illness or fasting—we are sometimes better off, because we do not sin in ways we might have otherwise.

The second kind of fear is fear of pain or punishment (the word "pain" has both meanings in Julian's English):

> The second is the fear of pain [punishment], in which a man is stirred and awakened from the sleep of sin. For he is not able at the time to perceive the soft comfort of the Holy Spirit, until he has undergone this fear of pain—or of physical death and of spiritual enemies—and understands it. And this fear stirs us to seek comfort and mercy from God, and enables us to have contrition by the blessed touching of the Holy Spirit. (ch. 74)

Julian seems to have in mind here the situation in which we fall ill, and are faced with the sudden prospect of death—and, we imagine, of hell and torment from our "spiritual enemies." It works this way: sometimes an individual is quite comfortable pursuing a sinful life, which (by its nature) is destructive and leads to everlasting separation from God; however, this life of wanton sin is suddenly interrupted by the prospect of great pain, or even death. The idea of dying and being cast into hell prompts this person to turn to God in prayer, and to seek everlasting life. In this sense the teaching of the Church about eternal damnation is entirely beneficial and true, even though God does not *blame* the sinner; for terror is the natural consequence of separation from God.

The third is a kind of fear which in itself is definitely not from God, but which can be turned to good. It is lack of trust in the goodness of God, and would also include a lack of confidence in ourselves:

> The third is fear full of doubt. Insofar as doubt-filled fear leads us to despair, God wishes to have it turned into love in us, through the experience of love. That is to say, that the bitterness of doubt be turned into the sweetness of kind love, by grace. For it can never please our Lord that his servants doubt in his goodness. (ch. 74)

This kind of fear is significant to Julian, because it masquerades for religion. There are persons who never doubt the *power* of God (that God is "almighty"), and who therefore give the appearance of piety; however, they doubt the *goodness* of God, and in truth are without any faith at all. This kind of fear always leads to despair, because we believe that we do not deserve the love of God, and therefore have incurred God's wrath. Since God is almighty, to believe only in divine wrath is the worst kind of despair possible. Often we see it in the bitterness of persons who believe that they have served God well in this life, but without being rewarded adequately. They work hard to keep the rules which they perceive to be "religion;" and when they fail (as is inevitable in a life of sin) they become bitter, and constantly critical of others whom, they think, are not as good as they themselves. It is actually this kind of fear or despair which is generally described as "faith" by persons who do not know the infilling of the Holy Spirit, but who believe that Christianity is a religion of rules or the terror of being sent to hell by an angry God. In the end, it leads to the pain which is in hell.

Finally, there is a kind of fear which is proper to the human being who knows God. It is also "fear," although it is opposite to the terror which we have just described. In contrast to the other kinds of fear, it comes from a genuine awareness of the nature of God. It is a genuine respect for God's holiness, accompanied by a knowledge of our sin, revealed in the light of divine love. Because the soul knows that God is only love, the feelings of terror and of despair which might otherwise have been produced melt into a "soft" or "gentle" respect for God's awesome power:

> There is no fear in us that fully pleases God, except reverent fear. And it is very soft, for the more we have it the less we actually feel it, because of the sweetness of love. (ch. 74)

Julian then observes that proper "dread" of God's holiness always accompanies faith or love of God, simply because we are creatures and God is Creator. It is right that we should respect God because of divine holiness. Faith, in fact, is never genuine without this deep respect for the Love of God:

Love and fear are like brothers, and they are both rooted in
us by the goodness of our maker. They will never be taken
away from us, forever. We have love by nature, and we
have love by grace; we also have fear by nature, and we
have fear by grace. It is proper to the Lordship and the
Fatherhood of God, that he should be feared; just as it
belongs to his goodness to be loved. And it is our duty, as
his servants and children, to fear him; just as it is our duty
because of his goodness to love him. And although this
reverent fear and love cannot be separated from each other,
nevertheless they are not the same thing. They have two
different natures and ways of working. However, neither of
them may be had without the other. (ch. 70)

Julian goes on to explain that whoever loves God, also
experiences "dread"—even though it is not felt as terror or
naked fear. She then describes the false kind of piety which
does not have any of the love of God in it, but which comes
"under the color of holiness." These can easily be recognized
by their fruits: those kinds of fear which have the effect of
turning us away from God, in terror, are never good; they are
either wrong, or "mixed with wrong." On the other hand,
those kinds of fear which cause us to turn to God, just as a
child flees in moments of fright to its mother, are good. Julian
recommends that we learn to tell them apart, and refuse the
wrong ones as not from God.

Four Kinds of Grace
Counterbalancing the four kinds of fear which operate in
our lives, there are four "manners of goodness" in which God
works to heal us. In her experience of the sixteenth revelation,
Julian was made aware of the true nature of her own sin, and
of the operation of fear in her life. At the same time, she says,
God did not show her the areas of her sin directly, but (as we
have seen) only in light of his own grace. Therefore, we do not
need to despair. The context of this life is sin, but the context
of sin is divine love.
As a part of her revelation, Julian learns that there are four
things which God wishes for us to know about the operation
of divine grace in our lives:

> It is his will that we have knowledge of four things: The first
> is that he is our ground, in whom we have all our life and
> being. The second is that he keeps us powerfully and mer-
> cifully, in the time that we are in our sin, and among all our
> enemies who have fallen on us (*i.e.*, in those times that we
> are so much more in peril because we have given them the
> opportunity to attack us, and do not even know our own
> need).

> The third is how courteously he keeps us and makes us to
> know that we have gone amiss. The fourth is how steadfastly
> he waits for us, and does not change his cheerful expression.
> For he wants us to be turned to him and joined to him in
> love, as he is to us. In this way, by this gracious knowledge,
> we may see our sin profitably, without despair. (ch. 78)

These four provide a summary of Julian's understanding of
divine grace. Its first assumption is that God is the "ground" of
everything; therefore we do not need to be afraid. The second
point relates especially to the work of the incarnate Son, who
has overcome the Enemy in the place where we are attacked—
that is, in our humanity. We are unable to comprehend the
real extent of our danger; but the Lord keeps us safe, when we
do not even know about it. The third relates to the special
work of the Holy Spirit: he "keeps" us and teaches us.
Together, these echo the words which Julian learned earlier
about the relationship of God to space and time: "I made it, I
love it, I keep it." The fourth is a kind of summary of them all:
that God does not change in his judgment of us, which judgment is merciful and dependable. Recalling once more the fall
of the servant, Julian sees that the lord's whole purpose is to
raise the servant so that he may be glorified. It was not the
lord's wish that the servant should fall; but since the "hole" of
evil was there, the lord reached down into the place of evil and
death to rescue him.

To turn towards this Lord is faith. It means, for Julian, that
we stop looking at our own failings, and begin to look towards
the compassion of God. This, for Julian, is the whole point of
the gospel. The consequence of it all is that we learn not to
give in to despair, which often accompanies the recognition of

our own sin. Although sin is hateful in God's sight, it would be wrong to feel abjectly lost because of sin; or to believe that God cannot rescue us even from hell. There is as mentioned the danger of false piety, in which the soul is always cast down or constantly sour about the world, or bitter against God because of the suffering which the soul has had to undergo. The "Christian" who gives this dark and foreboding picture of God is not yet aware of the meaning of the birth of Christ . The "pious" soul who constantly desires to escape this world in order to be with God in heaven, is not yet aware of the love of God the creator who desires for us to enjoy this life which is to come:

> Before this time I had a great longing, and desire, to be delivered by God's grace from this world and from this life; for I often contemplated the woe that is here, and the well-being and blessedness which is there. And even if there had been no suffering in this life, but only the absence of our Lord, I sometimes thought that it was more than I could bear. And this caused me to mourn and actively to long [for heaven]. And also my own wretchedness, laziness and weakness made me desire not to live and to work as I needed to.

> To all this our courteous Lord answered, to give me comfort and patience, with these words:

> "You will suddenly be taken from all your pains, from all your sickness, from all your disease and from all your woe. And you shall come up above, and you shall have me for your reward. And you shall be filled full of love and of joy. And you shall never have any kind of pain, nor misery, nor lack anything you may want, but will always have joy and bliss without end. So why should it grieve you to suffer for a little while, seeing that it is my will and for my glory?" (ch. 64)

Both falling and rising, then, are part of the life of faith. In falling, we learn of our own weakness in sin and our need to depend upon the grace of God. In rising up again, we learn of the love and compassion of God, who desires for us not to fall in sin. We should turn our attention not to the falling itself—

lest we fall even harder and more often, into despair—but to
the mercy and kindness of God:

> If there is any lover [of God] living on this earth who is
> continually kept from falling, I do not know about it, for it
> was not shown to me. But this was shown: that in falling
> and in rising we are always preciously kept in the same love.
> For in seeing God, we do not fall; and in contemplating
> ourselves we cannot stand. (ch. 82)

8

Five Joys:
Given Love, which is "Virtue"

The third kind of love which Julian saw in her revelations is the love of God which is shared, or what we ordinarily think of as the "virtue" of love in human beings. It is the love which we give to one another in ordinary life and which itself is a gift from the Holy Spirit to us, at work in us. For Julian, the "virtue" of love is an enjoyment of the presence of God in the circumstances in which we live, and in the people whom we meet. The soul who loves God and trusts in the kindness of God, learns to recognize God at work in everything. Such a soul stops complaining about suffering and failures and sins, and turns her attention instead to the joy and goodness of God. She enjoys the immediate presence of God, and enjoys God in all things. This joy, really the enjoyment of life itself, is drawn from the life of the Trinity— who is Joy. To know this joy and to share it is, quite simply, what we think of as "love" in this life.

Joy in God
Earlier we saw that Julian was shown three "heavens" in God (the ninth revelation, described in chapters 22-23). All three of these "heavens" Julian understood to be expressed in the humanity of Christ, for our sake; and all three of these were "love." Later, however, Julian describes them again as "joy," because love and joy are actually the same: love is the enjoyment of others, which is found in God, and which we share when we "love."

Julian uses three synonyms to describe her vision of joy in the Trinity: "joy," "bliss," and "delight," corresponding to the work of the three Persons within the Trinity (ch. 23). These remind us that the nature of joy is intimate sharing, which is defined by the Being of God. The Trinity is the source of what we mean by "joy," because in the Trinity there is the complete expression of ecstatic love (love *going out* of itself). It is "ecstatic" because in the Being of God, each divine Person is constantly and eternally going out of himself into the others. It is what Julian calls "endless delight."

We have also seen that the greatest joy to be found in God is not merely the self-expression of joy which is *within* the Trinity, but the love of God which has gone out of himself in creation and also in the incarnation of the Son of God—which two acts of God are really only one "act" from the divine point of view. God created humanity to be one with God, and in the same moment God became one with humanity. Now Julian extends this idea to say that the greatest joy in God is not merely in creating and sharing humanity, but in suffering for the sake of humanity; for true joy is compassionate, and true compassion is ultimately always joyful:

> For truly it is the greatest joy that can be, as I see it, that he who is highest and mightiest, noblest and worthiest, is also lowest and gentlest, most humble and courteous. . .

> For the perfect fulness of joy that we shall have, as I see it, is this marvelous courtesy and humility of our Father, who is our Maker in our Lord Jesus Christ—who is our Brother and our Savior. (ch. 7)

Julian identifies "joy" with the person of Jesus Christ, and notes that he himself is "bliss" with relation to his divine nature, even while he is in suffering and pain in his human nature:

> We know in our faith—and it was also showed in all the revelations—that Jesus Christ is both God and man. In respect to his Godhead he is himself the highest bliss, and always was so from without-beginning—just as he shall be without end: the same endless bliss which can never be increased or diminished. (ch. 31)

At the same time, the deepest sense of joy in Christ relates not merely to the endless bliss which he shares with the Father in heaven, but with his deliberate choice to suffer, in compassion, for our sakes: The eighth, ninth, tenth, and eleventh showings are completely given over to this theme. Julian sees it in an extended vision of Jesus on the cross, in which Julian is frightened by the graphic portrayal of his wounds, and by her experience of the deep pain of the cross. Just as she expects to see Jesus die, he does not—but looks at her with "cheer," and asks her this question:

> Then our good Lord said, "Are you completely satisfied that I suffered for you?" I said, "Yes, good Lord, by your mercy. Yes! Good Lord, may you be blessed!"

> Then Jesus, our good Lord, said, "If you are completely satisfied, then I am satisfied. It is a joy, a blessing and an endless delight to me that I ever suffered the passion for you. And if I could suffer more, I would suffer more." (ch. 22)

The particular source of joy for Christ is the role of *choice* in his suffering. Julian learns here that he enjoyed his role as savior because he took it upon himself, deliberately:

> And I, beholding all this by grace, saw that his love for our soul was so strong that he deliberately chose it, with great desire, and patiently suffered it with satisfaction. (ch. 20)

And again, Jesus speaks to her of his own joy in dying:

> "Look and see that I loved you so much, long before I ever died for you, that I wanted to die for you. And now I have died for you, and have suffered as willingly as possible. And now all my bitter pains and all my hard work has been turned into an everlasting joy and blessing.

> "And as for you, how could you possibly pray for anything at all that pleases me, that I would not very gladly grant it to you? For my pleasure is your holiness and your endless joy and bliss with me." (ch. 24)

The nature of joy, finally, is that it does not notice the extent of its own suffering, because it is immersed in others. True joy is to choose to serve others, for their sakes—in which we "set at nothing" our own pain, and even cease to be aware of it:

> This was a singular source of wonder to me, and a vision of great delight... It is, as I said, such a great blessing to Jesus that he sets at nothing his hard labor and his passion, and his cruel and shameful death. (ch. 22)

Looking at Jesus' face, then, Julian does not see sorrow or self-pity. Even when Jesus observes her thinking about the sorrow of his mother, who stood beneath the cross, he reacts with joy to think of her love:

> His countenance full of mirth and joy, our Lord looked down on the right side and brought to mind our Lady ... (ch. 25)

The Divine Laughter

An amusing interlude in Julian's *Revelations* is her description of the fifth revelation, in which she learned that the "fiend" had been overcome in the passion of Christ. Put just this way, we might not find it that amusing—for we are used to dry theological analyses and somber hymns about the suffering of the Lord to pay for our sins. Julian's vision was quite different, however. She saw the "foul fiend" soundly trounced by a cheerful Jesus. The fiend's undoing was his own wicked plot to overcome humanity in Adam's fall. Every wicked thing which the fiend might do was, in Julian's vision, turned into a blessing in the grace of God. In this way his "might" was turned into "unmight." The result of the vision was that Julian started to laugh uncontrollably—something which, she understood, the Lord would like to see Christians do a little more often.

The vision was amusing in itself. First, Julian was allowed to review, for a few moments, all that she had seen before. Then a voice formed in her soul, saying "With this the fiend is overcome." She assumed that the Lord was referring to the crucifixion. Then came a comical review of Satan's power:

In this, our Lord showed that his passion is the undoing of the fiend. God showed that the fiend still has the same malice that he had before the incarnation; but the harder he tries, the more he sees that all of those souls who were intended for salvation continually escape him, gloriously by the precious passion of Christ. And that is his sorrow; and he is most evilly afflicted by it!

For everything that God allows him to do turns into joy, and brings him shame and woe. And he has as much sorrow when God allows him to work, as when he can't work. And that is because he can never do as well as he would like, for all his power is firmly in God's hands. (ch. 13)

Julian learns that in all this, there is no malice or wrath in God—not even towards Satan. On the other hand, God "scorns" the malice of the fiend by letting it defeat itself. God intends for us to do the same:

Also I saw the Lord scorn his malice and bring his "unmight" to nothing. And he wants us to do the same.

Because of this vision I started laughing heartily, and that made all my friends who were with me start laughing too, and their laughter delighted me. I thought I would like for all my fellow-Christians to be there, to see what I was seeing, because then they would laugh with me. But I did not see Christ laughing. For I understood that we should laugh in order to comfort ourselves and to enjoy God, because the devil has been overcome. (ch. 13)

Analyzing the vision later, in a more somber mood, Julian concluded that three things were operating here: a joke (relating to the fiend's "unmight"—that the harder he worked, the more he saw his efforts turn into the joy of those who love God); scorn, in which we are to ignore the work of Satan—scorning it—and concentrate rather on enjoying God; and a serious matter (which Julian calls an "earnest"), the point of which is that the power of evil—which is horrible enough—has indeed been overcome through the passion of Christ. Because it has been overcome, we are able to enjoy the love of

God. And indeed, God's will is that we would learn to laugh at the "unmight" of evil, since it has been defeated. In this, we are able to enjoy God and bring blessing to our own lives.

Finally, Julian sees this "divine laughter" in a vision of Jesus as the Bridegroom, presiding in heaven at his own wedding. In the sixth revelation (ch. 14), Julian has a vision of the parable of the great banquet.[1] The Lord is "reigning royally" in his house,

> ...filling it full of joy and mirth. He himself was endlessly gladdening and cheering up his dearest friends, in a most friendly [homely] and courteous way, with a marvelous song about endless love in his own fair, blessed countenance: which glorious countenance of the Godhead completely fills the heavens with joy and bliss. (ch. 14)

Julian notes in this vision that Jesus is so busy acting as a cheerful host that he does not have time to sit down, but moves continually among the guests, making them enjoy themselves. This vision represented, for her, the nature of our reward in heaven, which is an eternal joy. Furthermore, the degree of "bliss" we experience in heaven is not related to how much we have done. Although, she says, everyone will know how old we are in heaven, and how long we have served God in this life, nevertheless

> God showed three degrees of bliss that every soul shall have in heaven, who has served God willingly in any degree at all. (ch. 14)

The three degrees of bliss are God's gratitude for our service on earth; his active thanks to us for what we have done; and the fact that we will enjoy him endlessly in heaven. Julian reiterates that all three degrees of bliss are for everyone who knows the love of God at all:

> For I saw that whenever, or at whatever age, a man or woman is truly turned to God, even for one day of service and for God's eternal will, he will have all these degrees of bliss. (ch. 14)

The whole purpose of God, then, is for us to enjoy him, not only endlessly but also in this life—sharing in the divine laughter which is always taking place at his banqueting table.

Five Kinds of Suffering, Five Kinds of Joy

In the remainder of her visions, Julian sees over and over again that suffering in this life will inevitably turn to joy—our own joy and that of others—if we are willing to turn it over to God. In so doing, we love God, and ourselves in God, and we show love to others—which is "virtue." The starting point for this theological observation is the passion of Christ, in which she notes five dimensions of his suffering. These then correspond to five kinds of joy which are in God.

In the same showing in which Julian saw the three "heavens" in God (the ninth revelation), she also saw five degrees of suffering in Christ. They were all revealed in her physical vision of the crucifixion:

> For our Lord showed me his passion in five ways: of which the first is the bleeding of his head; the second is the discoloring of his face; the third is the copious bleeding of his body, from the deep cuts of the scourging; the fourth is the deep drying-out [*or*, "dying"]. These four are the pains of the passion, as I said. And the fifth is this one, which was showed for the joy and the bliss of the passion: for it is God's will that we have a true delight with him in our salvation, and he wants us to be mightily comforted and strengthened in it. And so he wants us to be merrily preoccupied with his grace...(ch. 23)

For the fifth manner of suffering, Julian may have in mind the vision which immediately preceded, in which Jesus said to her that he had suffered as much as possible—for if it had been possible to suffer more, he would have (ch. 22). At the same time it seems that her meaning could be the continuous compassion of God which is in heaven; for God sees that we are cheerless, which is a pain to him. His purpose is rather that we should enjoy his love especially in view of the fact that he himself enjoys winning us back from the demons. Too many Christians view the passion of Christ with a dark and cheerless countenance. It is not God's view of it at all, for it is to him a "delight and a joy."

As if to emphasize this point, Julian now speaks of five ways in which God has "rejoiced" in us. These correspond in number to the five ways in which Julian saw Christ suffer on the cross, but they also represent the ways in which God has worked from eternity to bring love into our lives, and us into God:

> And then I saw that God rejoices that he is our Father: and God rejoices that he is our Mother; and God rejoices that he is our true Spouse, and our soul his beloved wife; and Christ rejoices that he is our Brother; and Jesus rejoices that he is our Savior.

> These are five high joys, as I understand it, in which he wills of us who are being saved to rejoice.

Enjoying God for God's Sake

Throughout her showings, Julian is taught that joy is the chief purpose of life. God created us out of joy, so that we would enjoy him and share in the joy which is the Trinity. Julian makes the point that "love" and "joy" always accompany one another, because the love which is in God and is God, is ecstatic love. This ecstasy is what we call "joy." Every soul really longs for the joy for which we were created, which is in effect a longing for God who is the source of joy and who is Joy. The soul, then, cannot be satisfied by anything less than God:

> And therefore we may ask anything from our Lover that we want. . . but we will never stop wanting and loving, until we have him in the fulness of joy. (ch. 6)

It is the true rest of the soul to rest in God, which is "bliss":

> After this our Lord revealed himself even more glorified (if I saw it correctly) than I had seen him before. In this I was taught that our soul shall never have rest until it comes into him, knowing that he is the fulness of joy: humble, courteous and blissful—true life. (ch. 26)

Joy cannot be ours, however, unless we love all that God loves. This becomes possible only when we accept all things in the assurance that God's judgments are right, and when we cease to blame God, others, or ourselves for what we perceive as failures in this life:

> But we cannot be blissfully secure in having this endless joy until we are completely at peace, and in love: that is to say, fully pleased with God and with all his works and with all his judgments; and loving and peaceable with ourselves and with our fellow-Christians, and with all that God loves— which is what Love desires. This is what God's goodness does in us... He is continually working to bring us into endless peace. (ch. 49)

And in summary,

> ...the fulness of joy is to see God in all things. (ch. 35)

The whole point of Julian's revelations is that we are meant to receive God's divine joy here, in this life. It is a deep tranquility which involves resignation to what God does, beyond what we can see or reason. At the same time, in the light of faith we begin to see that what God does is reasonable and right. Contrary to what many "religious" people would say, the bliss of heaven is not the negation of all that we know in this life, but its fulfillment. We may quote again Julian's teaching that:

> Then we shall all come into our Lord, knowing ourselves clearly and possessing God fully. We shall also be completely possessed by God, forever, seeing him in truth; and fully touching him, delectably smelling him, sweetly tasting him. Then we shall all see him face to face, familiarly and completely. And the creatures that have been created, shall see and eternally gaze upon God, who is their maker. (ch. 43)

Five Ways of Working: Towards a Life of Hope
Although the soul's deepest desire, for which it was created, is to know the joy of God, this life is "mixed." The truth is that

however hard we might try, we find ourselves depressed by the unhappy events of life and by our own failures. For the soul who loves God, this depression is offset by the desire to know God better; but that, in turn, can take the direction of self-condemnation, when we fear that we have not served God well enough. The final solution is not to deny that we have these feelings, but to confront them in hope. Hope is to admit that we are *incomplete*. We are infants, growing towards maturity; we are on a pilgrimage, the goal of which is divine joy and therefore, the fulness of human potential.

As Julian's showings taught her more about her own self, she could perceive five dimensions of life at work in her at once. These embrace both joy and sorrow, falling down and rising again, in a tension which is the substance of this life. Her experience of hope is that of deep tranquility, knowing that God is at work in all things:

> ... I felt in myself five things at work, as follows: Rejoicing ["enjoying"], sorrow, desire, dread, and sure hope. "Rejoicing," because God gave me to understand and to know that it was he, himself, whom I saw; "sorrow" because of my failures; "desire" because I wanted to see him ever more and more, understanding and knowing that we shall never have complete rest until we see him truly and clearly in heaven; "fear" because it seemed to me in all this time that the vision might cease, and then I would be left to myself. "Sure hope" was in the endless love that I saw would be kept by his mercy, and brought to endless bliss.
>
> But enjoying the vision, with this sure hope in his merciful safe-keeping, gave me a feeling of comfort—so that the mourning and the fear were not very painful.(ch. 47)

Julian concludes that the visions which she was receiving, and which gave her a deep sense of hope in the midst of her fear and depression, would probably not continue in this life. She would, therefore, have to learn to enjoy God even without the experience of supernatural visions, and even in the darkest periods of her life. And this, she reasoned, was for her own good, so that she might learn to depend upon God fully in everything. The bottom line of her struggle, then, is "hope": a sure trust in the principle that God is divine Love, and that God is at work in all things.

Passionless-ness: the Maturity of Hope

As love grows in us, we grow emotionally. Julian learns that in this process of growth, the emotion of fear begins to shrink and hope grows. It is what we may call "passionless-ness": the soul begins to lose its agitation over circumstances and inner fears, and begins to live in tranquility grounded in deep trust and love. The "passions" of this life begin to disappear, to be replaced by sure relationships which define love, joy, and peace.

Julian received special insight into this side of divine love when she inquired into the well-being of a loved one (ch. 35). At this point her visions suddenly stopped altogether, causing her to reflect that it is not God's will for us to try to judge our spiritual progress or that of any other individual. In her description of this lesson, Julian touches on what is traditionally known within Christian spirituality as *apatheia*, that is, being "without-passion."[2] After being told not to inquire into the spiritual well-being of others, Julian defines *apatheia* this way:

> I consented, and there I learned that is a greater glory to God for us to know everything in general, than to show a preference for any one thing in particular. And if I would act wisely according to this teaching, I would not be moved to gladness by any one thing at all. For "all shall be well," and the fulness of joy is to see God in all things. (ch. 35)

Once again, Julian's teaching has to be understood carefully. Although her concept of passionless-ness is consistent with the traditional teaching of the Church, it is very different from what we may have encountered today as "tranquility" or being "without-passion" in other spiritual disciplines outside the Church.

First, Julian's experience of tranquility does not come from a deep encounter with her own soul. There is no "well of tranquility" there, as has been depicted in other forms of spirituality. For Julian, in fact, her soul appeared to her as a dry desert (ch. 51), which gave her more cause for alarm and anxiety than for comfort. The deep well of tranquility which she encountered was specifically in Christ, our Mother, whom she understood to be at work in all things. Passionless-ness, then, stems from faith in the incarnate God, and not from any other kind of reflection.

Second, Julian's experience of peace and hope and joy, which renders her unmoved to gladness by specific things, does not mean that she is detached from the things of this world altogether. She is not detached from this world at all, in fact, but is actually learning just the opposite. For her, inner peace stems from the encounter with God at work in all things. It is, therefore, *an engagement with everything in this world*, loving it as God loves it, for the sake of God who is at work there. However, in the light of her visions of Christ as the center of all things, she learns not to take anything in this world as ultimately significant. Here is a paradox which, in a sense, cannot be appreciated outside Julian's mystical experience itself. It is that, in view of God's love, all things are infinitely valuable and all that exists has ultimate worth (because God made it, God loves it, and God keeps it); but that, on the other hand, reality is not determined by the things of this life, because all that exists has its being only as it shares in the Being which is God's. Therefore, we are to be moved to gladness not so much by particular things—which change and ultimately decay—but by the delight which we have in God at work in particular things and in all things in general. It is God who gives joy, because joy is God.

Finally, to be "passionless" does not mean, for Julian, having no feeling or emotions at all, nor being insensible in this life. In some spiritual disciplines, it is taught that the disciple must learn to be insensate, totally unmoved by circumstances or by the things of this life: not hearing, not seeing, not tasting, and so on. For Julian the opposite will be true. The one who loves God will know deep joy and deep sorrow, will hear and see, taste, smell, and touch—but in a new and more significant way. Now, joy is the fruit of an encounter with God, which surpasses any kind of happiness which might be had in this life, in any other way. It is the encounter of the soul with the true Self, who is Christ. Sorrow, too, is an encounter with

Christ, in the experience of deep contrition and compassion. The senses are, in a sense, heightened by the infilling of the Holy Spirit—a process which will be complete only when we gain a glorified body, in the state of bliss.

Rejoicing: the Response of Love

Finally, the whole purpose of creation is to return the joy which is in God. The fact of creation is itself a joy to God, because God "rejoices" in it and "enjoys" it, as Julian learns in her showings. However, all things are created with the capacity to return the joy which is in God. Human beings, who are created in the image and likeness of God, have this capacity more than any other—for, as we have seen, humanity is the highest of the natures which God has created, and in humanity all the "kinds" are joined together.

In this, Julian learns that joy is essentially a *response*. Being loved, for example, creates in us a sense of well-being and of love in return which cannot be had in any other way. Joy, too, is basically a response to love. It is *enjoyment*—which, in Julian's English, is the same as "rejoicing." We experience joy when we encounter the One who is the source of joy:

> "I am he. I am he. I am he who is highest, and I am he whom you love. I am he who delights you. I am he who serves you. I am what you are looking for. I am the one you desire. I am what you mean. I am that which is everything. I am what Holy Church preaches and teaches to you. And I am the one who has shown myself to you here."
>
> The number of his words passes all my wits, and all my understanding and all my ability; and they are the highest, as I see it. For in them is comprehended—I can't say what, except that the joy that I saw in the showing of them surpasses everything that my heart can think, or that the soul could desire. (ch. 26)

Earlier, we said that Julian saw five "high joys" in God—all of which express in some way the relationship which God has to us. Now she sees five ways in which the soul responds, in the "working" of the Holy Spirit. This response carries the soul beyond itself, because it is more than we could desire:

> These are five high joys, as I understand it, in which he wills
> for us who are being saved to rejoice: praising him, thanking
> him, loving him, and endlessly blessing him. (ch. 52)

God prompts us to rejoice in God, which is to "enjoy" him.
This rejoicing should describe the whole Christian life in general. It does not mean that we can expect never to feel hardship
or sorrow, but that our whole character is turned to God in
joy. However, the general attitude of rejoicing is always expressed in the encounter with specific things: we locate the
presence of God *there*, and rejoice in it. Julian notes that the
general response of "rejoicing" also has specific character, in
these ways: in praise, in thanksgiving, in showing love, and in
blessing. Julian's word "blessing" is an especially interesting
term because it is the same as the word for "bliss," but
outward-turned: "giving bliss," that is, "blissing." It has the
connotations of giving praise, bestowing a blessing, thanking,
enjoying. The Biblical terms for "blessing," in both Hebrew
and Greek, also carry the same meanings—that is, of praise,
thanksgiving, blessing, joy. (These terms, incidentally, give us
the name for the Christian rite of Holy Communion, which is
traditionally known as "eucharist," from Greek *eucharistia*,
"blessing.")[3] The heart of the Christian experience, then, is a
double blessing, one which works toward us first, and which is
then returned, in mutual joy.

It is typical of Julian's theological approach that all the
ways in which she sees the soul relating to God may also be
applied to the ways in which the soul relates to others in this
life. When we know the joy of God, we are able to praise
others and not blame them; to thank them for whatever they
might have done to us, as an outworking of God's will for us;
to demonstrate love; to bless others continually for who they
are. This will be true even when we perceive others to be "out"
of God's will; for God is at work in everything which is done,
even when we are individually disobedient, and even when
there are others who persecute us, for example, as servants of
the "fiend." We can give blessing in all things specifically,
because we understand God to be at work in all things generally.

In these ways, the joy which we have in God produces joy in

others. It is what we call the "virtue" of love: love which is given. In the end, it is simply the mystery of God at work in us:

> ...suddenly the Trinity filled my heart full of the highest joy. And I understood that this is how it will be in heaven without end, for all who shall come there. (ch. 4)

9

Six Ways of Prayer:
Becoming One with God

Faith is the attitude of the soul which is turned towards God in all things, and particularly in the times of hardship and suffering. It is to trust that the kindness of God can turn failure into joy, and to look for the kindness of God at work in all things. The means by which the soul grows in faith is prayer. Prayer is the exercise of faith, and in prayer the soul finds true rest. Prayer is therefore delightful to God, especially when it means that we lose the artificialities of this life in order to learn the humility of God:

> And also our good Lord showed that it is the greatest pleasure to him that a simple soul come to him nakedly, plainly and humbly. This is the natural desire of the soul, through the touching of the Holy spirit, as I am given to understand in this showing. (ch. 5)

For Julian, the positive effects of prayer cannot be overstated. She says boldly that:

> Prayer unites the soul to God. (ch. 43)

It is important that Julian does not say, "some kinds of prayer unite the soul to God"—as though we could practice certain techniques which would help us to achieve mystical union. Rather, prayer—all prayer in general, our own prayers in particular—leads to oneness with God, who is the source of prayer.

If we say that prayer unites the soul to God, however, we must understand at the same time what Julian means by "prayer." For her, it is more than an activity which we undertake now and then, perhaps to please God or because we have certain needs. Prayer is, for Julian, our whole life in the presence of God. We could say, more especially, that "prayer" means to live in the presence of God, who is actually at work in all things. Thus, prayer is not what we do just when we are speaking to God, but how we live in the presence of God. In that sense there is neither "spiritual" life nor "secular" life; but only persons who live consciously in the presence of God, delighting in him, and persons who do not know God, or who are threatened by his presence. For the soul that loves God, then, life itself becomes prayer, so that prayer and life cannot be separated.

As we explore Julian's concept of prayer, we bear in mind that she spent much of her life—perhaps more than fifty years of it—in the practice of intentional prayer. Although she does not tell us anything about her method of prayer, we may gather, from the fact that she was an anchoress, that she spent many hours each day in absolute seclusion and silence. We know, too, that she practiced certain prayer-disciplines which were typical of her time: singing the Psalms, meditating on scriptures, praying through the great themes of the faith (creation, incarnation, resurrection and so on), as well as praying the burial office each day, to remind her that she was dead to her sins. All these methods of prayer would have led up to the practice of silence: a kind of prayer in which the mind iteslf is stilled, and the soul looks upon the grace of God in stillness and awe.

Julian speaks of "beholding" God, and of seeking God—evidently two different experiences in prayer, of "seeing" and "seeking." It is not clear, however, whether "seeing" (i.e. contemplating) involved supernatural visions or not. She does not tell us definitely whether she experienced any visions after her original sixteen showings, though she does seem to have had occasional supernatural experiences through the rest of her life, which she calls "touchings."

In this she follows an unwritten rule in the practice of Christian spirituality, that the *techniques* of prayer are never discussed as if they were the *substance* of prayer. Julian tells us nothing at all about her way of prayer because for her, prayer itself is a grace which comes from the Holy Spirit.

Finally, Julian suggests that the highest form of prayer is really not to pray. This does not mean that we do not turn to God, but that the soul learns not to struggle with its own ideas of prayer or of what God desires from it. True prayer is a gift of God which wells up from deep inside, as a response to the love of God. Thus, when Julian speaks of prayer, it is of a response to God which God has created in the soul, and which the soul only shares in the gift of divine love.

The Ladder of Prayer

Before analyzing Julian's own concept of prayer, it is helpful to sketch in a background, once more, of how it may have been understood by Julian's "even-Christians" for whom she wrote. We have already seen that in Julian's day spiritual growth was said to take place in a steady progression upwards, on the so-called "ladder of perfection." We said that Julian appears to reject this popular image, because for her spiritual progress takes place through a whole lifetime of falling down in sin, and rising up again in the mercy of God. In Julian's understanding, we "grow" spiritually even when we think that we are not growing, and perhaps most when we feel that we have failed altogether.

In the same way, Julian offers an alternative to the way in which prayer was generally understood by her contemporaries. The "ladder" image of spiritual growth is important here, because the "ladder" was inevitably thought of as stages in prayer itself. While different writers might depict the rungs of the ladder in different ways, in general it could be thought of in terms of different kinds of prayer disciplines, and experiences in prayer, leading from simple prayers to the deep prayer of silence, or contemplation.

In this scheme, the lowest rungs of the ladder represented the idea that prayer is "asking God for things." Here prayer tends to be a one-way conversation, in which we talk to God rather than engage in listening or learning. The soul would be concerned here mainly with the physical necessities of life—house and home, food and drink, health and prosperity—without much thought for the things of heaven or even for other persons in this life.

Somewhat higher on the ladder would come prayers of contrition, intercessions, and spiritual requests. Still higher would be the more mature grasp of prayer which includes a measure of silence: listening and learning become possible, and the soul is no longer exclusively preoccupied with itself. Here, prayers also begin to include praise and adoration, without so much thought for the things of this world and certainly not for one's own needs. A model for prayer at this level would be the psalms, in which the method of prayer would include "psalmody"—singing the words of the psalms— and meditation, in which the mind would be fixed on certain passages of scripture or mysteries of the faith.

Finally, at the top of the ladder would be prayers of inner silence and contemplation, in which the soul is preoccupied with God alone. As the soul nears the top, she begins to long for an escape from this life into the life of heaven, and for the unmediated vision of the face of God. Here, life becomes as it were "all prayer," and prayer itself ceases to be so much an activity of the soul, as a form of rest in the grace of God. Such prayer is said to be "infused" by the Holy Spirit, rather than requiring hard effort. It may be accompanied by unusual experiences, in the rare individual, such as moments of ecstasy in which the soul goes out of itself into the presence of God, no longer sensible of the things in this world or even of itself. In time there might even be, in the soul which has become "pure," a "beatific vision" in which the soul glimpses the uncreated light of God's own all-surpassing Being; leading, at last, to mystical union of the soul to God.

As we might expect, progress up this ladder was said to require both hard work on the part of the individual, and continual practice—accompanied, of course, by divine grace. The idea was to shut out as many distractions from prayer as possible. Usually, for the serious person, this would mean undertaking a number of disciplines, including fasting, penances, and so forth, designed to decrease the influence of the flesh and to fix the mind on the things of heaven. Naturally, the higher rungs were understood to be reserved for those who had devoted their whole lives to prayer alone: the monks and nuns, for the most part, and especially the men of prayer (women, it was held, would have difficulty reaching the highest levels unless they could become "male" in their souls, through extraordinary work and determination). For those who deliberately engaged in the constant "warfare" of prayer, in its battle against the flesh, the final goal was never supposed to be out of sight: to become totally absorbed in prayer without distraction; to find union with God through prayer and so to escape the corruption of this world.

It was debated from time to time whether in this last stage, it is really possible for the created soul to *see* God or not. Some theologians held that a so-called "beatific vision" would indeed be possible, although the surpassing brightness of God would carry one beyond all speech and thought, and might appear to be a kind of "darkness" to the soul still living in mortal flesh. Others held that the pure essence of the Godhead would never be visible in this life, not even to the most advanced souls, simply because the Being of God is inaccessible to the creature: "no one has ever seen God."[1]

Some texts indicate that the earliest men and women to teach extensively about Christian prayer outside the New Testament, the so-called Desert Fathers and Mothers of the fourth and fifth centuries, understood "warfare" to be something which could and should be practiced by every Christian, in any walk of life. While not everyone might enter into the special kind of spiritual battles faced by the monks and solitaries of the desert, nevertheless the calling of each person could be seen as the place in which holiness would be worked out "in fear and trembling." In the intervening centuries, however, prayer seems to have been understood more and more as reserved, somehow, for those who learned it within the monastic life. It was, after all, their special "work."

To say this is, of course, an oversimplification; but at the same time, it would appear that in Julian's lifetime—especially in England—there was a popular movement to give prayer back, so to speak, into the hands of the laity. We have already mentioned that Walter Hilton, Julian's contemporary, wrote his book, *On the Mixed Life*, for the situation of a nobleman who wished to deepen in prayer without having to become a monk; and another popular book of the time, the *Layfolks' Prayer Book*, addressed the question of a prayer-discipline for the ordinary believer. Julian, in any case, sees prayer as the interaction between the soul and God, which takes place in every station in life; and she regards all kinds of prayer as equally important and equally powerful in the working-out of divine love in this life.

In general, as against the "ladder" concept of prayer, Julian makes three important points: first, all kinds of prayer are valuable, and serve to unite the soul to God; second, prayer is something which God brings about in us in our daily lives, rather than something which we can achieve through special efforts on our part; and third, the whole life of faith is the life of prayer—including those times when prayer seems difficult and dry, and when we engage in prayer only because we wish to obey God. In the end true prayer is not to "pray" at all: for true prayer is to yield to the Holy Spirit, and to allow the Spirit of God to pray within us. This kind of prayer is available to every Christian soul, whether young or old in faith, because prayer is a gift of God.

"I Am the Ground"

Ordinarily when we think of prayer, the first thing to come to mind is "asking for things," which Julian calls "beseeching." We may know that this is not the full extent of prayer, but it is certainly the most natural and, usually, the first kind of prayer which we experience in life. In the "ladder" scheme of prayer, this kind would appear near the bottom. For Julian, however, it is no less wonderful than any other kind of prayer. In fact, it may illustrate better than anything else the true nature of prayer as it springs from God and returns to God.

There are three important points to be learned here, even about the simplest and most childlike prayers. Julian outlines them as follows:

> Our Lord God desires for us to have a right understanding specifically of three things that belong to prayer. The first is by whom, and how, our prayers originate. He shows by whom, when he says, "I am the ground;" and how, by his

goodness; for he says, "First of all, it is my will." The second is to know in what manner and how we should use our time for prayer; that is, that our will should be turned to our Lord's will, in joy. The third is to know the fruit and the end of prayer: that is, to be oned and like to our Lord in everything. (ch. 42)

For the first point, Julian refers to her vision in which Jesus says to her, "I am the ground of your beseeching." Jesus is himself the source of prayer, which is given both because it is his will and because of his goodness. The second point is that, in prayer, our will is turned to God's will for our own benefit. The third point is that all prayer serves to unite us to God and to draw us into the image of God. While these three points are straightforward in themselves, Julian elaborates them in the *Revelations* to help us understand how to apply these principles in the specific practice of prayer.

What Prayer Is Not

If we take Julian's teaching seriously, it will become clear that some of what we think of as "prayer" is not really beneficial to the soul. Julian does not say that in her understanding God forbids these things, but that they show a lack of knowledge of the love of God, and of the true nature of prayer. There are several things, then, that prayer is not.

1. Prayer is not "changing God's mind."

We have already seen the principle that God does not change. At the same time, Julian recognizes that God has given us the possibility to pray for things and to intercede. It is, in fact, God's will for us to do this—the first point which God revealed to Julian about prayer ("First of all, it is my will," ch. 42). There is a mystery here, because on the one hand God does not change his mind; but on the other hand, God has commanded us to ask for things so that we can receive them. It will indeed sometimes appear that we have changed God's mind, because our prayers have been answered. We can even imagine situations in which prayer seems to change the course of events; and in one sense, they have—because God has given us this means of sharing in the course of events.

Julian's answer to this mystery is two-fold. First, our purpose in prayer is not to change God's mind, but to adapt our own will to God's will. Second, it is true that God has determined in advance what is best for us and what is good to give to us. Therefore, God prompts us to ask for what we need, so that God might give it—and therefore encourage us. By answering prayer, God also gives us the opportunity to share in the working out of events in this life. It is a sign of the humility of God. We will explore the way in which God answers prayer in a moment, but meantime we note that in prayer, "our will should be turned to our Lord's will, in joy" (ch. 42). Prayer is the soul seeking God, to know his will.

2. Prayer is not asking "in the right way."

It is sometimes our impression that we have to pray in the "right" ways, if God is to answer our prayers. But this idea really denies the love of God, and also God's power. If we believe that God will only hear us when we use the right techniques or the right kind of language, then we believe that we can control God. Prayer becomes a kind of manipulation of God, in which we try to impress him for the sake of gain. At the same time, we doubt the true power of God—because we believe that God *cannot* act unless we fulfill certain conditions first.

In Julian's day, this idea appeared especially in the practice, which must have been widespread, of praying by "means." This practice meant that the penitent would name before God those things which seemed to have "merit" in God's eyes: for example, the cross of Jesus, or Mary his mother, or his own blood, and so on. Julian points out that to approach God in this way is really to fear God in the wrong sense; that is, we do not fully appreciate the depth of God's love. She has this to say:

> The purpose of this showing was, as I understand it, to teach our soul wisely to cling to the goodness of God. At that moment our customary way of praying was brought to mind: how, because we did not understand and know his love, we used to employ many "means." Then I saw that surely it is more glory to God, and much more delightful, if

we faithfully pray to God himself, of his goodness—and there cling to his grace, with a true understanding and steadfast faith—than if we used all the "means" that the heart could think of. For if we invoke all these "means," it is too small, and not fully glorifying to God. For the whole is in his goodness, and nothing is lacking there. (ch. 6)

Julian suggests that it pleases God for us to seek him and to worship him by mentioning these things, but at the same time we must recognize that none of them has any power in itself. The good which is in anything is the goodness of God, which is to say, God's love:

We pray to God by his holy flesh and his precious blood, his holy passion, his most dear death and wounds; but all the blessed kindness, the endless life, that we have from all this is his own goodness.

And we pray to him for love of the sweet mother who bore him, but all the help that we have from her is of his own goodness. And we pray to him by the holy cross on which he died, but all the virtue and all the help that we have from the cross is from his own goodness. And in the same way, all the help that we have from special saints, and all the company of heaven, the dear love and unending friendship which we have from them—it is from his goodness. (ch. 6)

She concludes that God, of his goodness, has ordained all these things to help us; indeed, our salvation came about only because the Son of God was born of Mary, died on the cross and so on, so that the most important "means" of salvation is in his own human nature. However, we are to understand that it is more important to trust in God's love than to pray through the saints or for the sake of anything which God has used to bring about our salvation:

Therefore it pleases him that we seek him and worship him through these various "means"—but understanding and knowing that he is the good which is in them all. For the highest prayer is to the goodness of God, which comes down to us, in the lowest part of our need. (ch. 6)

3. Prayer is not always the activity of speaking to God.

If God is the source, or "ground" of prayer, and if God prompts us to pray so that we might turn our will to God's will, then it follows that the first step in prayer is learning what is the will of God. Prayer is not always speaking to God, but also involves listening to God and resting in God. In the end, prayer is not the *activity* of saying and doing things which we believe will be pleasing to God. Rather, it is to recognize what God desires from us, in repentance and humility; and to learn of the goodness of God. In this sense, prayer is simply resting in God. Ultimately, all prayer aims toward this one goal, for the soul to know God and to rest in God's love. The goal of prayer, then, is to receive God—which is not the activity of the soul, but its true rest .

Julian illustrates this principle in the midst of her vision of the tiny "point" or hazelnut, which represented all that exists (the first revelation). She learns in this vision that there is no true rest for the soul in anything that has been created. Much prayer is the result of our spiritual agitation with things in the world, trying to work out things which cannot be resolved— because they are not God's will. In these times of distress we have not really prayed at all: we have suffered agitation, we have complained, and out of anxiety have gone through the motions of speaking to God without really believing in God's goodness; but we have not *received* God.

As Julian describes her insights in this section of her book, she suddenly breaks into prayer, in the midst of her narrative. We can imagine that as she dictated this passage to a scribe, she became lost in worship, and began to pray for God's own presence:

> God, of your goodness, give to me yourself. For you are enough for me, and I may not ask for anything less than would fully glorify you. And if I ask for anything less, I will always desire more; for only in you do I have everything. (ch. 5)

Prayer, then, is to listen to God and to look for the signs of

God's presence, and to receive God in humility—coming to him "nakedly, plainly and humbly," which is the natural desire of the soul.

Two Conditions of Prayer

We have seen that for Julian, it is not very important how we pray. Nevertheless, Julian sees two "conditions" for prayer which are necessary, if we are to see the fruit of prayer. It is not that God's power to act is limited by what we do or do not do in prayer, but that sometimes we approach God without any faith. In these times, we cannot see the answers to prayer which God has provided; and we do not bend our will to God's. The result is that we find prayer fruitless or "dry," and we doubt the goodness of God.

Julian says that the two conditions for prayer are to pray rightly, and to have sure faith (ch. 41). "Right" prayer means praying, as mentioned, in accordance with the will of God, which we can know in Jesus Christ and through the ministry of the Holy Spirit. God cannot be not-God, and therefore cannot answer prayer which calls for God to dishonor his own goodness. Sure faith is also a practical matter: we should pray really believing that God intends to give us what is best for us. If we do not have this kind of faith, there is no point in prayer at all. When we pray without faith, we conclude that God has not heard us—whereas the problem lies in us, and not in God:

> Yet often our trust is not full, for we are not sure that God hears us, as we think, because of our unworthiness, and because we do not feel anything [when we pray]. Often we are just as barren and dry after praying, as we were before. But this, our own feelings—our foolishness—is because of our weakness. That, at least, is what I have felt in myself. (ch. 41)

A key requisite for prayer, then, is faith. Julian suggests that our faith should be as large as we can imagine it. Our prayers, too, should be big—for with great faith come great prayers:

> For this is our Lord's will: that our prayer and our faith be just the same, large. For if we do not trust as much as we

pray, we fail to glorify our Lord in our prayer; and also, we
waste time and give pain to ourselves. (ch. 42)

To pray at all is to exercise faith, and faith grows in the
exercise of prayer. Julian points out that we cannot know the
extent of God's love if we do not call upon God to love us,
trusting that he will. And because God is patient with us, we
do not need to fear praying in the wrong ways. In those
instances during the showings when Julian did not show trust,
or when she said things which were displeasing to God, she
was not blamed or rebuked; but the showings stopped for a
time, and Jesus was silent. In these times, Julian learned that
she had stepped out of God's will. Sure trust, then, means
continuing to pray when we "hear" nothing, and increasing
(not decreasing) in our trust that God hears us and desires to
give us what is best for us.

Six Ways of Prayer
Now we are ready to look at six kinds of prayer which
Julian discusses in the *Revelations*. These may be thought of
as six dimensions of prayer, rather than as stages in prayer or
as separate events; for each one leads to the others, and all
together form the whole of what we call "prayer." Nor can we
say that the soul should move on from one kind of prayer to
another as if they were rungs on the ladder. All the various
ways of prayer are part of the life of any soul who loves God.
All of them are "natural" to the soul who has come into an
awareness of divine love, through the ministry of the Holy
Spirit. None is better than any of the others, as Julian sees it;
but all afford us the opportunity to draw closer to God.
The six ways of prayer are as follows:

1. The Prayer of Seeking (Desiring)
The first dimension of prayer is seeking God. Julian calls it
"kind yearning," that is, the natural desire of the soul for God.
It will be clear that not all persons consciously long for God,
because one effect of sin is to dull our awareness of this deep
need in the soul. Nevertheless, it is the nature of the soul to
need God, whether we know it or not. We can say that one
ministry of the Holy Spirit is to create in us a sense of need, so
that we turn to God in prayer. In the beginning, we may not

be aware that we are praying *for God*, because we are simply asking for things in this life. However, since God does everything that is done, any prayer at all for things in this world is also a prayer for God to act in our lives. It is therefore a prayer for God himself. Moreover, we pray because we desire peace, or "rest for the soul." There is no peace in the things of this world; so the soul turns to God, seeking the peace which can come only from divine love.

Whenever we turn to God at all, it is because the soul is seeking for this divine rest. Jesus tells Julian that it is he, himself, for whom we seek whenever we pray, and not necessarily the created things for which we are praying:

> "I am he. I am he. I am he who is highest, and I am he whom you love. I am he who delights you. I am he who serves you. I am what you are looking for. I am the one you desire. I am what you mean. I am that which is everything..." (ch. 26)

We have already seen that this discovery made such a profound impression on Julian that she could not tell about it without lapsing into prayer spontaneously, which prayer was recorded by her scribe:

> God, of your goodness give to me yourself; for you are enough for me, and I may ask nothing less...(ch. 5)

The desire which we have for God is partly due to the fact that in this life we do not see perfectly. In her vision of Jesus' face in the third showing, Julian found herself annoyed that she could not see more clearly. She was answered,

> "If God wants to show you more, he will be your light. You do not need anything but him." For I saw him, and I sought him. (ch. 10)

Part of our pilgrimage on Earth is to seek God more fully. Prayer is our means of seeking God. God prompts it, and God is delighted with it.

And this vision was a lesson to my understanding, that the continual seeking of the soul for God pleases him greatly. For it [the soul] may do no more than seek, suffer and trust. This is brought about in the souls who have it, by the Holy Spirit: finding God clearly is the gift of his special grace, and comes only when he wills. So seeking with faith, hope and love pleases our Lord, and finding pleases the soul and fills it full of joy.

And so I was taught in my understanding that seeking is as good as seeing, during the time that he allows the soul to work at it. It is God's will that we seek him until we see him, for in this way God will show himself to us, by his special grace, whenever he wills. (ch. 10)

2. The Prayer of Asking (Beseeching)

The second kind of prayer is that in which we ask for things, or actually plead or even "beg" (Julian's term "beseeching" implies all of these). Here we may be asking for many different kinds of things, from our daily needs to spiritual things such as enlightenment or even for God himself. In Julian's view, what is important is not first of all what we ask for, but the fact that we are calling upon God for something. To call upon God at all draws the soul nearer to God, and invites God to act in our lives.

Julian suggests that in prayer, we should be specific in the things for which we ask. We should not pray abstractly, because this shows a lack of sure trust; and because God cannot answer prayers abstractly, simply because the world is itself concrete, and not abstract. In prayer we should ask first for mercy and grace—knowing that (by the very fact that we are praying) we have already received God's mercy and grace. Then we yield ourselves to the Holy Spirit, who prompts us to pray specifically for the things which God desires to give us:

> . . . prayer is a witness that the soul is willing what God wills. This comforts the conscience and enables man to come to grace. And so he teaches us to pray, and mightily to trust that we shall have it; for he looks upon us in love, and will make us partners in his good deeds. And so he

> prompts us to pray for whatever he desires to do, for which
> prayers and good will he desires to reward us and to give us
> endless repayment. (ch. 43)

Julian explains at some length in these paragraphs that an important principle in prayer is to seek God's will first, and then to ask in sure faith. Seeing such prayers answered specifically builds our faith, and draws us closer to God. Part of this way of prayer is believing, without any doubt, that everything which God has created, was created in order to serve us. God has already taken care of our needs, and in prayer we are given the opportunity to see how God's gifts are worked out in our lives, as if we actually shared in bringing them about. Julian reckons that three things must be true of our own faith before we can regularly see specific prayers answered in this way: 1) We believe that God has created all things good, out of his love; 2) We believe that we have been saved in Jesus Christ; and 3) We believe that God has given us everything in creation to serve us, in love; therefore we have authority over the things of this world. When we pray, it is as if God said to us:

> "Look and see that I did all this before you prayed for it;
> and now there you are, and you are praying to me." (ch. 42)

Finally, it is not merely that we *can* pray specifically for things in this world, but that God commands us to do it.

> It is his will that we should pray for all the things that our
> Lord has ordained to do, either for particular things or for
> everything in general. (ch. 42)

To do so will create joy in us, which is a foretaste of the joy which is in heaven. We should notice especially here Julian's three principles of prayer, which apply whenever we ask God for anything. We must first believe that this creation is good, and that God means for us to enjoy it; otherwise, it is foolish to pray for anything, and in any case we would not appreciate God's answer. We believe that we have been delivered from the sickness of sin, in Christ; and we take our position as the highest point in creation, for which everything else has been created. These points are entirely practical in our daily experience of prayer.

Taking Julian's teaching so far, let us apply it in the case of a typical example of "beseeching" prayer: in this case, a prayer for healing. Julian has noticed that when we fall ill, there is a tendency to believe that God is punishing us with our sickness. (We may even believe that this is unfair, because we are not aware that we have "sinned.") Because we do not really trust that God desires to heal us, we do not ask for healing in prayer. Finally, we may believe that in this life we are supposed to experience only hardship and misery, because "real" life is in heaven. Julian's teaching in the showings suggests that all three of these attitudes are mistaken, and prevent us from knowing the fruit of prayer.

First, it is not true that God punishes us by making us fall ill. (We have seen that, in Julian's view, suffering is a "given" in this life; however, God may "lay" something on us to strengthen our faith or to deepen us, which is not due to any particular sin on our part.) In the situation of suffering we should, rather, turn to God to seek what God is doing in the situation: healing us, causing us to grow spiritually, giving us the opportunity to exercise authority over our own impatience, or providing an opportunity for witness to his own glory, as we are made well again. Then we believe that God has created us in his image, in order to enjoy this life. We cannot pray for healing if we believe that his life is dreary, and that we are simply to suffer through it without any enjoyment of what God has made.

The next step is to recognize that we have been healed (or "made whole") in Christ. Feelings of guilt and unworthiness do not come from God, and do not allow us to pray with confidence. It is true that we are guilty and unworthy; but it is also true that in Christ we are set free from anxiety over our guilt. God desires simply for us to grow in the image of his Son, and to ask for whatever he desires to give us. This delights God, and it also blesses us.

Finally, we recognize that the things of this world are made in order to serve us; we are the "crown" of creation, and God is keeping creation because of his love for us. In light of this great love of God, we do not need to believe that we are merely subject to the changes and chances of life. We are whatever God desires for us to be. In prayer, then, we approach God—who does all things—asking boldly for healing or for his perfect will in the situation of our illness. Our prayers are large, because our faith is large: we know that God has already worked out the answer to the prayer before we prayed. We enter into prayer, then, with an excitement and expectancy, eager (with "kind yearning") to see God at work in this situation. We pray with sure faith that "all shall be well, and all shall be well, and all shall be well."

Sometimes it is the case that we do not immediately see the results of our prayer. In this instance, Julian suggests that we persist in prayer, and recognize that this is the most important time for prayer. Perhaps our soul is still agitated by the things of the world, and has not really prepared herself to receive what God is doing; therefore it is time to couple the prayer of "beseeching" with the prayer of "yearning" for God, to know what is his will and purpose:

> I know well that the more the soul sees of God, the more the soul desires him, by his grace. But when we do not see him, we feel the need to pray—because of our failure and inability to receive Jesus. For when the soul is in turmoil, troubled and left to herself because of unrest, then it is time to pray to make herself supple and receptive to God. But she cannot, by any manner of prayer, make God receptive to her—for he is always the same in love. (ch. 43)

Julian's whole understanding of this kind of prayer is summed up in Jesus' words to her, where he says that he is the "ground" of prayer:

> "I am the ground of your asking. First, it is my will for you to have it; and since I made you desire it, and I made you ask for it and you are asking for it, then how could it be that you should not have what you are asking for?" (ch. 41)

Prayer is prompted by God, the Holy Spirit, so that it might return to God. We trust the Father to do all things for us, knowing that we have been brought into communion with the

Father through the Son. Prayer, then, is asking God to act, and knowing that God has answered our prayer already.

3. The Prayer of Thanksgiving

The third kind of prayer which is prompted by the Holy Spirit is thanksgiving. It is the natural result of prayer with faith, because following prayer there is, Julian says, great reward. It is not merely that we receive what we ask for (sometimes we will not) but that we have the joy of working with God, in the things that God is doing. The soul who seeks to be near to God therefore rejoices in prayer, and gives thanks for what has happened as the fruit of prayer.

Julian points out that this way of prayer can never remain silent. When a soul is giving thanks, there are shouts of joy. Julian experienced this herself during the visions, when she found herself shouting, "Lord, bless us!"—much to the dismay, no doubt, of those in the room who thought that she was dead. In the same way, a "dead" soul can be given life in the Holy Spirit, and awakened to thanksgiving. Julian recalls that in her initial experience of the love of God in her visions, she was moved to prayer—as we all are, when we have been touched by the Holy Spirit:

> Another thing which belongs to prayer is thanksgiving. Thanksgiving is a new, interior knowledge, turning ourselves with great reverence and holy fear, with all our might to the work that our good Lord stirs us to—inwardly rejoicing and giving thanks. And sometimes, because of the abundance of it, it breaks out with a loud voice and says, "Good Lord, have mercy! Blessed may you be!" (ch. 41)

Genuine praise, however, is more than words. It does not depend merely on the outward circumstances in which we find ourselves, but is a deliberate choice to know the joy which is in God. Thanksgiving is grounded in the promises which we have in God's word, of salvation and eternal love:

> And at other times, when the heart is dry and we do not feel anything, or else is tempted by our enemy, then it is driven by reason and by grace to cry out to our Lord with a loud

voice, recalling his blessed passion and his great goodness. And the power of our Lord's word pierces the soul and quickens the heart, and begins it to working properly again by his grace, and makes it to pray blissfully and truly, rejoicing in our Lord. This is a truly blessed thanksgiving, in his sight. (ch. 41)

As Julian points out here, the nature of thanksgiving is to confess the wisdom of God, and to rehearse the things which God has already done for us in Christ. The soul who loves God knows that God is at work even when there is no evidence of God's works, by our judgment, and even when our will does not conform to God's will. True prayer begins and ends with thanksgiving. In heaven we will see why:

And therefore, when the judgment is given and we are all brought up above, we will see clearly in God the secrets which now are hidden from us. Then none of us shall be stirred to say of anything, "Lord if it had been thus and so, then it would have been well." For we shall say with a loud voice, "Lord, blessed may you be! For it *is* thus and so, and it is good. And now we see truly that everything is done as it was ordained, before anything was made." (ch. 85)

Finally, thanksgiving is a reflection of the joy which is in God. It is the intention of God to "thank" us when we are in heaven, to reward us for the suffering which we experienced in this life. Julian's vision of this "thanking" is of a great feast or banquet, at which the Lord presides and honors those who have been faithful:

After this our Lord said, "I thank you for your trouble, particularly in your youth." And in this my understanding was lifted up to heaven, where I saw our Lord in his own house, in which he had called all his dearest servants and friends to a great feast. I did not see the Lord take a seat in his own house, but I saw him royally reigning in his house, filling it full of joy and mirth. He himself was endlessly gladdening and cheering up his dearest friends in a most friendly and courteous way . . . (ch. 14)

By entering into praise, we have a foretaste of the feast to come. Thanksgiving, then, grows out of the desire for God, and the prayer which boldly asks for God to act in our lives.

4. The Prayer of "Working"

There is another dimension of prayer which is precious to God and which, in one sense, is even more delightful to God than those which we have seen so far. Julian calls it "working" or "travail," that is, prayer which seems like hard work to us, because we enter into it only out of obedience to God. Jesus says to Julian,

> "Pray inwardly, though you find no satisfaction in it. For it is profitable, even if you do not feel it, though you see nothing, yes, and even when you think you cannot do it. For in dryness and barrenness, in sickness and in feebleness, then your prayers are most pleasant to me, though you think that it gives you but little satisfaction. In this way all your life is prayer in my sight." (ch. 41)

Julian develops this insight to say that God desires for us to pray continuously ("he covets our continuous prayer") and accepts this kind of prayer as good labor on our part regardless how we feel about it. This is our "work," for which we will be rewarded in heaven. The reward is Jesus himself. In her description of this kind of prayer, Julian jumps ahead to say that later, in the fifteenth revelation, Jesus promised to take the soul out of the context of pain and hard labor:

> "And you will come up above, and you will have me for your reward; and you will be filled full of joy and bliss." (ch. 64)

5. The Prayer of Beholding

The purpose of all prayer is to unite the soul to God. There is a kind of prayer, however, in which we are especially drawn into the will of God. It is a prayer of silence, in which we are listening to the word of God and looking to him, without any activity on our part. Eventually, this kind of prayer gives way to an interior mental silence, in which we are not thinking about the word of God, but simply hearing it; not analyzing the way in which God is working, but contemplating his glory.

Julian calls this kind of prayer "beholding." We remember that the first dimension of prayer is "seeking," which is the natural desire of the soul for God. Julian says that "I saw him, and I sought him." The prayer of "beholding" is the fruit of seeking God, but it is still prayer: standing in the presence of God, not communicating anything but only receiving.

The prayer of "beholding" requires time. It cannot be done quickly, and it cannot be achieved by any exercises on our part. Like all prayer, it is a gift, and we cannot think of it in terms of a technique or a form of deliberate activity of the soul. Julian discovered several times in her showings that she was overwhelmed with the appearance of Jesus' goodness, so that she could not speak or even take it in. She found later that she could not adequately describe what she had experienced at these times. The experience surpassed all language. One of these experiences involved her vision of her own soul, which is the dwelling-place of God:

> Then our Lord opened my spiritual eyes and showed me my soul in the midst of my heart. I saw the soul so large, as it were an endless world, and as if it were a blissful kingdom... In the midst of that city sits our Lord Jesus, God and man, a fair person of large stature, highest bishop, most solemn king, most glorious Lord... (ch. 67; Pch. 68)

This vision rendered Julian speechless, and she learned that in such visions the soul is actually changed by what it sees:

> This was a delectable sight, and a restful showing—[to know] that it will be this way eternally. And to behold this while we are still here, is fully pleasing to God and of great benefit to us. And the soul that contemplates it becomes like that which is contemplated, and is made one in rest and peace. (ch. 68)

The key phrase is that "the soul that contemplates it becomes like that which is contemplated." Julian points out that we become like what we contemplate in prayer. This principle is actually true in any situation in life: if we contemplate violence, we become violent; if we contemplate the truth of God, we take on the qualities of God—peace, joy, love—which we see there. We remember, meanwhile, that for Julian there is no question of contemplating abstract *ideas* of "peace" or "joy" or "love." She is looking into the face of Jesus during the visions themselves, and she recommends that we continue to pray in this way. We do not attempt to empty the mind in order to contemplate what is beyond us. Rather, we look in silence at what God has already given us to see, in Jesus Christ. In this sense, the incarnation of the Son of God makes prayer possible; for without it, we would be unable to contemplate the mysteries of God at all, having nothing to "see."

In this kind of prayer there will be no words. Whereas other forms of prayer which she describes involve speech or images of speech—"yearning," "asking," "thanking"—in this kind of prayer the images all involve sight, in silence: "contemplating" ("beholding"), "seeking," "looking," and God's "showing." It also involves "waiting" upon God, without any activity on the part of the soul. A clear example of this kind of prayer appears in the eighth showing, in which Julian is learning about compassion in the crucifixion. She begins to feel what Jesus feels, and to know the inner spiritual experience of compassion.

We have seen that in this showing she expected to see Jesus die, a sight which she wanted to avoid. Suddenly, however, his face was transfigured from death into life, from darkness into brilliant light. The change took place as she gazed into his face. This change actually brought about a change in Julian, although nothing was said at the time:

> Just at the moment that I thought, from his appearance, that his life could last no longer, and a vision of his end would have to be, suddenly—as I looked at the same cross— he changed his blessed countenance. The changing of his blessed appearance changed mine, and I was as glad and merry as possible. (ch. 21)

It is not clear whether, in Julian's description of this kind of prayer, she has in mind actual visions, or if she is thinking rather of a kind of contemplative prayer in which nothing appears either to the eyes or to the inward, spiritual "eye." It is clear from her *Revelations* that she did experience visions of various kinds even after the sixteen revelations had ended. She says, for example, that

> ...thus I saw that whenever we see needs for which we pray, our good Lord follows us, helping our desire...

> It is then that we may, with his sweet grace and our own meek continual prayers, come into him now in this life, with many special "touchings" of sweet spiritual visions and feelings, measured out to us as our simplicity can bear it. And this is wrought, and will be, by the grace of the Holy Spirit, until we die in yearning for love. And then we shall all come into our Lord... (ch. 43)

Ultimately, the object of the soul—to see God—is partially filled in this kind of prayer. Julian makes it clear that she does not accept the idea of "beatific vision," if it is meant that the created soul might look into the uncreated Being of God. She suggests that supernatural visions of the glory of God are measured out in part, as we can receive them:

> ...for no man may see God and live afterwards, that is to say, in this mortal life. But when he, of his special grace, wills to show himself here, he strengthens the creature above itself, and he measures out the vision according to his own will, as it is profitable at the time. (ch. 43)

6. The Prayer of Enjoying

The final way of prayer which Julian describes is "enjoying." This word may sometimes be translated "rejoicing," except that when she uses it with relation to prayer, she is speaking technically of a special experience which does not involve any deliberate prayer on our part. We may say that this kind of prayer is, in a sense, beyond prayer: the soul experiences it only by "not-praying," in a sense which is difficult to explain but which is very real and important to the Christian experience of prayer. It does not mean abstaining from prayer, but rather, a release of the soul into the Spirit of God, such that the soul is no longer aware of itself, or of prayer, or of anything else but God. Prayer ceases here, in the sense that the soul sees no need for any deliberate activity. It is a foretaste of the union which is ours with God in heaven, eternally.

The prayer of "enjoying" is an extension of the contemplative prayer which we have just described, and takes place when the soul has been seeking God. It is not the result of the soul's activity, as Julian sees it, but a grace from God to the soul who is prepared for it. It depends entirely upon the will of God:

> But when our courteous Lord, by his special grace, reveals himself to our soul, we have what we desire. And then we do not see, during this time, that we have any need to pray. All our intent and all our might is fixed wholly upon the contemplation of him. And this is a high, ineffable prayer, as I see it.

> For the whole reason for prayer is made one in the vision and contemplation of him to whom we pray, marvelously enjoying him with holy dread, and such great sweetness and delight in him that we cannot pray at all, or only as he stirs us to at the time. And I know well that the more the soul sees of God, the more it desires him, by his grace. (ch. 43)

Although Julian does not elaborate, we can assume that she understood this kind of prayer to be more rare, and of short duration. She explains that it cannot be continuous in this life, or else we would be preoccupied with the wonder of the experience rather than with God:

> And yet in all this I beheld, in the vision of God, that this kind of vision cannot be continuous in this life, for the sake of his own glory and to the increase of our own eternal joy. And therefore we often fail to see him, and then we fall into ourselves, and then we find no feelings of compassion— nothing but contrariness in ourselves. . .(ch. 47)

In this experience of "returning" to ourselves, in our own sin, we find it necessary to repent; and the prayer of "natural yearning" for God begins over again, and the soul begins once again to pray deliberately in the desire to be one with God. The circle of prayer is complete.

After the experience of her supernatural showings, Julian took the vow of anchoress and spent her entire life in the pursuit of prayer. It is significant that she did not become a total recluse, however, but remained in daily contact with those people who sought her counsel or who needed prayer. For the prayer of enjoying God means that we enjoy all that God has made, for the sake of God:

> And that is a gracious gift, in the working of which we love God for himself and ourselves in God, and all that God loves, for God. (ch. 84)

Epilogue

Let us Pray Altogether:
Seven Virtues in the Christian Life

All life is a process of growing up. As children, we grow physically, in an obvious way. As adults, we continue to grow and to change in our soul. Julian says of this process of growth that it never ends in this life. We are all children:

> ...there is no higher state in this life than childhood, in weakness and failure of strength and of understanding, until the time that our gracious Mother has brought us up to our Father's bliss. (ch. 63)

The virtue that we have in this life is to live kindly, as a child, loving its Mother and looking to him in the time of our need.

There are some souls who never really grow in this time of childhood. They turn inward upon themselves, consumed with guilt and blame, until they begin to hate this life and all that God has made. They seek to deny this life and to escape it, if possible—shutting themselves off from God and from creation, and even from themselves. Filled with "contrariness," they look for what is wrong in others, and they blame themselves for the wrongs which they perceive in their own lives. Eventually they cut themselves off from the possibility of loving, because they do not receive love. They are separated from God, and from their soul.

There are others souls who are growing into maturity in this life, especially through the experience of humiliation. They suffer in this life, but their suffering is more and more an occasion for joy: learning humility, upbuilding others who suffer in like ways, and sharing in the unifying power of the crucifixion itself. As they learn to become "smaller" (in pride and ambition), their interest in God and what God has made becomes larger. They are turned outward, in curiosity and joy. The result of this outward-turning is that they look for the hand of God in everything and in everyone, and rejoice in everything, even when it is painful and undesirable—except in sin, which they hate. They may appear, in the sight of others, to be foolish—because they accept suffering without complaint, and even welcome it; and because they seem to be blissfully unaware of the harsh "realities" of life, including their own wrongdoing and the shortcomings of the world around them. The inner pain of contrition, compassion, and deep longing for God which they experience constantly is hidden. It is evident only in their attitude of self-emptiness and silence in the place of punishment and blame. They themselves do not blame others or themselves, because they have found union with God, and God does not blame.

This is the lesson which Julian received in her sixteen showings of divine love. Granted the opportunity to live past the experience of a "mortal illness, Julian's life undoubtedly became very different from what it was before. She shares her experience with us so that we might be spared the pain of learning her lessons as she did—in intense suffering and with the loss of pride which Julian herself evidently underwent in the ordeal. She tells us that she wrestled particularly with certain patterns of sin in her own life: of complaint and laziness, despair and impatience, and a feeling of pious self-importance which often marks false religion. The showings replaced all these with patterns of true humility and joy which are in God, and which are divine Love itself.

In our summary of Julian's insights into the nature of divine love, we have "counted" through six dimensions of that love. We saw that God is One, a unity of love in himself; and that the whole purpose of God's creation is to be one with God. We saw then that Julian's visions were given in "two," literally and figuratively; and that we ourselves are "two" in our sensuality here in this life—in knowing what is right but in not doing it, in our separation from God and from one another, in the fragmentation which is typical of this life, in the pain of sin which is despair. We saw that the "two" can be reconciled in Christ, our divine Mother, who works with us in nature, mercy and grace to draw us into himself: "knitting" us to the Being of God in three ways. Then the four-fold nature of divine love was shown in the patience with which our Lord sustains us during our "falling down" in sin, converting our fears to faith through gentle persistence and courteous love. Next, the five-fold joy which is in God became clear to the soul who loves God, mirrored in the five-fold way in which we experience joy and faith in this life. Finally, we saw that there are six ways of prayer in response to the prompting of the Holy Spirit, drawing us into unity with God in this life.

Julian never really spells out the "seven" which follows from these six dimensions of divine love which she saw in her showings. The seven are a thread which runs through the whole of the *Revelations* and which continues in our lives after we have shared with Julian her vision of divine love. For Julian, this last dimension of divine love is the fulfillment of "love which is given," the virtue of love which becomes typical of the soul who loves God. Here we see that the "virtue" of love is really seven virtues, which mirror the life of Christ, who is the image of the unseen God.

The seven virtues which Julian describes in the *Revelations* are these: humility, kindness, compassion; peacefulness, faithfulness, wisdom; and true "oneing" with God. There are other qualities which, as we have seen, describe the life of faith in Christ—in particular, contrition and joy, patience and long-suffering—but we may say that they are incorporated in the seven virtues which are found in a true relationship with God in Christ. As Julian sees it, these fulfill our capacity as human beings, and they describe the "normal" human life as it can be in the context of an evil world. In eternal life they will not change, but simply be fulfilled; for here we have a beginning, which is intended to continue forever in the timeless love which is in God and which is God.

The seven virtues which together are the one "virtue" of love, are to be found in the Church on Earth. This Church is the body of Christ, and is Christ:

> . . . for it is his holy Church [or, "he is holy Church"]. He is
> the ground, he is the substance, he is the teaching, he is the
> teacher, he is the lesson, he is the reward towards which
> every kind soul is traveling. And this is known and shall be
> known to every soul to whom the Holy Spirit declares it.
> (ch. 34)

The purpose of the Church, which is made up of all those
souls who are being saved, is to be the presence of Christ for
each soul individually; and to nourish and encourage us in this
life as we grow in Christ.

The Church, Our Mother

Julian understands the seven virtues, which are one in love,
to be signs of faith. They are, therefore, characteristics of the
true Church of Christ, that is, all those souls who love him and
who are being changed into his likeness, through the operation
of the Holy Spirit. We must be careful to note that they are
not the *only* signs of faith; for example, humility may be
found outside the Church, and humility in itself does not
mean faithful following of Jesus Christ (we have seen that for
Julian, faith is always centered in the incarnate Son of God).
On the other hand, the soul who truly loves God will always
learn to be humble, because humility is the nature of God.

We have said that, furthermore, Julian's visions were only
of those souls "who are being saved." Her concern is to describe
the process of salvation or atonement in Christ, and not to
probe the workings of the Spirit of God outside the Church
itself. At the same time, Julian is fully aware that the Church
as we see it is not perfect, for two reasons: first, not everyone
who is baptized is necessarily a "lover of Christ" or a "soul
who is being saved" (ch. 32); and second, the Church itself is
made up of Christians who will continue to sin in this life, even
though the Spirit of God has taught them to hate sin and to
love God. The "virtues" of faithful love are therefore not inevitably present at all times in every Christian soul. For this reason
the Church, like every human soul, is "double:" it is a con-
gregation of sinful human beings who love God; and it is the
mystical body of Christ on Earth, which incorporates every
soul who loves him and which, in the eyes of God, is holy and
glorified.

Julian's vision, then, is of the "hidden" Church on Earth. This secret Church is not hidden in the sense that we do not know what it is, or where it meets, but in the sense that is is pure and holy only in the secret judgment of God, who sees the souls of the faithful in light of Christ. Only God knows which souls are called to salvation; we do not make such judgments because we cannot. Julian asserts that the Church itself is preserved pure and holy in the calling of God, even though Christians taken individually, will sin in this life:

> And he desires for us to take ourselves mightily to the faith of Holy Church, and there to find our dearest Mother, the solace of true understanding with the blessed communion of all [the saints]. For a single person may often be broken, as it seems to himself; but the whole body of Holy Church was never broken, nor ever shall be, without end. And therefore it is a sure thing, good and gracious, to will, meekly and mightily, to be sustained by our Mother, Holy Church, and joined to her—that is, Christ Jesus. (ch. 61)

In an earlier vision, Julian had seen the blood of Jesus flow from the cross up to heaven and down into hell, more plentiful than the waters of the sea and more beneficial to wash us clean than the purest waters of the earth (the fourth revelation). It was a vision of the "harrowing of hell," in which Christ set free all the souls there who had been destined to belong to him.[1] Now Julian compares this washing to the water of baptism, in which the blood of Jesus washes us free from sin:

> For the flood of mercy that is his dearest blood and precious water is plentiful enough to make us fair and clean. The blessed wound of our Savior is open, and delights in healing us; the sweet gracious hands of our Mother are ready and diligent around us, for he in all this working, uses the office of a kind nurse, who has nothing to do but to tend to the salvation of her child. (ch. 61)

Christ, then, is our Mother; and the Church, who is Christ himself, is our Mother on earth. Julian describes herself as a "daughter of Holy Church." At the same time, the Church is within herself: for the Church, who is Christ, dwells in her own soul and is hidden there. The Church is the place where we are nourished by Christ, our Mother; it is his "breast." At the same time, it is hidden in our own "breast," where Christ himself dwells:

> Here we may see that we are all bound to God by nature, and we are all bound to God by grace. Here we may see, too, that we do not need to seek far away to know the nature of everything, but to Holy Church—into our Mother's breast, which is to say, into our own soul, where our Lord dwells. And there we shall find everything...(ch. 62)

This understanding of the Church, as hidden in our own breast where Christ himself dwells, is not to be taken by us individually to mean that we are without sin or holy in this life:

> And there we shall find everything: now, in faith and in understanding; and afterwards, truly in himself, clearly , in bliss. But let no man or woman take this to apply to himself individually, for then it would not be true. It is true in general...(ch. 62)

The nourishment which we receive from the Church, at the "breast" of our Mother Christ, is through the teaching of the Church. At the same time, it is through the sacramental life of the Church. The number of sacraments—seven—corresponds to the virtues which we receive in Christ:

> Also in our faith come the seven sacraments, each following the other in the order which God has ordained for us; and all kinds of virtues. For the same virtues that we have received in our substance, are given to us in nature, by the goodness of God. The same virtues, by the working of mercy are given to us by grace, through the renewal of the Holy Spirit. These virtues and gifts are treasured for us in Jesus Christ...(ch. 57)

The sacrament of Holy Communion is Christ feeding us with himself, as a mother nurses her child at the breast:

> A mother may give her child to suck her milk, but our precious Mother Jesus feeds us with himself. He feeds us courteously and tenderly with the Blessed Sacrament which is the precious food of life itself. This is what he meant in the blessed words where he said, "I am what Holy Church preaches and teaches you"—which is to say, "All the health and the life of the sacraments, all the virtue and grace of my word, all the goodness that is ordained in Holy Church for you—I am all of it." (ch. 60)

However, when our mother nurses us at her breast, we remain outside her, as a separate soul. It is not true of our relationship with our Mother Christ, however; for we live in Christ, and as members of the Church, we are his body on earth:

> A mother may hold her child tenderly to her breast, but our tender Mother Jesus can easily lead us into his blessed breast, through his dear wounded side. . . (ch. 60)

We are, then, mystically incorporated into Christ, through our relationship with the Church. As we have seen before, Julian reckons that because of this relationship there is a sense in which we are never "born" out of Christ, our Mother. The Church acts as his womb, protecting us and nourishing us in this life:

> And our Savior is our true Mother, in whom we are endlessly born; and we shall never come out of him. (ch. 57)

As we examined Julian's concept of "falling and rising," however, we saw that each soul-to be-saved is, as an individual, made to grow spiritually in this life through the experience of trials and suffering, as well as in the experiences of joy and blessing. In the same way, the Church as a whole will be severely tried. In one passage, Julian seems to speak prophetically, more than a century before the Protestant Reformation, when she says that

> ...in this I was filled partly with compassion for all my fellow Christians. For those well, well beloved people that shall be saved—that is to say, God's servants, Holy Church—shall be shaken in sorrow and anguish and tribulation in this world, as men shake a cloth in the wind. (ch. 28)

Julian is taught in this that the Church will survive, and its anguish will be seen as a great reason for thanksgiving in heaven as the Church is finally glorified. But the Church has not yet been glorified on Earth:

> For with respect to being our Head, Christ is glorified and impassible. But with respect to his body, in which all his members are knit together, he is not yet glorified and impassible. (ch. 31)

The Church, therefore, is even now in its period of trial and suffering. It suffers in contrition, compassion, and true longing to be with God in heaven. Until that time, it remains on Earth as our Mother, which is the body of Christ on Earth. The church will suffer with Christ, as on the cross, until it joins him in eternal glory.

"Let Us Pray"

Julian perceived that the Church is the presence of Christ on Earth. The model for the Church, then, is Christ himself. The body of Christ is crucified—torn, bleeding, and the object of hatred—but the body of Christ is also risen and glorified. In this life, the Church itself is also torn apart and wounded by sin; but it is also risen with Christ, and glorified by his Holy Spirit. Julian urges us to take ourselves to the Church where we might find truth, and our own soul; for we cannot know ourselves until we know the One who has made us, and in whom human nature itself is preserved whole and clean in a world of darkness and suffering. She urges us, too, to pray together:

> For love's sake, let us all pray together to God, with God's working: thanking, trusting, and enjoying. for our good Lord desires to be prayed to in this way...(ch. 86)

Julian's words here have a double meaning. She means that we should pray *together with God's working*; for, as she goes on to say, he is the ground of our prayer. Prayer, then, should spring from the Holy Spirit of God, and she urges us to learn what is his will and to pray accordingly. At the same time, her words may be translated, "let us all pray together. . . . " She is asking the Church, for the sake of God's love, to pray as one to the God who is at work in us, and who is perfectly One in love. These words are timely for the Church today, as the Church continues to suffer division from within as well as persecution from without. Prayer is the first work of the Church; but it is prayer which is worked out in love, not only for God but for all that God has made.

Julian's book ends with the notation that she has just begun, by God's grace, but has not finished. She asks the reader, then, to trust in God and to enjoy God in prayer. Her desire is that we might be perfectly one in the compassionate love of God, shared with us in our human nature which belongs to the incarnate Son of God, and made real in our own lives through the ministry of the Holy Spirit. But how could we achieve this unity which Julian desires for us?

In the *Revelations* there are many implications for the practical Christian life, in prayer, faith, personal spiritual discipline, and so on. It would be unprofitable, however, to work them all out on paper, as if they were a set of rules for the soul to follow in order to live, somehow, successfully. Julian's point is that all that we need is already given to us in Christ. He is life itself; he is the source of genuine peace, of goodness, of ability, of what we call "love." He is both the teaching and the Teacher. He teaches us himself, through the ministration of the Holy Spirit. And he is ours in prayer, coming to live—with the Father and the Spirit—in the deepest recesses of our own soul.

Of his gifts to us, we have seen that there are three, given through nature, mercy, and grace. They are faith, hope, and love: faith, because in the faith of the Church we meet God and so come to know our own human nature; hope, because in hope we do not despair, and so fall more deeply into the wounds of sin; love, because the being of God is love, and God desires to live in us and to love in us. The greatest of these is love:

From the time that it was shown to me, I often desired to understand what was our Lord's meaning. And fifteen years later, and more, I was answered in spiritual understanding, saying: "Do you want to know your Lord's meaning in this thing? Know it well. Love was his meaning. Who showed it to you? Love. What did he show you? Love. Why did he show it? For love. Hold yourself in it, and you shall understand and know more of the same; but you will never understand or know anything else in it, forever." (ch. 86)

To have an understanding of love is a great gift. To live in love is greater. Julian herself made a beginning in love, as she learned about the kindness which is in God and which is God. For us it is enough, too, to make a beginning; for "seeking is as good as beholding" in this life, and we are but beginners on the Way. It is good for us to end with Julian's admonition in mind:

For love's sake, let us all pray together. . .

Notes

Introduction

[1]That Julian actually died during this illness has not been the standard interpretation, but is suggested by her own account of events afterwards. In the Shorter Version of the Revelations, Ch. X, she reports that her mother stepped forward to check her eyes, or to close them (how to translate the text is not clear), believing "that I was dead already, or else had just died." This caused some consternation to Julian, either because her vision of the cross was temporarily hampered by her mother's actions, or else because Julian did not want, to be given up for dead.

In this and other references to her own death it is not always clear whether she means that she had actually died, or merely that she was "thought to have died." In any case, she describes graphically the experience of death including gradual paralysis, difficulty in breathing, a strange kind of pain (in which she thought that she was separating from her body), and the horrible experience of attempting to communicate with people in the room who could not hear her, nor see what she was seeing. In this her experience seems parallel to that of St. Teresa of Ávila, in that both women had their eyes closed by bystanders in the belief they had actually died.

[2]Prohibitions from wearing colorful clothing, visiting members of the opposite sex, etc., were, of course, ideal. The fact that they are frequently mentioned in sermons and admonitions suggests that they were abused. In one contemporary account, layfolk complain that certain nuns are slipping out of their convents to visit the taverns, dressed in bright colors and provocative clothes; and even that they have danced through the night with monks (Power, pp. 341-393 and *passim*).

[3]Since Julian never refers to the scriptures in Latin, it seems likely that she knew them (and her prayers) in English—probably in the form of an English missal. This version is taken from *The Prymer or Lay Folks Prayer Book*, which was contemporary with Julian (Littlehales, pp. 37 ff.).

[4]The so-called "Office of the Dead," here given in a modernized version. This Office, which was important to the anchoress' vow to be "dead to the world," includes all or part of more than thirty Psalms, the Magnificat, and passages from the book of Job. Many of the anchoress' daily prayers include these or similar words.

[5]Cf. James 1:13-17. The "privative" theory of evil (that evil tends toward non-being) was argued by Augustine against the Manicheans, who held that there is both a good god and an evil god. Augustine may have borrowed his concept from the philosopher Plotinus and the Neoplatonists; he rejected, however, the popular Neoplatonic argument that matter itself is evil. The Christian view, rather, was that evil is at work in a "fallen" world. Hence the common observation that nature is always tending towards chaos and disorder, or "nothingness" (the phenomenon known in modern physics as

the "law of entropy"). That evil is *mē-on*, "not-being," is held uniformly by the Eastern Fathers. Cf. Athanasius, *On the Incarnation*, 4: "What is evil is not, but what is good, is."

[6]Ch. 12, 32. This popular belief had its origin in Augustine's *Enchiridion* (published in modern editions as *Faith, Hope and Charity*), 9:28-30. Although Julian seems to assume that it is a point of faith for her readers, it was never actually defined as part of the dogma of the Catholic Church. Anselm, however, refers to it as common knowledge in *Cur Deus Homo* (*Why God Became Man*), Book I, Ch. 16.

[7]Cf. Isaiah 49:1, 15, 66:11-13, etc. The theme of the divine Motherhood in scripture and in Christian theology and spirituality has been explored by several scholars in recent years. See pp. 161ff. below, and Bibliography. Evidently the idea of "Christ our Mother" was not uncommon in Julian's time.

[8]MS Sloane 2499.

[9]Cf. Athanasius, *On the Incarnation*, 57: "Whoever would understand the mind of those who speak of God must begin by washing and cleansing his soul by his manner of living." As in later Christian spirituality, the reference to "washing" implies baptism.

[10]Galatians 2:20. Cf. Romans 8:9-10, 1 Corinthians 6:16-19, 2 Corinthians 6:16, Colossians 3:3 etc. For the following see 2 Peter 1:3-4, John ch. 14-15.

[11]The four "Doctors" of the Church popularly recognized in the fourteenth century were Ambrose, Augustine, Jerome and Gregory. It has sometimes been suggested that in Ch. 79 of the *Revelations* there is a direct quotation from Gregory's *Life of St. Benedict*, a point which is further taken to indicate that Julian may have been a Benedictine nun. However, the passage in question contains only a fragment of a sentence which could be attributed to Gregory ("And so in the [experience of] fear I have *something of meekness, which saves me from presumption. . .*" etc.). In any case the same passage from Gregory is quoted in the *Ancrene Riwle*, albeit in Latin. Julian would have been familiar with the *Riwle*. Cf. *CE*, p. 704, n. 19.

Attempts by various writers in recent years to demonstrate in Julian a first-hand knowledge of numerous patristic, scholastic and mystical texts remain unconvincing. No direct quotations from extra-biblical sources have been positively identified in the *Revelations*, although Julian seems familiar with the content of much traditional Catholic theology. She was, of course, acquainted with the main points of Augustinian thought as it had become part of her cultural and religious heritage.

[12]Cf. Pelphrey, "The Trinity in Julian of Norwich"; and *Love*, pp. 69 ff. and *passim*. Julian's trinitarian theology and mysticism seem reminiscent of the works of Sts. Maximus the Confessor, Symeon the New Theologian, Gregory Palamas, and others.

[13]Selections from the *Revelations* appear as the first entry in the relatively new *Norton Anthology of Literature by Women: The Tradition in English* (Gilbert, Sandra and Susan Gruber [ed.], New York and London: W.W. Norton and Co., 1985). This may be seen as a major step forward, in view of the fact that Julian's name does not even appear in most standard anthologies, including the *Norton Anthology of English Literature*, upon which teachers of English literature have customarily relied.

[14]For this and the following, see CE pp. 1-10 and *Show* pp. 21-22.

[15]Julian makes frequent oblique references to scripture, but without citing her sources. In the two exceptions, she refers to the speaker rather than to the appropriate book in the Bible, certainly not to chapter and verse, e.g. "As Saint Paul says. . ." etc.

Julian's use of the Pauline epistles may indicate a source which had been translated into English. The "Paues Bible," a 14th-century New Testament and most certainly a Lollard translation, seems to have a deliberate predilection for the Pauline epistles.

(See Paues, Anna, *A Fourteenth Century Biblical Version*, Cambridge: Cambridge University Press, 1904). Julian's use of the Lollard term "New Law" for "New Testament" (ch. 38) may further indicate a Lollard association. (For information about the Lollards and the availability of English translations of the Bible in Julian's time, see both of Deansley's works in the Bibliography, below.)

[16]The phrase "all shall be well," for which Julian is perhaps best known, occurs in some manuscripts of Hilton's *Ladder [or Scale] of Perfection*, Book I:33 (cf. Underhill, p. 75). Kirchberger (p. 135) suggests that Hilton may have had Julian's *Revelations* in mind in another instance, in which sin is likened to a "blackening" of the soul represented by the darkening of Jesus' face during the Passion (*Revelations* ch. 10; Walter Hilton's *Goad of Love*, Ch. 20).

[17]Julian returns to this point several times, e.g., in Ch. 70 where she refers to the use of the crucifix during the time of her own visions, and to her continuing awareness of the passion itself. While she agrees with the *Cloud* author that the soul could never be satisified by anything beneath God, she argues that God (whom we cannot see) is known to the soul only in the incarnation of the Son of God (whom we can see). Thus she rejects the practices of entering into contemplative prayer without the use of any visual image (including the crucified Christ) or through the use of one-word "mantras." Both had been advocated by the *Cloud*, ch. 7 (Walsh, p. 132). Julian's insistence on this point may indicate that she was familiar with the *Cloud* author or at least had his works in mind when she wrote the *Revelations*.

[18]This list is taken from Meech, S.B. and Hope Emily Allen (ed.), *The Book of Margery Kempe*, Oxford: Humphrey Milford (Early English Text Society), 1940, p. lx.

[19]Merton, Thomas, *Conjectures of a Guilty Bystander*, New York: Image Books, Doubleday and Co. 1968, pp. 211-212.

[20]See Seton, Anya, *Katherine*, Boston: Houghton Mifflin Co., 1954; and Bishop, Michael, "Close Encounters with the Deity," *Isaac Asimov's Science Fiction Magizine*, Vol. 10 No. 3 (March, 1968), pp. 102-110.

[21]Eliot, T.S., *Collected Poems 1909-1962*, London: Faber and Faber, 1963.

[22]Butler-Bowden, pp. 71 ff.

Notes, Chapter 1

[1]For the sake of brevity, details have been omitted from this synopsis of the tale. The ultimate source for Chaucer's version, from which he made a translation into English, has not been positively identified. However, like sources—especially for the Prologue to the tale—contain numerous references to theological points which are mentioned in passing by Julian, e.g. that the Virgin is at once "daughter and parent" (of God), that the Son "wore for himself the vestment of our salvation," etc. The tale, called the *Passio S. Caeciliae*, was part of the *Legenda aurea* ("Golden Legend"), compilation of legends which circulated popularly in Europe. Cf. Bryan, W.F. and Germaine Dempster (ed.), *Sources and Analogues of Chaucer's Canterbury Tales*, Chicago: The University of Chicago Press, 1941.

[2]Cf. The New Catholic Encylopedia, Vol. XI, pp. 73 ff. (New York, 1967).

[3]Bernard of Clairvaux, "On the Love of God"; and "On the Three Ways in which We Love God" (*Sermon XX on the Song of Songs*).

Notes, Chapter 3

[1]Students did not necessarily learn to write. In modern times we associate the skills of reading and writing as though the two must be learned simultaneously. This is not actually the case, as modern teachers of literacy can attest; certainly it was not the case in the Middle Ages, when English was just emerging as a written language. Layfolk would have been able to recognize certain symbols in context (e.g. in the market-place) without possessing the ability to form letters or to spell. A difference, further-more, existed between the spoken and written grammar, such that common folk would have hesitated to put their colloquial speech (mixed with Saxon) into writing, lest they appear "lewd" and ignorant. (A similar distinction exists today in Chinese, in which speakers of the Cantonese dialect cannot write down their speech; and although they can read Mandarin characters, do not pronounce them in the Mandarin way— which "reading" language in turn is not the same as spoken Cantonese.) It is likely that in Julian's day most lay Christians had a familiarity with Latin phrases found in the Mass (and therefore in the scriptures), which they knew by heart, although they could not speak Latin and would not have been able to write the Latin phrases down, or possibly read them.

[2]On this point the present writer is inclined to take Julian's words at face value. For the opposite interpretation—that Julian was herself familiar with theological texts which, if available at all were available only in Latin—see Colledge and Walsh (CE and *Show, passim*). Colledge and Walsh take Julian's words to be a literary conven-tion, used even by notables such as Chaucer.

To argue that Julian was indeed schooled in the classic texts requires the double assumption that she received a unique education for a woman of her time (including mastery of Latin) and that the relevant texts were available to her, if they could be found in Norwich at all. Both assumptions seem at least questionable in view of historical evidence regarding education and the availability of theological texts in the English conventual houses of the time. (cf. Deansley, *The Lollard Bible*, p. 206 and pp. 110-116; and Power, pp. 240 ff.).

It has been pointed out that Julian's sudden exclamation in Ch. 4, *Benedicite domine!* ("God bless!") is ungrammatical; it should be *dominus*. The mistake would be not untypical on the part of uneducated layfolk; however, it may not be Julian's (it appears only in the Sloane MSS). Colledge and Walsh (CE p. 211, n. 17) point out that Julian may actually have said something else, e.g. *Benedicite et benedictus es domine*.

Notes, Chapter 4

[1]The phrase may ultimately be traced to Augustine, as follows: "Therefore seek not to understand that you may believe, but believe that you may understand" (*On the Gospel of St. John*, XXIX:6;). However, it is a major theme in Anselm's works. Anselm's *Proslogion* was originally entitled *Fides quaerens intellectum*, "Faith seeking understanding." Anselm writes, ". . . I have written the following treatise, in the person of one who strives to lift his mind to the contemplation of God, and seeks to understand what he believes" (Preface to the *Prosloqion*).

[2]Suggested by Sr. Ritamary Bradley.

[3]On this point Julian appears to echo St. Thomas Aquinas. Cf. the *Summa*, Part I, Question 8, Art. 1, Repl. Obj. 2.

[4]The idea that all souls were created at once and are subsequently "released" into bodies through time, predates Christianity. It was never embraced by the Church, although it was put forward by Origen or his students in the 3rd century. Subsequently condemned as heresy, the idea tended to recur in medieval Neoplatonism. Another medieval heresy was the notion that creation is co-eternal with God (i.e. that God was always creating from eternity) because it takes place in the timelessness of God.

[5]Julian neatly summarizes the Christian doctrine of the Trinity which had been defined by Augustine in various works (cf. *On the Trinity*, I, viii, 17-18; and Books VI and VII). However, she avoids the tendency, evident in Augustine and subsequent Western theologians, to view the Trinity more in terms of psychological, rather than ontological, reality (i.e. as "personalities" in the Godhead rather than as objective "Persons").

[6]Cf. Malachi 3:6; James 1:17. That Julian knew the text of James rather than merely its contents is indicated by her interview with Margery Kempe (*p. 60*, above) in which she refers to the passage in James 1:6-8, although without indicating ner source.

[7]The somewhat awkward term *perichoresis* did not come into use in Christian theology before the 4th century. However, the idea itself was in evidence much earlier. Julian reproduces the manner in which the term was introduced by the Eastern Fathers, e.g. Athanasius, John of Damascus, and Maximus the Confessor. For an account of its history in trinitarian theology cf. Kelly, pp. 402-409.

[8]So-called "process theology" is identified with the philosophical/theological school this century originating in the teaching of A.N. Whitehead (1861-1947), Charles Hartshorne (1897-), and W.M. Pittenger (1905).

Notes, Chapter 5

[1]Medieval manuscript art can be "read" according to certain conventional symbols, which are probably only poorly understood today. Thus, Christ in judgment wears a cloak "as blue as the sky," as Julian says.

[2]Cf. Matthew 17:1-8 and parallels; Revelation 4:3, 19, etc. The enthronement of the risen Christ is frequently depicted in medieval Christian art. It is interesting that in Julian's vision, Jesus' new robe combines all the colors of the rainbow. White light is, of course, a combination of all the colors in the prism.

³The phrase, reminiscent of Romans 5:20, appears in the *praeconium paschale*, or the Blessing of the Paschal Candle, on Easter Eve. It was probably in liturgical use in Julian's time. The idea is, however, typical of Augustinian thought and perhaps an underlying theme in the *Confessions*. Thomas Aquinas quotes from the Easter Eve liturgy in the *Summa*, Part III, Q. 1, Art. 3, Repl. Obj. 3 before going on to say that "...God allows evils to happen in order to bring a greater good therefrom."

⁴Cf. Mark 13:32.

Notes, Chapter 6

¹Cf. Mark 15:40-41; Luke 23:27-29.

²Modern readers will be unsure whether to understand the "Holy Vernicle" as historical reality or merely as the subject of legend. Julian, however, believes it to be a genuine relic in possession of the Church of Rome; although whether she believes it to be still on display for contemporary pilgrims is not clear from the text.

There is surprising evidence that the legendary veil may be identified with the cloth which today is known as the "Shroud of Turin." The features of the face on the Shroud, though indistinct and present in a "negative" image, are strikingly similar in detail to those of Jesus' face as it began to appear in Eastern and later, Western, Christian iconography soon after the 6th century. This corresponds to the discovery in 525 AD of a cloth in the walls of the city of Edessa (now Urfa, Turkey) which bore on it an image later revered as the "true likeness" of Christ. This "portrait not made by hands," as it was known, became the subject of much attention throughout Christendom, called the "Holy Mandylion" (from the Arabic word for "veil"). The cloth was later removed to Constantinople, where it was kept from 944 until 1204. It then disappeared during the sack of the city by crusaders from western Europe.

The Shroud of Turin, meanwhile, is known to have existed in Europe from 1357, exactly contemporary with Julian. It is interesting that in Julian's day the "Holy Vernicle" (or "Veil") was said to be the kerchief of St. Veronica. The name "Veronica" may be a corruption of the Latin phrase for "true likeness," as the portrait was identified. That Veronica's Veil may have been the Shroud of Turin would account for the tradition, which is known to Julian, that the portrait was indistinct or "murky," and that it was "not made by hands," i.e. not a painting but an impression upon the cloth. If the Shroud were displayed with a fold just beneath the imprint of the face, it would give the impression of containing only a smudged facial image. Scholars suggest that it was so displayed as the "Holy Mandylion." (Cf. Stevenson, Kenneth, and Gary Häbermas, *Verdict on the Shroud: Evidence for the Death and Resurrection of Jesus Christ*, Ann Arbor, Michigan: Servant Books, 1981, pp. 13-31 and photo inserts.)

³Cf. Genesis 1:26

⁴Cf. Romans 5:12-21, 1 Corinthians 15:20-23. Augustine develops the content of the image of the Trinity in the human soul in *On the Trinity*, Book X, Ch. 11-12. He identifies the "made Trinity" with the properties of memory, reason (or understanding) and will. Irenaeus' doctrine of Christ as the "new Adam," which was echoed by Anselm, appears in *Work Against Heresies*, Book V, 1-2 and 19-20.

⁵Cf. Matthew 2 3:37

⁶Cf. 1 Thessalonians 2:7; 1 Corinthians 15:9; Galatians 4:27, Romans 8:19.

⁷Ward, Sr. Benedicta (tr.), *The Prayers and Meditations of St. Anselm*, Harmondsworth: Penguin Books, 1973, pp. 123, 260 ff.

⁸*Ancrene Riwle*, Part IV (Salu, p. 102).

⁹It has been suggested that Julian derived the image from the works of St. Mechtild, St. Bridget of Sweden, or St. Catherine of Siena, among others. However, the availability of the texts in question remains a problem. Julian need not have borrowed from other writers in any case, since the theme was part of the spirituality in her day.

¹⁰An alternative reading of the text has been suggested, however, as follows: ". . . it may not verely be seyde of none ne to none but of hym and to *hym* that is very mother of lyfe and of alle" (CE, p. 598; italics added).

The theme of Mary as taking the role of Eve in the New Covenant would not have been unfamiliar to Julian. It is graphically portrayed in traditional icons of the resurrection (the Harrowing of Hell, in Eastern iconography) where Mary is customarily depicted as Eve, the "mother of all" because she is the mother of Christ, in whom humanity has re-birth. Cf. Genesis 3:20.

¹¹Cf. John 4:24.

¹²*Ladder of Perfection*, Book II, Ch. 13.

¹³Paul's argument—that in his inner being he delights in God's law, while at the same time in his sinful nature he does what he knows to be wrong—seems to apply only to the soul of faith. Julian, at least, understands the passage in this way, where the "inner being" is identified with Christ living in the soul-to-be-saved. However, in Thomist theology a double nature is ascribed to humanity in general (cf. the *Summa*, Part III, Q.1, Art. 3, Reply Obj. 3). Julian is consistently misunderstood on this point even today, to imply that all human beings have a "divine will" implanted deep within which only needs to be discovered and expressed.

¹⁴Cf. Ephesians 4:12; Colossians 2:1. Hilton uses the image of "knitting" in the *Ladder*, Book I Ch. 12 (although the term does not appear in all editions; cf. Underhill, p. 25), and in the *Goad of Love*, Ch. 1.

¹⁵Julian compares the dying body of Christ, with its drying out in the wind, to a cloth being hung out to dry (ch. 17). This recalls the medieval metaphor, much used by Julian, of human nature as a cloth or tunic which the Son of God put on (the "skirt" worn by Adam in Julian's vision, Ch. 51).

¹⁶Genesis 2:7.

¹⁷Julian describes the events of Matthew 27:45, 51-53, together with the account in Acts 17 of Paul's sermon at the Areopagus (Mars' Hill), in Athens. The latter event is significant to her because it was the subject of popular legend relating to Dionysius, the "Areopagite" mentioned in Acts 17:34. This Dionysius was identified with the "St. Denys" whose mystical treatise had recently been translated into English as the *Hid Divinity*, and upon which the *Cloud of Unknowing* was based. In a complex series of confusions, the same "St. Denys" was said to have established a mission in France (later the Monastery of St. -Denis) and to have had his head cut off, after which he miraculously continued to live. Thus at least three persons, living in different centuries, combine to make the "St. Denys" known to Julian.

Notes, Chapter 7

[1]Cf. Genesis 28:10-22.

[2]Galatians 5:9; 1 John 5:16-17. Julian refers to "venial sins" (ch. 52) and develops a lengthy explanation of how she conceives sin to be "mortal" even in the life of the believer (ch. 72).

[3]In Ch. 76 Julian refers to her own particular temptations to "sloth" and "wasting of time." She probably has in mind the kind of listless depression commonly known to ascetics as "accidie," warned against in the *Ancrene Riwle* (Salu, p. 93).

[4]Julian refers to Romans 8:35 ("Who shall separate us from the love of Christ?" etc.) and Matthew 14:30 and 8:25. She has actually confused two separate events in her reference to Peter's words, since it was not Peter but the disciples who said, "Lord, save us" etc. Not surprisingly, in this—one of only two attempts at direct quotation from scripture in the *Revelations*—Julian clearly does not have the actual text in front of her. (In the other instance, in Ch. X of the Shorter Version, Julian paraphrases a portion of Philippians 2:5, which she identifies as "a saying of St. Paul.")

[5]The extended reference to St. John of Beverley has been taken as an argument for the date of May 8 rather than May 13, 1373 for Julian's visions. St. John's feast date would have fallen on the day before. However, the reference does not occur in the Shorter Version, and was perhaps included later on because of recent local devotion to the new saint, who may have been contemporary with Julian. It is not conclusive evidence for the date of Julian's vision. Cf. Reynolds (AMR), p. 315.

Notes, Chapter 8

[1]Cf. Matthew 22:1-14.

[2]Cf. 2 Peter 1:4

[3]The traditional Greek term translates the Hebrew *berakah*, the term for the "blessing" prayer of the Seder or Passover meal, which begins "Blessed are you, O Lord our God," etc.

Notes, Chapter 9

[1]Cf. Exodus 33:20, referred to in Ch. 43 of the *Revelations* and John 1:18.

Epilogue

[1]Cf. 1 Peter 3:18-21, where the image of Christ's descent into hell is juxtaposed with that of washing in the waters of baptism.

Select Bibliography

Editions of the Revelations (arranged chronologically)

Collins, Henry, ed., *Revelations of Divine Love Shewed to a Devout Anchoress by Name, Mother Julian of Norwich*, Thomas Richardson and Sons, London, 1877. (From Sloane MS. 2499.)

Warrack, Grace, ed., *Revelations of Divine Love*, Methuen and Co., London, 1901 (1907 edition). (From Sloane MS. 2499.) Referred to as Warrack.

Tyrrell, George, ed., *XVI Revelations of Divine Love Shewed to Mother Juliana of Norwich 1373*, Kegan Paul, Trench, Trübner and Co. Ltd., 1902. (From Paris MS.)

Harford, Dundas, ed., *Comfortable Words for Christ's Lovers, Being the Visions and Voices Vouchsafed to Lady Julian Recluse at Norwich in 1373*, H. R. Allenson, London, 1911. (From Shorter Version, Brit. Mus. Add. MS. 37790) Referred to as Harford.

Hudleston, Dom Roger, O.S.B., ed., *Revelations of Divine Love*, Burns Oates and Washbourne Ltd., London 1927. (From Sloane MS. 2499) Referred to as Hudleston.

Reynolds, Frances (Sister Anna Maria, C.P.), *An Edition of Ms. Sloane 2499 of Sixteen Revelations of Divine Love by Julian of Norwich*, unpublished M.A. thesis, University of Leeds, 1947.

Chambers, P. Franklin, ed., *Juliana of Norwich: An Introductory Appreciation and an Interpretive Anthology*, Victor Gollancz Ltd., London, 1955. (Selections from all known MSS.) Referred to as Chambers.

Reynolds, Frances (Sister Anna Maria, C.P.), *A Critical Edition of the Revelations of Julian of Norwich (1342 - c. 1416), Prepared From All Known Manuscripts*, unpublished Ph.D. thesis, Leeds University, 1956. Referred to as AMR.

Reynolds, Anna Maria, C. P., *Julian of Norwich: A Shewing of God's Love,* Sheed and Ward, London, 1958 (1974 edition). (From Shorter Version, Brit. Mus. Add. MS. 37790.) Referred to as SGL.

Walsh, James, S.J., ed., *Revelations of Divine Love*, Anthony Clarke Books, Glasgow, 1961 (1973 edition). (From Sloane MSS. 2499 and 3705, and Paris MS.) Referred to as J.W. or Walsh.

Wolters, Clifton, ed., *Revelations of Divine Love*, Penguin Books, Harmondsworth, 1966 (1973 edition). (From *Sloane MS. 2499.) Referred to as C.W. or Wolters.*

Glasscoe, Marion, ed., *Julian of Norwich: A Revelation of Love*, University of Exeter, 1976. (From Sloane *MS2499 with alternate readings, from S2 and P.)*

DelMastro, M.L., ed., Revelations of Divine Love, Image Books, Garden City, New York, 1977. (From Sloane MS 2499 with Sloane MS 3705 as a corrective "where necessary").

Colledge, Edmund, O.S.A. and James Walsh, S.J., ed., *Julian of Norwich: Showings,* Paulist Press, New York, 1978 (Longer Version, using all available MSS). Referred to as "Show."

Colledge, Edmund, O.S.A. and James Walsh, S.J., ed., *A Book of Showings to the Anchoress Julian of Norwich* (two volumes), Pontifical Institute of Medieval Studies, Toronto, 1978 (Critical edition of both versions from all available MSS). Referred to as CE.

Life and Religion in Medieval England

Deansley, Margaret, *The History of the Medieval Church 590-1500*, London: Methuen and Co., 1925.

——————, (ed.) *The Lollard Bible*, Cambridge: Cambridge University Press, 1920.

Littlehales, Henry (ed.), *The Prymer or Lay Folks' Prayer Book*, London: Early English Text Society, Kegan Paul, Trench, Trübner and Co., 1895.

The Anchorite Tradition

Power, Eileen, *Medieval English Nunneries c. 1275-1535*, Cambridge: Cambridge University Press, 1922.

Salu, M.B. (tr.), *The Ancrene Riwle*, London: Burns and Oates, 1955.

Writers and Mystics of the Middle Ages

Butler-Bowden, William (tr.), *The Book of Margery Kempe*, London: Jonathan Cape, 1936.

Kirchberger, Clare (ed.), *The Goad of Love*, London: Faber and Faber, 1951.

Knowles, Dom David, *The English Mystical Tradition*, New York: Harper Brothers, 1961.

Underhill, Evelyn (ed.), *The Scale of Perfection*, London: John M. Watkins, 1948.

Walsh, James (tr.), *The Cloud of Unknowing*, New York: Paulist Press, 1981.

The Patristic Background

Kelly, J.N.D., *Early Christian Doctrines*, London: Adam and Charles Black, 1973.

Rolt, C.E. (tr.) *Dionysius the Areopagite on the Divine Names and the Mystical Theology*, London: Society for the Promotion of Christian Knowledge, 1920.

Feminine Imagery in Medieval Mysticism

Bradley, Ritamary, "Mysticism in the Motherhood Similitude of Julian of Norwich," *Studia Mystica* 8 (Summer, 1985), pp. 4-14.

Bynum, Caroline, *Jesus as Mother: Studies in the Spirituality of the High Middle Ages,* Berkeley: University of California Press, 1982.

Lagorio, Valerie, "Variations on the Theme of God's Motherhood in Medieval English Mystical and Devotional Writings," *Studia Mystica* 8 (Summer 1985), pp. 15-37.

Studies in Julian's Theology

Llewelyn, Robert (ed.), *Julian: Woman of our Day,* London: Darton, Longman and Todd, 1986.

_____, *With Pity Not With Blame*, London: Darton, Longman and Todd, 1983.

Pelphrey, Brant, *Love Was His Meaning: The Theology and Mysticism of Julian of Norwich*, Salzburg: Institut fu³r Anglistik and Amerikanistik, Universita³t Salzburg, 1982. (Referred to above as *Love*).